MEDITERRANEAN COOKERY

ALSO BY CLAUDIA RODEN

A Book of Middle Eastern Food

Everything Tastes Better Outdoors

The Good Food of Italy—Region by Region

These Are Borzoi Books
Published in New York by
Alfred A. Knopf, Inc.

MEDITERRANEAN COOKERY

Claudia Roden

ALFRED A. KNOPF   NEW YORK   1992

For Clare Brigstocke

THIS IS A BORZOI BOOK PUBLISHED BY ALFRED A. KNOPF, INC.

This work was originally published in hardcover in Great
Britain by BBC Books, London, and in the United States
by Alfred A. Knopf, Inc., New York, in 1987.

Library of Congress Cataloging-in-Publication Data

Roden, Claudia.   Mediterranean cookery.
Includes index.
1. Cookery, Mediterranean. I. Title.
TX725.M35R63   1987   641.59'1822   87-45231
ISBN 0-394-54434-X
ISBN 0-679-72835-X (pbk.)

Manufactured in Italy

First American Paperback Edition

The Publishers would like to thank the following suppliers for
loaning items for photography: David Mellor; Divertimenti;
Elizabeth David; General Trading Company; Harrods;
Moroccan Embassy; Moroccan National Tourist Office.
Thanks are also due to Hyams and Cockerton, Nine Elms;
Mr. and Mrs. Hegerty of Hope End Country House Hotel,
Ledbury; Brian Portch of Portch and Sons (Fishmongers),
Chiswick; and Mr. and Mrs. Fahri of Topkapi Restaurant,
Marylebone, for their help in providing ingredients.

A NOTE ON THE TYPE

The text of this book was set in a digitized version of Bembo,
a well-known Monotype face. Named for Pietro Bembo, the
celebrated Renaissance writer and humanist scholar who was
made a cardinal and served as secretary to Pope Leo X, the
original cutting of Bembo was made by Francesco Griffo of
Bologna only a few years after Columbus discovered America.
   Sturdy, well balanced, and finely proportioned, Bembo is a
face of rare beauty, extremely legible in all of its sizes.

This book was composed by Ace Filmsetting Ltd., Frome,
England. Color separations were made by Technik Lithoplates
Ltd., Berkhamsted, Herts, and Gilchrist Brothers Ltd.,
Leeds, England. The printing and binding were done by
Officine Grafiche di Verona, Arnoldo Mondadori Editore,
Verona, Italy.
Designed by Julian Holland with Martin Smillie.
Introduction, location, and recipe photography by
Alex Dufort. Still life photography by
Sue Atkinson.
Line drawings by Nicholas Hall.

Contents

Acknowledgements

Working on this book has been fascinating, challenging and enjoyable because it grew out of my involvement in the BBC television series *Mediterranean Cookery*, which was filmed by Maddalena Fagandini and Clare Brigstocke in seven countries during 1986.

Clare was also my editor on the book and responsible for seeing it through at every stage. My greatest debt is to her. I cannot thank her enough for the way she made it all happen and for the boundless enthusiasm and passion she brought to the project.

Maddalena has given me invaluable help with the Italian recipes and I am also very greatful for the research she did on wine. I also wish to thank Helen Moir of the TV production team for all that she has done. Working with the team was part of the pleasure.

The book benefited greatly from the help and advice of the BBC Publications staff, Nigel Bradley and Jennie Allen, as well as Sue Conder, the copy editor, and Carole Handslip and Clare Gordon Smith, who did the cooking for the photographs. I have special affectionate thanks for Alan Davidson for his kind advice, and Alicia Ríos who has been wonderful and overwhelmingly generous with her rich fund of Spanish lore and recipes. I thank all the people who have appeared in the television series. Their names are mentioned in the recipes they provided.

My research in the area has been going on for many years and a great many people have helped me with recipes and information which form the bulk and backbone of the book. There were so many that I cannot name everyone but I take the opportunity here of expressing my gratitude to them all. Those to whom I am particularly indebted are: Mannana Alami, Massimo Alberini, Pablo Amate, Nayra Atiya, Asma el Bakri, Raymonde Bendaoud, Khadija Bensdira, Esther Bensimol, Henri Boccara, Yolande Bona, Guillermina Botaya, Martine Bourdon-Williams, Yvette Brieunne, Frédéric Brun, Carles Camós, Manuel Carrillo Diaz, Carmen Casas, Alec Chanda, Franca Colonna Romano, Jaume Font, the Freixenet family, Khadija Boutaleb Ghallab, Rudolph Crewe, Feyzi and Nevin Halici, Ans Hey, Malika Laraichi, Elise Madon, Suzie Magaziner, June Marinos, Fernando Ossorio, Stelios Platanos, Victoria Roque, Jeremy Round, Dody Sabbah, the Slaoui family, Sue Tassios, Nezha Torres, Mohammed Torres, Penelope and Claudio Vita Finzi, Aydin Yilmaz, Theodore Zeldin, Sami Zubaida.

I thank most particularly Patrick Gooch of Foods from Spain who invited me on the television reconnaissance trip to Spain, and Maria José Sevilla Taylor who accompanied us and made it a most memorable and happy experience. I also have special thanks for Gulsen Kahraman of the Turkish Tourist Office for sending me on a magnificent gastronomic trip to Turkey. Both Maria José and Gulsen have also been extremely generous in many other ways.

I am grateful to Dottore Massimo d'Amico and Gian Franco Spaggiari of the Italian Trade Centre, Abouchita Hajouji of the Moroccan Tourist Office, Pauline Hallam of the French Tourist Board, Catherine Menac'h of Food and Wine from France, Jean Ferniot of the Institut des Arts Culinaires in Paris, Pascale Hervé of the Nice Tourist Office, Mrs Hara Vlachaki of the National Tourist Organisation of Greece in Athens and Philip Diamond of Covent Garden Fishmongers, London, for their kind help. And, of course, I thank my children, Simon, Nadia and Anna, and my parents, Nelly and Cesar, for their support.

I have consulted many cookery books; the main ones are listed in the bibliography, but Jane Grigson's splendid *Vegetable Book* and her *Fruit Book* have been especially useful.

My interest in food was inspired by Elizabeth David's *A Book of Mediterranean Food* and it has remained my favourite book.

Preface

The aim of this book was to look for the traditional home cooking of the Mediterranean and to pick the gems. The recipes were in the main collected on the spot in the different countries. They are the fruit of several years' travel and research in the area as well as my involvement in the BBC Television series *Mediterranean Cookery*.

The recipes come mostly from women who cook for their families. When I travel it is not restaurants that I explore. Starting with a few addresses and telephone numbers I go from one home kitchen to another, passed on from one woman to another. Even the professional chefs featured in this book have given the kind of things people cook at home. In Italy restaurants were once ashamed of doing simple local food but now they are proud of it and say that simple food is best and that playing around with it does not improve it. Spanish chefs are now doing their best to recover their lost culture from the phoney tourist cuisine which had almost destroyed it in the last decades. In the South of France I have gone to restaurants where chefs have resisted the temptation to produce *nouvelle cuisine* and still offer traditional regional foods. The recipes are a true record of their dishes. I have tried them all and made them work in a way that reflects my taste, but as they are cooked locally and without embellishments or additions. I have not been concerned with fashions nor with restaurant food. When you come to make them they should taste as they do in the Mediterranean. The only change I have made in interpreting them was to reduce the quantity of animal fat and sometimes also of oil when it was not vital to the success of a dish.

I have not attempted to be comprehensive but have tried rather to offer a balanced selection of dishes which you would want to adopt for every day and for entertaining. The choice is very personal. It represents the kind of food I love – full of flavour, interesting and wholesome, and which can be made without too much effort and expense. A good part of the dishes – those which are featured in the television series – were decided on with the people who cooked them. They are all much loved and popular though they are not necessarily well known. You will find that several well known dishes are missing and that some countries are hardly represented. Since many dishes can be found in several countries as variations on a theme I have tried to pick only the best among them to avoid overlap and repetition. The best were usually the simplest.

Wherever I have been in the Mediterranean, in every country, when I asked people to explain how they cooked they always protested that it was impossible to do so and that I had to watch them and taste. On one occasion in Morocco the husband exclaimed: 'How could you possibly communicate in words what my wife has learnt from her mother and her relatives and their cooks, and which she has perfected over fifty years of cooking?' But you can, and if the results are not exactly like this wonderful lady's, they can still be splendid.

I have used metric units as my standard measurements. The imperial equivalents are exact when it is important, as with breads and pastries, otherwise they are a close approximation. Use the measures, temperatures and timing as a guide but do not abandon your judgement, initiative and good sense and, above all, your taste. It is impossible to give foolproof measures and instructions which cover every eventuality. You may have several things in your oven at the same time so that some of the shelves may not receive very much heat. A very large lemon could have little juice, or it may have plenty but not be sharp at all. Your garlic may be young or old, your aubergine bitter or not. Nature is like that. What is sharp or spicy or delicate for me may not be so for you; we all have different ideas about what is crisp or golden or brown so it is unlikely that your dish will turn out exactly like mine or even that it will come out exactly the same each time. But it is precisely that personal touch, that knack for doing things which is what cooking is about. You will have to learn to trust your taste and to be confident about your judgement even if you have never eaten the dish before.

With Mediterranean food, flavour is all-important and you must keep tasting and adjusting the seasoning as you go along. Like tuning a musical instrument, you must play it by ear. Flavours should be strong but they should not dominate. Always use fresh herbs, if possible, and spices which have not lost their scent. Mediterranean food is aromatic, sometimes spicy, occasionally peppery, but the natural flavours of the main ingredients should never be drowned or masked.

Throughout the book olive oil is used for salads and for dishes to be eaten cold and also for frying fish. Everywhere else I prefer to use sunflower oil but you can substitute safflower or any light vegetable oil. I use size 2 eggs for most dishes including those which require large eggs. When flour is mentioned I mean plain flour but you can usually substitute strong flour. For pepper, unless white pepper is specified, use freshly ground black peppercorns. When a bunch of parsley is called for, use the continental flat-leafed variety which is now widely available, especially at Indian and Greek grocers and be very generous with it. Depending on the dish, a large bunch may mean from 50 g (2 oz) to 125 g (4 oz). I have only been specific where the weight is particularly crucial.

Wherever possible use fresh tomatoes. When they are not at their best a pinch of sugar improves their flavour. But it is better to use a very good quality of canned plum tomatoes, such as Italian ones, than fresh ones with a poor taste.

You will find some inconsistencies. For instance, I do not usually mind tomato seeds so I have not bothered to say 'de-seed' unless the person who gave me the recipe has specified it. Some people do not think it necessary to salt aubergines to rid them of their bitter juices because they like the bitterness. I do so out of habit but it is only important if the aubergines are to be deep-fried so that they absorb less oil.

To enter into the spirit of Mediterranean eating you must enjoy food, but you must also treat it seriously, beginning with the planning, through shopping, peeling, chopping and cooking, to the sitting down at table. Shopping is particularly important. You must get good-quality ingredients in good condition, and you may have to feel and smell them to be sure of that. There is added pleasure when they are in season and at their best.

To plan a meal you may like to choose an all-Spanish or an all-Moroccan menu, for instance, but you can also put together dishes from different countries – they mix very well and you will have more choice and flexibility.

The French have a saying 'le plaisir de la table commence par celui des yeux' (the pleasure of the table starts with pleasing the eye). The food must look appealing and appetising. It is difficult to improve on the beauty of an artichoke or of a seafood mixture but you can make the most of brilliantly coloured vegetables and interesting combinations of ingredients to make an attractive presentation. Garnish in the traditional Mediterranean way with chopped herbs, toasted almonds, raisins and pine-nuts or black and green olives. You can also colour with saffron, dust with cumin or paprika, dribble with oil, let the stew acquire a deep burgundy colour and brown a dish until it glows warmly. The presentation must be beautiful in a simple and natural way, not fussy, fiddly or effete.

On the whole, you do not need complex expensive wines to drink with simple hearty dishes. When food is strongly flavoured and aromatic it needs simple robust wines with character and quality which can stand up to the flavours and support them. You may like to serve the local wines with the food of the same region. We have indicated throughout the book some which are usually available here. For France, Spain and Italy we have only included wines of the Mediterranean regions for reasons of space.

My hope is that when you have used the book for some time you will be able to conjure up a meal with a Mediterranean flavour with whatever is in the house and without feeling bound to a recipe. And when you sit down to eat do so in a happy and relaxed mood. It should be a ceremony and a celebration. The Mediterraneans have a reputation for easy-going *joie de vivre* and the table is the best place for you to start cultivating one.

Claudia Roden
January 1987

Right: Orange grove in Greece

Mare Nostrum – *Our Sea*

Holidays in Alexandria were a round of swimming and fishing expeditions, afternoon ice-creams on the corniche, horse carriage rides and picnics at sea. We were always with a large group of relatives and friends because everyone enjoyed company more than anything else and no one could bear to be alone. Every night a crowd of children from Alexandria joined those from Cairo at the hotel. We formed a giant circle in a dark, jasmin-scented corner of the garden and played *bouteille*. Someone went into the centre, twirled a bottle and kissed the person it pointed to.

In our eyes Alexandria was a city of great romances. Compared to the serious and prudish Cairo it was a pleasure-seeking society. *Le Journal d'Egypte* kept us in touch with the goings-on in a page devoted to *la seconde capitale – les potins d'Alexandrie* ('the second capital – gossip from Alexandria'). Alexandria was different from Cairo. It lived under a different climate with different trees and flowers and it had a different atmosphere. As soon as you arrived you felt the exuberant light-hearted mood in the cafés along the seafront. The wealthy Greek community which we were told had been there since Alexander the Great set the social tone and Italian architects determined its appearance with yellow and pink painted buildings and villas. It was more Europeanised and you could hear many languages in the street. Alexandria was part of another world – one to which Marseilles and Barcelona, Genoa, Athens and Algiers, Beirut and Tangiers also belonged, and it had a culture of its own. This culture was so powerful that the whole country was influenced as though the sea was its centre of gravity.

Egypt during my childhood had a large cosmopolitan Mediterranean society where French was the *lingua franca* and people spoke as many as six languages. It was a mosaic of minorities in which Greeks, Italians, Jews, Armenians, Syrian Christians, Lebanese, Maltese and British and French expatriates lived amongst the Copts and the Muslim upper classes. My own Jewish community was also subdivided. I belonged in part to the *Halabis* who came from Aleppo in Syria and also to the Sephardi Jews who originated in Spain and Portugal. They were called *Espagnolis* or the *Kekeres* because of the way they asked '¿*Que quieres?*' ('What do you want?'). Although their ancestors had left these countries in the fifteenth century and they had spent some hundreds of years in Turkey, the Sephardi Jews continued to speak ancient Castilian and their dialect *ladino*.

The culinary palette in this environment was as large as the linguistic one. There were few purely

Egyptian vendor selling ful midames

To most people in Europe and America the Mediterranean belongs to Spain, France and Italy and to Greece. To me in my early years it belonged to Egypt where I was born.

When I was a child and living in Cairo we spent summers in Alexandria to escape the heat. We drove on the desert road with a band of relatives in a convoy of cars singing '*Alouette gentille alouette*' and '*O my darling Clementine*'. We passed the salt pans and suddenly the sea was there, deep blue, seemingly drunk with joy under the azure sky. We screamed and cheered at the glory of it.

Our first stop was at Xenophon, a Greek fish restaurant in the district called Mex. It was wooden, on stilts, and the sea came running in underneath. We lingered over an assortment of appetisers accompanied by arak and coca cola while lobster, prawns, sea urchins and all kinds of fish and sea food were prepared. Sometimes we pushed further to the Casino Chatby where there were acrobats, magicians, belly dancers and couples doing Spanish and ballroom dancing, and where the beach underneath was divided into separate sections for men and for women. We shared a flat with our cousins or we stayed at the Beau Rivage Hotel.

Right: Tamarind syrup being sold on a Cairo street

Olive grove on the Greek island of Paros

Egyptian dishes and these were mostly peasant foods such as *falafel, ful midames* and *melokhia* soup. The cooking of the cities and of the upper classes was mainly Turkish because the country had been part of the Ottoman Empire and the court at the time of King Farouk was Turkish. The grocers and small restaurants were Greek, and there was also French and Italian cooking because all eyes were turned towards Europe. In my own home we ate Syrian and Turkish food, as well as Spanish dishes dating from the Inquisition. There was a kind of symbiosis between the communities although everyone kept to their own ways.

After the 1956 Suez crisis which resulted in the expulsion of the French and British nationals and the departure of the Jews from Egypt, my extended family was dispersed. I had been to school in Paris for three years but was by then studying art in London. Now London has become my home, but in the Mediterranean I also feel happy and at ease like a fish in its natural waters. I have discovered that if you belong to any part of the Mediterranean you are never a stranger along its shores. The entire region, which links sixteen or so countries around the sea,

framed in the north by mountains and in the south by the desert, is a world of its own with something of the same climate and vegetation and something of a common way of life.

*　　*　　*

Geographers tell us that the Mediterranean zone coincides with the limit of the olive tree. But it has such a strong identity and it makes such a vivid impression that you do not need olive trees or fig trees or vines to recognise where you are. When visitors to France and Spain, in particular, drive towards the sea they say that the sensation at a certain point is of opening a door and entering another world. And they have, for despite the contrasts – there are bays and inlets, peninsulas and islands, mountains, plains and deserts – the Mediterranean has something which makes it different from anywhere else on earth.

Have you not been there? Everywhere it is dry with hot summers and mild winters, with rare but violent rainstorms and strong winds. The scenery is idyllic, the still blue sea and luminous sky and colours fading into pastel tints in the dazzling light, the earth grey and ochre, the houses white or rose or rusty gold. It is so dry that the luxurious vegetation is pale, not vivid green. Against it the different reds of the winter roses and of the geraniums and bougainvilia which

Mountains of fresh beans in the Cours Saleya, Nice

come out in the spring are electrifying. When you are there it seems natural that landscapes should have crept into medieval Italian painting and that Cézanne should have worked in Provence.

The area has its own characteristic smells. In the north and west you are greeted by the scent of lavender, thyme and rosemary and a whole variety of wild herbs, by the odour of fig trees and Aleppo pines basking in the sun and of smouldering leaves and vine prunings. In the east and the south there are the enchanting smells of orange and lemon blossom in winter and jasmine in summer. The heavy burnt aroma of lamb roasting on aloewood wafts through the streets mingling with incense and the perfumes of the spice shop.

The food too has a personality of its own, very sensual and strongly flavoured. The northern and Christian Mediterranean make lavish use of herbs and wine while spices and perfumes characterise the southern and eastern part. Food is cooked in olive oil, grilled over charcoal, long-simmered (the French call it *la cuisine mijotée*) and deep-fried. Sauces are thickened with bread, ground almonds or walnuts or emulsified with egg. There is a curious feeling of *déjà vu* about the octopus stew in Greece and the octopus stew in Provence, the same *aubergine caviare* in Provence as in Turkey and so many similar versions of fish soup and *ratatouille*, rice pudding and almond

pastries. There are thick omelettes, stuffed vegetables and sweet fritters everywhere; sauces begin with onions and garlic fried with tomatoes and dishes are garnished with raisins and pine-nuts.

One of the characteristics of Mediterranean cooking which is often remarked on is its sobriety. On the whole the Mediterranean is an impoverished rural world whose food is simple and rooted in the soil. The reality behind the charm of the region is one of hardship and poverty and constant struggle where everything is gained by painful effort. The soil is generally poor and often stony and shallow and only a small part can be cultivated. The weather is capricious with the constant threat from drought, landslides and storms. Crops are at the mercy of unstable elements and if the soil is not protected by crops it is swallowed by the desert or by the wilderness.

I often stay with friends in Lacoste, a medieval village perched on a hilltop in the Vaucluse in the South of France where everything seems radiant. But when I ask the farmers how they are, I am invariably told *'C'est la catastrophe!'* Either the south wind blew just before harvest time and the crops dried out, or they were attacked by frost or the rains carried away the seed. When the morrow is uncertain you have to be careful and frugal.

Why then does everyone enthuse about the heavenly raw materials of Mediterranean cooking? Because, despite the difficulties, when the conditions are right the result is so good that it is hardly credible. The entire region lives by agriculture. Lands under cultivation are scattered between great stretches of scrub and forest, both on plains and on mountain slopes. The soil is not suitable for agriculture on a large scale, but it is good for vegetable gardens and for tree crops. The produce of gardens and orchards is extraordinarily rich and varied and when it is added to the produce of the sea and of pastoralism it amounts to a superlative list of ingredients.

Both the olive and the vine are classic types of Mediterranean vegetation which require little moisture. Their long roots which seek out water deep into the soil also help them resist the wind's attack. In the past, wheat, maize and barley were important cereal crops which were sometimes rotated with chick peas, lentils and broad beans. But the grain fields have receded to make way for fruit groves and market gardens and for specialised single-crop cultivation.

Although much of the Mediterranean has remained attached to the idea of smallholders growing a variety of crops for the local market, the trend now is for specialised and mass-produced cultivation directed towards the export market. Some areas concentrate entirely on a single crop, such as rice in Egypt, olives in Tunisia, Spain and Italy, wheat and barley in Morocco, lemons in Sicily and oranges in Spain and Morocco, while many of the plains are covered by a sea of vines. And the industrialised wine and oil productions account for nearly all of the world's olive oil and three quarters of the world's trade in wine. Since the 1950s the agriculture of EEC countries has been considerably subsidised, and new technnology is widespread.

With not enough humidity nor much space for cattle raising, there is little of the butter and cream and large quantities of meat characteristic of the cooking of northern Europe. On the whole the area is sheep and goat country and stock-raising is restricted to smaller animals such as pigs and rabbits, as well as chicken and game birds which do not require fodder nor much attention. Fish and seafood are much vaunted, much loved and very highly prized. But although the variety is extraordinary, yields can be disappointing.

Right: Dried-fruit seller in the Fez medina

The cooking, like everything about Mediterranean life, is linked to the land and to the sea. And it is the combination of frugality and fruitfulness with little meat, butter and cream and an abundance of grain, vegetables, pulses, fruit, nuts and fish which gives it a unique rustic and healthy quality. But cooking is also linked to the past.

*   *   *

The Mediterranean has a glittering past which brought refinement and sophistication to the kitchen. As all the countries shared their past, this too has been a source of unity. Since ancient times there has always been intense activity around this little inland sea. Its enviable position as highway and crossroads between Europe, Africa and Asia, its natural beauty and kindly climate gave it an early importance and attracted all kinds of invaders who spread across the entire region and left their mark on the cooking as well as on the landscape.

Phoenicians created ports and established trading posts. They introduced the present-day methods of lagoon fishing, they exploited salt pans and also planted trees – it was they who first brought pomegranates. From the seventh century BC the Greeks founded colonies on the coasts and islands. They planted vineyards, orchards and olive groves on terraced foothills, grew grain on plains and used mountain forests for grazing, all of which became typical of Mediterranean agriculture. All the fish soups are part of their legacy. In the sixth century BC

Etruscans were planting vines and cutting canals to irrigate them.

The Roman imprint on the landscape, the famous classical triad of wheat, olive oil and wine, which has been the most extensive and durable, started in the second century AD. The Romans planted limes, elms, poplars and olive trees on the foothills, let the vines climb over the olive trees and planted cereals on the plains, all of which remain models of Mediterranean land use. In the kitchen they popularised the pestle and mortar and beehive outdoor bread ovens. In the seventh century much of the Mediterranean came under the Byzantine Empire which was based in Constantinople and whose mercantile power established regional trade and gave a lasting character to many coastal cities. These ancient colonisations endowed the region with a basic spirit and a cultural affinity of which cooking is a part.

But the greatest contribution to the cooking of the Mediterranean came with the spread of Islam and the Arabisation of the area. By the eighth century an Islamic empire had spread right across the region through Sicily, southern Italy and all the way to Spain where the Arabs (known as Saracens and Moors) stayed for 700 years. Many countries adopted the Muslim religion and the entire Mediterranean submitted to the influence of its civilisation. The western

Hill-side vineyards and wheat fields in Italy

Mediterranean (Spain and Sicily) was conquered by armies led by generals from the east while the soldiery was recruited in North Africa and later dynasties were centred in Morocco.

Persia was one of the first countries to be converted to Islam and the Arabs absorbed the Persians' love of fruit trees along with the notion that paradise was an orchard. They turned the Mediterranean into a vast orchard as well as a vegetable garden. They introduced many new crops such as mulberries, rice, sugar cane, apricots and oranges (the Romans had known only bitter oranges) and reintroduced lemons and pomegranates which had disappeared since Roman times. They also brought dates and bananas, artichokes and spinach, aubergines, saffron and buckwheat. All these needed watering and the Arabs installed irrigation techniques which continue to be used today.

In the Golden Age of Islam cooking reached the level of an art. Gastronomy was esteemed and the refinement of pleasure and the search for the most delicious combinations of foods became a preoccupation of the upper classes. Many of the exquisite dishes which were developed in the courts of the Caliphs gradually appeared all over the Mediterranean and they can still be found there now. These dishes combined Arab peasant foods based on wheat, pulses and vegetables with the nomadic desert diet of dates, sheep and dairy produce and the refined and exotic foods from ancient Persia. Islam meant the absence of the pig and prevalence of the goat and sheep, but it did not prevent the cultivation of the vine.

The Arabs brought the art of making sorbets and flaky pastry, ways of distilling alcohol, new methods of preserving fruit and vegetables and of salting fish. They introduced all kinds of dishes including savoury pies, meats grilled on skewers, rice dishes, meat stews with fruit, milk and rice puddings and fritters bathed in syrup.

In the thirteenth century the influences started to come from the West, especially from Spain. The kingdom of Catalunya expanded into the Mediterranean, conquering Sicily, Sardinia and Naples, and by the fourteenth century its influence penetrated Italy and the South of France into the Roussillon and Languedoc. Catalans had developed an elaborate and unique cuisine based on a mixture of Roman, Germanic and Arab styles, essentially Christian because it used pork and pork fat. They used fragrant olive oil, garlic and herbs, had a penchant for saffron and spices and the sweet and sour, combined fruit with meats and used almonds and fried onions generously. They also made great use of eggs, mushrooms and asparagus, spinach and aubergines and of the fantastic sea food which was at their disposal. The Catalans loved sauces and refined the techniques of thickening them with egg yolks, bread or nuts using the pestle and mortar.

The expulsion of the Moors after the reconquest of Spain had an enormous impact on Morocco and North

Barcelona market

Africa where the returning *Moriscos* brought Andalusian dishes to cities like Tetouan and Fez and caused a renaissance in the kitchen.

A new force came on the scene with the Turkish conquests which began in 1453 with the fall of Constantinople. The Ottoman Empire expanded over half of the Mediterranean until the end of the nineteenth century. Fierce and war-like by nature, the original nomadic Turks had little culinary sophistication. But as the Ottoman Empire grew, the Sultans' courts became notorious for their luxury and devotion to the pleasures of the table. A rich and refined style of cooking emerged at the palace of Topkapi in Istanbul. It developed from the amalgam of traditions of the conquered territories and combined Chinese and Mongolian influences with Persian, Arab and Greek ones.

On the days the Divan (cabinet) met the imperial kitchens served 4000 to 5000 people, including the Sultan, the women of the Royal Harem and the eunuchs, and up to 10 000 people on special occasions such as the visit of a foreign ambassador. The strict rules which were adopted at the palace of Topkapi so that chefs could train apprentices and assistants formed the basis of a classic Ottoman cuisine which spread from the Danube to the tip of the Arabian Peninsula, and from the Balkans to the shores of North Africa. It was brought to Bulgaria and Romania, Serbia, Yugoslavia, Hungary and Greece, Cyprus, Crete and parts of Russia, as well as to most of the Arab world, by the battalions of cooks who marched with the conquering armies or who accompanied the ruling élites which established themselves in various pockets of the Empire. Kebabs, meat balls, pilafs, stuffed vine leaves and all kinds of stuffed vegetables, yogurt dishes, little pies, vegetables cooked in olive oil, nutty pastries soaked in syrup – all these were left on Mediterranean tables when the Empire collapsed.

The Mediterranean was the centre of the world until the dawn of the seventh century. The voyages of Columbus and Vasco da Gama are supposed to have ruined it by robbing it of its role as a trade route. But these explorers brought back from the New World many of the ingredients which now characterise Mediterranean cooking. Tomatoes and peppers came via Mexico. Maize, potatoes, sweet potatoes, peanuts,

Traditional bread-baking outside Cairo

string beans, pumpkins, Jerusalem artichokes, pineapples, chocolate and vanilla are among the new crops that came from the Americas. All these, and turkeys too, came into Spain and Italy and swept towards the East, affecting all the cuisines in the most dramatic way. The western Mediterranean countries began to play an increasingly important cultural role and eventually, when the Ottoman Empire crumbled and the countries of North Africa and the Levant became colonies and semi-colonies, their influence was all-important.

France in the eighteenth century was the most impressive country in Europe. Its ideas and the kind of refinements which the French cultivated were copied throughout the Mediterranean until the mid-twentieth century. French became the *lingua franca* in most countries and Paris was the centre for those who aspired to some kind of culture. From east to west the Mediterranean rich copied the ostentatious dishes of the French bourgeoisie with their sauces, creams and butters. French *haute cuisine* was the élitist taste.

*   *   *

Looking for the imprint of the past in the Mediterranean can be fascinating and helps to explain why a dish on one side of the sea is like another on the other side. But it is even more exciting to discover the extraordinary regional diversity of the area. For here unity does not mean uniformity. Obviously a Berber village clinging to a rock has a different way of interpreting a stew from a city like Granada. The Mediterranean has many faces: eastern and western, Christian and Muslim, one intimate with the sea, one with the desert, one which knows the mountains and one which looks beyond the olive trees at northern Europe, one which is rooted to the land, another which glitters with ancient grandeur. And regional cooking reflects them all.

There are broad major styles: Arab cooking, which is best represented in Syria and Lebanon; North African (Maghrebi) which is at its purest and most refined in Morocco; Turkish Ottoman which spreads over many countries; and the cooking of southern France, Italy and Spain. All these are divided and subdivided so that every city, every town, village and hamlet, even every family has its own special ways of cooking. You cannot imagine just how fiercely and jealously each place holds on to its dishes and how it protests their originality. It is as though the very identity of the people depended on the extra teaspoon of saffron or cumin. It was touching and curious for me, especially after having found the same foods in Istanbul as in Cairo and Jerusalem, to discover the little secrets which made every dish in every place so different.

Mediterranean society is family-based and that is where real Mediterranean cooking at its best is to be found. The home cooking of a society with strong family ties, large clans and women at home has none of the rigid rules of a professional *haute cuisine*. And when dishes are passed down in the family they are full of the little touches which make them both exquisite and individual.

I once asked a wrought-iron craftsman in Turkish Anatolia who builds pavilions in Seljuk and Ottoman styles, why he thought food in Turkey was regarded as being so important. He replied, 'What we enjoy most in life is being hospitable. That is all we have. You must not eat alone.' When he married off his daughter he invited 3000 people and sat them to eat in the garden, sixteen to a tray. Hospitality and gregariousness are deeply entrenched and offering food is what life is all about. In such circumstances you develop the art of pleasing and your food becomes very lovable.

We love the Mediterranean for the sea and the radiant light, for its colours and varied forms and a hundred warm intangible smells. We love it because of its spirit and because it was the home of the magnificent civilisations which lie at the heart of our own. But it is its foods which formed our tastes that are the easiest to love.

Ingredients

WE HAVE ALL become very interested in ingredients, appreciative of quality and ready to explore. And the trade has responded by being ever more adventurous with what they are prepared to stock. Mediterranean produce has been available here for a long time, but recently many new things, such as tiny baby artichokes, kohlrabi and different types of pumpkin, have begun to appear in our supermarkets. Basil, dill, coriander, mint and other fresh herbs are on the shelf throughout the summer, while all kinds of different pasta, rice, pulses and, in some places now, couscous and cracked wheat are permanently there. Small ethnic shops sell all kinds of goods not restricted to their own speciality. You can find Middle Eastern goods such as rose water, vine leaves, filo pastry and harissa paste in Indian or Italian shops (I found Egyptian *ful midames* in a local Chinese store) and Italian and Spanish specialities in Cypriot shops. A farm in Norfolk raises continental-type pigeons and many fishmongers are selling squid, octopus and a good variety of Mediterranean fish. Almost everything is obtainable and tempting enough to charm you into buying.

I hope that once you start cooking Mediterranean dishes you will want to adopt Mediterranean foods for everyday use, in which case you should stock up your larder with good-quality olive oil, rice, pasta, lentils, beans, chickpeas, dried fruit and nuts, tins of anchovy fillets, peeled tomatoes and tomato paste, and preserves such as olives and capers. Collect a good range of spices and aromatics and always have garlic, onions, lemons and tomatoes at hand. One of the most exciting things you can do when you travel is to buy new foods and bring them home. Knowing what people eat is a good way of becoming acquainted with a country and it is great fun to wander around the markets and specialist shops. Bring back local cured meats and cheeses (these are different from those produced for export) from France, Italy and Spain, dried vegetables, fruits and nuts from Turkey, preserved lemons and olives for your North African dishes and mildly hot romesco peppers for your Spanish ones. You will find that the spices you buy in Mediterranean markets have a stronger taste and aroma than you are accustomed to, and that rose and orange blossom essences are more powerful than the diluted ones you can buy here, so you will have to be careful and use less. Some things keep very well and will prolong the pleasures of your holidays for months.

The following section is a guide to Mediterranean ingredients, many of which will be familiar to you. Some, however, are not widely available here and you can look out for them when you go travelling.

Right: Fresh vine leaves

Vegetables

Vegetables have a very important place in Mediterranean cooking. Almost all are familiar to us in the UK and although they may not always have the same quality and freshness in our supermarkets we do have them all the year round.

Now that you are often allowed to rummage through vegetable stalls and even supermarket shelves it is important to learn how to recognise the best. Vegetables should always be firm – never soft and limp or tired-looking and damaged – and they must smell fresh and good. Skins should be shiny, not dry and wrinkled or blemished. This may seem obvious but it is surprising how many people are still afraid to feel and smell produce. Once you start taking a real interest in what you buy and become more adventurous, you can turn shopping into an art as well as a pleasure.

Asparagus
In the western Mediterranean asparagus grows wild in meadows and on sandy coasts and many species are cultivated. It should be firm and freshly gathered.

Aubergine
Aubergines are the most popular vegetable in the Mediterranean. There are many different kinds – long and round, big and small, with colours ranging from white through yellow and green to mauve, purple and black. The long purple-black one is widely available here. Medium-sized ones are good for stuffing, while tiny ones, white or mauve, are used for pickling whole and for making into jam. Large aubergines are cubed and used in stews, omelettes and gratin dishes or fried in slices or roasted whole. Buy them firm with a shiny unblemished and unwrinkled skin.

Artichoke
The only type of artichokes found in the UK are the common large globe artichokes. You only eat the heart, or bottom, and the little bit of flesh at the base of the leaves which you can nibble off when you pull the cooked leaves away from the heart. In the eastern Mediterranean most dishes deal only with the hearts pared of leaves and emptied of the hairy choke. Tiny globe artichokes can be eaten whole before the choke starts to grow although you need to remove the first row of leaves and cut off the dark tough tips and peel the stems. If they are very young you can eat them raw or marinated.

Beans
French (green) beans must be very fresh to be good. The tiny green ones have a delicious flavour. If they are young, beans only need to be topped and tailed but with older ones you will need to cut away the stringy edges. Unless they are very young large runner beans tend to be tough and stringy.

Broad beans
Young fresh broad beans can be so tender they can be eaten in the pod. Otherwise they need to be shelled. Quite often the tough outer skin of the bean also needs to be removed, especially by the end of the season. Frozen broad beans are an acceptable substitute for fresh ones.

Avocado
This was introduced into the area by Israel. The usual green avocado is ripe enough to eat when it yields slightly all over and becomes slightly patched with brown. It is a good idea to buy it hard and let it ripen at home for two or three days. (Refrigeration will slow down the ripening process.) There is also a dark purple-green, horny skinned variety, and a very small green one without a stone.

Beetroot
You can buy these raw or already cooked. They are mostly used for salads.

Red cabbage

Cardoon
This relative of the artichoke family is very popular in the Mediterranean but you cannot yet find it sold commercially in the UK. On the continent it is usually sold trimmed of the prickly outer stems and leaves. You eat the hearts or inner stalks.

Cabbage
White and Savoy cabbage are used in stews and for stuffing and red cabbage is occasionally used for salads.

Broccoli
There are purple, green and white flowering kinds of this Italian vegetable. The bright green one called calabrese (it was first grown in Calabria) is especially good and comes in larger clumps than the other two.

Carrot
In the East older carrots are preferred for their stronger flavour.

White cabbage

Cauliflower
In the Mediterranean this familiar vegetable is put into stews and cooked in fritter batter.

Savoy cabbage

Celeriac
This large hard round root from the celery family has a delicate flavour. It needs to be peeled and cut into pieces before cooking.

Celery
The leaves are used as a herb, the stalks are cooked or eaten raw.

Chicory

There are different kinds of wild and garden chicory. Besides the compact white cigar-shaped one (confusingly called endive in France) there is the Italian dark red and white variety called radicchio (see p. 26), and wild varieties which have green and curly leaves. They all have an agreeably bitter flavour which is stronger with the wild ones. They are eaten raw in salads and can also be cooked.

Cucumber

There are many different varieties of this vegetable which are widely used for salads. Apart from the familiar long smooth cucumbers, there are small ones used for pickling, and others with a rough, ridged skin.

Colocasia

This potato-like tuber has a delicate flavour. Like the potato it can be peeled and boiled, roasted in its jacket, mashed, fried in slices, or cooked in a stew. It is eaten mostly in the eastern Mediterranean.

Courgette

Young tiny courgettes can be cooked whole while medium ones are good for stuffing. In the East courgettes are hollowed out for stuffing, while in the West they are first cut lengthways in half. They do not need peeling – just trim the ends. The bright yellow courgette flowers are delicacies and can be stuffed, battered and deep-fried, or cooked in soup.

Dandelion

The leaves are used for salads or cooked like spinach. You can gather them young and fresh from the fields.

Endive

Confusingly called 'chicoree frisée' in France, the endive has a very pleasant, refreshingly bitter flavour. It can either be served raw in salads or cooked as a side vegetable. Batavian endive or escarole (scarole in French) has broader leaves.

Garlic

Garlic is often eaten as a side vegetable in France and Spain where it is baked whole in a hot oven, which causes it to acquire a delicious gentle flavour.

Jerusalem artichokes

As Jerusalem artichokes are knobbly and difficult to peel, try to pick out the smoothest ones. They have a beautiful taste, a little like that of globe artichokes although they are not related.

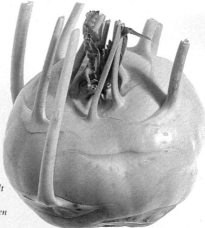

Fennel

Fennel has a delicate aniseed flavour and a fresh aroma. The feathery leaves are the most aromatic part. Wild fennel grows like a weed and is used as a herb.

Kohlrabi

This vegetable is a swollen stem, not a root. It can be peeled and sliced in salads, ot cut into sticks and cooked like turnips or celeriac. When it is young and tender it has an even better flavour and can be eaten raw in salads.

24

Lamb's lettuce
This plant is both cultivated in the Mediterranean and grows wild. The soft leaves go into salads and are also cooked.

Leeks
Leeks need to be cleaned thoroughly as the packed leaves contain a lot of grit. Chopped leeks are sometimes used for flavouring instead of onion or spring onions. Small thin leeks have the best flavour.

Lettuce
The usual Mediterranean salad is cos. Buy it crisp and fresh and look for a tight heart. Large leaves can be stuffed. Small closely packed lettuce are braised whole. Each country has other native varieties.

Mallow
The leaves, which have a viscous juice, are cooked or eaten raw in salad. Melokhia is the Arab name of a member of the mallow family which is popular in the Eastern Mediterranean. The chopped spinach-like leaf gives a jellied quality to a soup of which the Egyptians are fond.

Mange-tout peas
These are found mainly in France. The sweet and juicy pods only need to be topped and tailed before brief cooking.

Marrow
The flavour of marrow is not as attractive as that of courgette or pumpkin although it is part of the same family and is used in the same kinds of dishes.

Mushrooms
There are numerous species of mushrooms, both cultivated and wild. The delicious wild mushrooms such as cep (with small tight caps or with huge plate-sized ones), morel and girolle can be found in most Mediterranean markets and are now becoming more available in the UK. Choose fairly large cup-shaped mushrooms for stuffing.

Girolle

Morel

Field mushroom

Okra
This is one of the most popular vegetables of the eastern Mediterranean where it is called bamia. Other names for it are ladies' fingers and gumbo. The small and large varieties are equally good even if they have slightly blackened corners. The best way to find out if they are stringy and tough is to bite into one. To prepare, trim the calyx but do not slice into the okra as the mucilaginous juice will run out. This juice helps to make a rich jellied sauce.

Onions

The Mediterranean has many varieties of onions including the fresh white-bulbed ones, the smaller, more powerful ones, large Spanish and mild red Italian ones, shallots and spring onions. Many Mediterranean sauces and stews start with a base of chopped sautéed onions. They can also be braised, roasted, grilled or stuffed.

Peas

It is not easy to find peas young, small and sweet but this is the only way they are worth eating fresh. They are used more in the western Mediterranean. Frozen petits pois are better than large hard fresh peas.

Peppers

Peppers are one of the great vegetables of the Mediterranean. They give colour to the cooking with their brilliant shades. Red and yellow peppers are more mature and sweeter than green ones. Choose medium-sized ones for stuffing, small slim ones for frying whole and plump fleshy ones for grilling. Tiny chillies are very hot and peppery. Do not touch your face when you are cutting them as the juice stings the eyes and mouth very badly.

Pumpkin

Pumpkins are used all over the Mediterranean in a variety of both savoury and sweet dishes. They can be long or round, pale or dark green, yellow or orange, mottled or streaked. The kinds with orange-coloured flesh have a distinctive sweet flavour. The only way of knowing that a pumpkin is not going to be stringy or unpleasant in flavour is to taste a piece.

Potato

This vegetable is not served as a side dish in the Mediterranean as often as it is in Northern Europe and the Americas, but it is used as an ingredient in many dishes.

Radicchio

Radicchio is a type of chicory with a pleasant bitter taste. It is widely used in salads.

Radish

The usual round scarlet variety of radish can grow to a huge size in the Mediterranean. There are also other species including long violet, black and white radishes which usually have a more powerful taste. The strong flavour of radishes is an appetite-whetter so they make an ideal hors d'oeuvre. Radishes are served whole or chopped up in salads. Be sure that they are firm and crisp.

Salsify

The salsify, or oyster plant (a black variety is called scorzonera) comes from the western Mediterranean. It needs to be scraped and washed before using.

Sorrel

Sorrel grows mostly in France where it is used in salads, soups and sauces. There is both a wild and a garden variety. Both are sharp and lemony-tasting but the wild variety is more so.

Swiss chard

This is also called spinach beet because it belongs to the beetroot family. It is grown both for the green spinach-like leaves and the large white ribs which are the chards. The chards are considered the best part and the two are often cooked separately.

Spinach

This is one of the most common and popular vegetables and lends itself to many uses. There are different varieties with larger and smaller leaves.

Sweetcorn

Sweetcorn is a street food in the eastern Mediterranean; it is sold boiled in Israel, grilled on charcoal in Egypt.

Sweet potato

There are several different species of this tuber with white, yellow or pink flesh. The yellow one has the sweetest flavour. They are cooked like potatoes, ie boiled, roasted or fried.

Tomatoes

The most common are the large knobbly ones and the small long plum tomatoes. Use ripe tomatoes for cooking and firm, even slightly green ones for salad.

Truffles

The rich-flavoured French black (above) and Italian white truffles are the most expensive vegetables in the world. They are either eaten raw, sliced very thinly over a dish, or are used as a flavouring, e.g. in sauces.

Turnips

Look for small young turnips which have a delicate flavour.

Vine leaves

Young tender leaves are needed for the famous rice and meat stuffed vine leaves of the eastern Mediterranean. They are softened by poaching for a few seconds before they are filled. Larger ones are used to wrap fish and quails when they are cooked on charcoal. The ones sold in the UK packed in brine need to be soaked before using.

Fruit

In the Mediterranean the traditional and prestigious way to end a meal is with fruit. There are relatively few desserts besides fruit – puddings and pastries are usually reserved for special and festive occasions. I suppose it is difficult to match the pleasure given by a bowl of ripe fruit when there is such quality and variety.

Most cookery books neglect to champion fresh fruit as a dessert but I would like to sing its praise and urge you to serve it every day at home and also to make it a sweet course for your parties. Apart from being healthy and light, it is just right with Mediterranean food.

Other western Mediterranean ways of eating fruit include macerating it in wine or chopping it up in a fruit salad. Make one in the usual way by combining fruits with contrasting flavours, textures and colours, sprinkle with lemon or orange juice or a mixture of both and add a little caster sugar which will draw out the natural juices, softening the fruit and adding extra liquid. If you like, add some sweet liqueur, spirit or wine as well. In winter in the eastern Mediterranean an assortment of dried fruit such as apricots, figs, prunes, dates and raisins and sultanas is provided along with nuts for guests to pick at. It is the custom for people to stuff the fruits with walnuts or almonds and to present them solicitously to a neighbour at the table. Once, when I was eating with a Moroccan friend in Paris, she stuffed a dried fig with a piece of walnut and a tangerine segment and continued to feed me in this way to my great delight.

Fruit also has a very important place in the Mediterranean kitchen. Apart from its uses in the form of fruit juices and syrups, it is made into spoon sweets (see p. 57) and preserves, pastes, sweetmeats and winter compotes. In Italy they make luscious fruit sorbets and ice creams, while France specialises in tarts, candied fruits and fruits preserved in syrup or alcohol.

There is also a very old tradition of using fruit in savoury dishes. Apricots, dates and prunes are cooked with lamb, apples with pork, pears with goose and duck, quince with fish, lamb and pork. Raisins, usually partnered with pine-nuts, go into all kinds of dishes. Many of these fruit/meat combinations are a legacy of ancient Persia and appear particularly in the cuisine of Morocco and Tunisia.

Apricots
The musk-apricot has the best flavour. The white-fleshed clingstone is sharp while the peach apricot is fragrant, juicy and sweet. Eat them when they are ripe – slightly soft and deep orange.

Apples
Look out for the less common eating varieties. Both eating and cooking apples can be used for cooking.

Cherries
Taste these before buying as they vary so much. There are sweet and sour varieties, red and black and there are golden white ones and morellos.

Bananas
Buy them slightly underripe – still slightly greenish, so that you eat them when they are just right.

Cape gooseberries or physalis
Sweet and golden, these are also called Chinese lanterns because of the papery husks that cover them. For an elegant presentation pull the protective dry calyx away from the berry and let it crown the fruit like a winged bow.

Cherimoya
This is also called a custard apple because the sweet, scented white flesh is so creamy. Although the scaly skin looks hard and leathery it is soft and you must be careful not to squash the fruit. Eat the flesh with a spoon.

Dates
Fresh dates should be eaten quickly as they go sour. There are different varieties including dark brown, red and golden ones. They are deliciously soft and sweet and their smooth skins come off easily.

Figs
There are many fig varieties, green, gold, white, purple and mauve, and even the same variety can vary greatly in taste from fig to fig. The magnificent and sweet flavour is best when the fruit is slightly warm.

Grapefruit
Pink ones are sweeter than yellow ones.

Grapes
From green- and gold-skinned to red and blue-black, with or without seeds, grapes vary so much that you really must taste them before you buy them.

Guavas
These have a soft but gritty, salmon-coloured flesh with a strong scent and an unusual sharp flavour. They contain lots of little seeds which can be eaten.

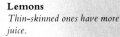

Lemons
Thin-skinned ones have more juice.

Limes
The flavour of the lime is stronger than that of the lemon but the two fruits can usually be used interchangeably.

Loquats
The flesh of loquats is tart, juicy and firm, but because the stone is large in proportion to the flesh it is not considered a very 'worthwhile' fruit.

Melons

The cantaloup varieties, Charantais and Ogen, and the musks, such as Galia, are strongly scented. The cheaper, pale-fleshed winter honeydew does not have as much flavour. Choose a melon that feels heavy for its size. If it is soft when you press it gently at the stalk end, it is ripe. It is best eaten chilled.

Mangoes

This is an exquisite fruit and makes a grand dessert. But some mangoes are stringy with a sort of turpentine flavour and, with the exception of the Alphonse variety, it is not always easy to tell when they are good. Eat them ripe. The best way to cut them is close to the long stone on both sides using a sharp knife. Note that it is difficult to get rid of the bright orange stains of the juice.

Medlars

Medlars grow wild and you cannot usually buy them. They need to be brown and over-ripe before you can eat the creamy flesh.

Mulberries

Mulberries are tart and juicy with a bright purple juice which leaves stains. You are more likely to pick them from the tree than find them in the shops.

Nectarines

Nectarines are like smooth-skinned peaches, but they are sweeter. They have white or yellow flesh.

Pears

The most usual varieties are Conference, Comice, Williams and Beurré Hardy. Buy them hard as they ripen very quickly and become too soft.

Oranges

There are many different kinds including the Valencia, Jaffa and navel orange. Blood oranges are sharper and the bitter Seville orange is used for flavouring and is made into preserves as are the miniature oranges called kumquats.

Peaches

Mediterranean peaches can be magnificent. White ones are said to taste better than orange ones but this is not always true. Really it is difficult to tell which will be good before you taste them.

Persimmons
Some varieties of this fruit have a metallic aftertaste if they are not ripe. The Israeli sharon type are sweet and delicious even when they are hard. You can either slice them or cut off the top and eat them with a spoon.

Plums
There are many varieties such as Victoria, Santa Rosa, blue plums and damsons. Mirabelles and greengages are the sweetest and most fragrant.

Pomeloes
These are like large, soft-skinned, sweet grapefruit.

Pomegranates
ut these open and scoop the pink juicy ds out into a bowl. They have more fume than flavour and are not as pleasant eat as they are to decorate a dish. The ce of sour pomegranates is used as a vouring in cooking.

Prickly pears or Barbary figs
This is the fruit of a kind of cactus plant and it is covered with the same kind of hairy thin spines as the cactus. The prickles are terribly difficult to get rid of but you can wash them off carefully under the tap. To peel the fruit, hold it using a fork or rubber gloves. The flesh is soft and orange with plenty of seeds which you can eat.

Strawberries
Although strawberries are mostly cultivated rather than wild in the Mediterranean, they are sweet, juicy and deliciously scented.

Quinces
There are a few golden varieties which make rare appearances in UK shops. They have a wonderful fragrance but they are too bitter to be eaten raw. The flesh turns pink and the flavour is magnificent when they are cooked in syrup, baked or made into preserves.

Rhubarb
The young pink stems of rhubarb are stewed.

Watermelon
Watermelons can have pale green or very dark skin but the flesh must be red and sweet. You cannot always tell if it is good and ripe but you can try tapping it and listening for a hollow sound. It is usual for vendors to cut out a small square piece as a sample. Serve them very cold.

Tangerines
Clementines are sweeter than satsumas.

Fish and seafood

Not many fish arrive here directly from the Mediterranean but nearly all Mediterranean varieties are now appearing in fishmongers in the UK. They are either imported fresh from countries such as Portugal, the Seychelle Islands and Brazil, or, in the case of red mullet and the once-despised monkfish, are caught in British waters. Generally, they are larger, fatter and vastly superior in texture and flavour to those caught in the Mediterranean because they come from richer seas and colder, less polluted waters. You can find almost everything in Britain if you know where to go and what to ask for, and not all of it is expensive. Some, but not all fish are available all year round. Others appear from time to time so you should be on the look out for the more interesting varieties. A few items, such as octopus and scampi, are quite acceptable frozen. Except for certain fish, like the legendary bony *rascasse* which gives a distinctive flavour to fish stocks, what you cannot find can usually be substituted for. So you have no excuse for not making Mediterranean fish dishes.

Do get into the habit of cooking fish. The more familiar you are with it, the more you will enjoy it. Try to buy fish and seafood the day you want to eat it because it spoils very quickly. When you buy fish it must be absolutely fresh and smell of the sea. The eyes must be bright and clear, the gills bright pink or red and the flesh firm. When you press it with your finger it should not leave an indentation and when you pick it up it should not flop. Shellfish and, if possible, crustaceans should be bought alive. Ask the fishmonger to scale, clean, fillet or skin fish; they should be happy to prepare it anyway you want it.

The fresh fish and seafood shown here are the ones commonly used on the Mediterranean coasts which are mostly available in the UK.

Anchovy
The oily flesh of the anchovy is very delicate and full of flavour. It is not easy to obtain fresh anchovies in the UK.

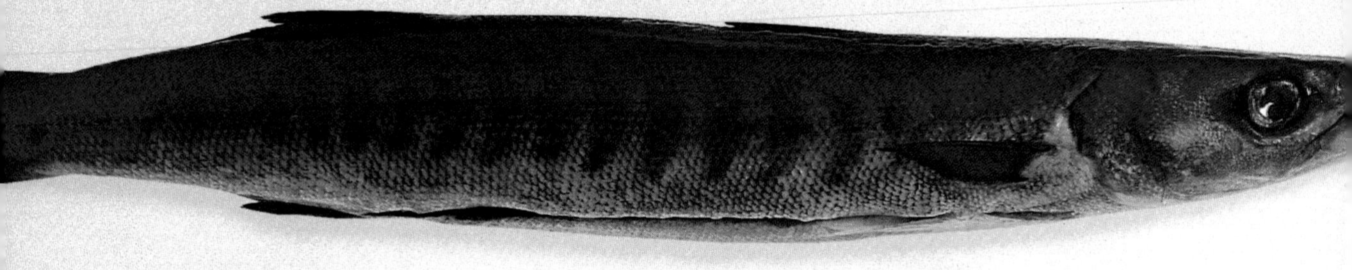

Barracuda
Its lean white flesh has a fine flavour.

Brill
This oval fish looks like turbot but it is cheaper and tastes even better – light and delicate with a firm white flesh. The spine needs to be trimmed and broken so that it does not curl up during cooking.

Clams
There are different kinds of both hard- and soft-shelled clams. The former, if large, can be rubbery unless marinated before cooking.

Cockles
Cockles are usually sold here pre-cooked. Try to avoid the ones steeped in vinegar.

Crab
There are several kinds of crab including spider crabs (illustrated) which have a strong sweetish flavour but not much flesh, and dull green, soft-shelled crabs. The white and dark meat of crabs have very different flavours. Try to buy them live and cook them yourself.

Cuttlefish
Cuttlefish are not as common here as their near relation, the squid. The beak, eyes and innards all need to be removed before cooking (see p. 145). The flesh is very sweet and needs little cooking.

Eel
There are different varieties of eel. The common eel starts its life in fresh water before moving out to sea, but both the conger and the moray eel are purely saltwater fish. The moray is considered to have the finest flavour in the eel family. Eels are usually bought alive and because they are so slippery they are difficult to handle.

Snails
There are different kinds and colours, large and small. Vineyard snails are the most popular. They must be purged (starved), preferably for three days, before they are eaten.

Frogs' legs
Often available ready-prepared at fishmongers, frog's legs taste a bit like chicken. The smaller they are, the better flavour they have.

Flounder
This is a delicious flat fish which can be substituted for sole.

Grey mullet
All varieties of grey mullet are long, slim, with a good-flavoured medium-firm flesh. As they shoal in river estuaries their gut cavity may smell and need to be washed well. The roe of one species is used to make poutargue *and* tarama.

Grouper
This fish with its firm, lean, well flavoured flesh is considered a delicacy. Get your fishmonger to remove its thick scales.

Hake
Though often small in size in the Mediterranean, hake can be very large here. It has a good flavour and a soft texture.

John Dory
Oval and flat, John Dory looks to be all bony head but the white flesh is highly regarded for its firm texture and delicious flavour. The black spot on either side is a distinguishing feature.

Lobster
The different species include spiny, or rock lobster (also called crawfish) which lacks the large claws of the common lobster. Dublin Bay prawns or Italian scampi, though smaller with less flesh, belong to the same family.

Mackerel
This delicious, cheap, strongly flavoured oily fish is widely available and very versatile.

Octopus
The flavour of octopus is in a league of its own. It is readily available in the UK, cleaned and tenderised (see p. 143).

Monkfish
The head of the monkfish is thought to be so ugly that fishmongers only display it already beheaded. The tail though, has the most wonderful firm and delicious flesh.

Mussels
Mussels are popular all over the Mediterranean. Cooking them is the easiest way of opening their shells but in Turkey they are sold raw already shelled. They need to be scrubbed and bearded before cooking.

Scallops
Scallops, though expensive, have a wonderful flavour and are very easy and quick to cook. Because the coral has a softer texture than the white scallop muscle it needs even less cooking time.

Prawns
There are different kinds of prawns found all over the Mediterranean – grey, rose, red and grey – including large fat-tailed ones and tiny ones.

Sardine
Fresh sardines are becoming more available in the UK.

Red mullet
*The colours of this highly esteemed fish range
from rosy red shot with gold to dark red. They
come in various sizes – mostly small, but the
bigger ones have an incomparable flavour if you
can get them. Small ones do not need gutting. The
liver of the red mullet is considered a delicacy.*

Scorpion fish
*This is the rascasse of bouillabaisse fame which, more than
any fish, is symbolic of the Mediterranean. Unfortunately
it is not yet widely available in the UK. It has little
edible flesh but is used for the special aroma it
gives to soup and stocks.*

Sea bass
*Sea bass is one of the noblest and most wonderful of all
Mediterranean fish. It has fine and delicate flesh of medium-firm
texture, few bones and a most remarkable sweet flavour.*

Sea bream
*This beautiful fish is highly esteemed in the
Mediterranean. Its white flesh is lean and flaky with
an exquisite taste. Of the many species, the best is
the gilt-head or royal bream with golden spots on the
cheeks and a golden crescent between the eyes.*

Sea urchin
These round prickly creatures are usually eaten raw. They are cut in half and their red coral is scooped out and eaten either on its own or with bread and lemon juice.

Sprat
A member of the herring family, the sprat has a lot of bones, like the sardine, but it has a pleasant flavour and is not as oily.

Shad
The shad is both a freshwater and a sea fish. It has plenty of bones but the soft and oily flesh is fat with a good rich flavour.

Skate
Skate (or ray) wings, with their long strands of bone and cartilage, are the only parts of this fish sold in the shops. Easy to cook, skate has a lean and firm flesh. It is the only fish which can be kept a little longer than usual in the refrigerator.

Sole
This widely available fish is highly regarded in the Mediterranean. It has firm, white, lean flesh and a delicate flavour.

Squid
The squid has an elongated body well suited to stuffing. For preparation, see p. 145.

Tuna
There are different kinds of tuna, of which the most common in the UK comes from a large species and is usually sold in steaks. All kinds have a firm, dark (almost meat-coloured) richly flavoured flesh. The best part is the stomach section which is tender and delicate.

Swordfish
Swordfish is usually sold in meaty steaks. Its flesh is pale pink and firm with a delicate flavour.

Whitebait
This is the name given to different kinds of very tiny baby fish which might include red or grey mullet.

Turbot
The white flesh of this highly regarded fish has an exquisite and subtle flavour.

Whiting
The flesh of the whiting is light and lean with a fine, flaky texture. It is very inexpensive here.

Dairy produce

Butter
Butter (unsalted) is used in hot dishes in Arab and Turkish cooking but is less commonly used elsewhere in the Mediterranean.

Clarified butter
Clarified butter, called *smen* or *samna* in the Arab world, is butter – usually made from buffalo's milk – which has been melted down and strained through thin muslin so that the impurities which cause butter to burn and to go stale are eliminated. It becomes rich and so strong that much less is needed than fresh butter. It has a distinctive taste and smell and keeps very well – often for many years.

Cream
Cream is not a cooking ingredient in the Mediterranean. It is not used in sauces, not even in southern France. However, there is a delicious Middle Eastern cream called *kaymak* made from buffalo's milk which is so thick that it has to be cut with a knife, and it is served with desserts and spoon sweets (see p. 57). The closest thing to kaymak here is clotted cream but whipped double cream is a good substitute.

Milk
Milk puddings made with ground rice, cornflour or semolina are a feature of Mediterranean and especially of Middle Eastern cooking. Provence is famous for its egg and milk flans, but otherwise there is not much cooking with milk.

Yogurt
Several countries boast of making the best yogurt. The best that I have eaten was in Turkey. It was made from buffalo's milk and was thick, creamy and sweet tasting. Yogurt plays an important part in Arab and Ottoman cooking but it has only just started to be used in North Africa. It is mostly used uncooked but if you need to heat it in a soup or stew you must 'stabilise' it first so that it does not curdle. To do this, beat in a tablespoonful of cornflour or a raw egg white (I use both for safety) and bring it slowly to the boil, stirring all the time in the same direction. When you feel it thickening it is ready to be used. You can now buy ewe's milk yogurt and thick, strained yogurt in the UK which are used in many dishes.

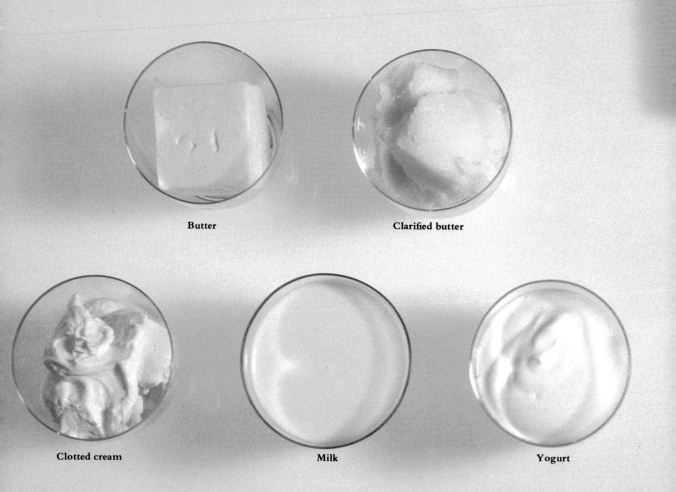

Butter   Clarified butter

Clotted cream   Milk   Yogurt

Cheese

Southern France and Italy have a large selection of cheeses for eating, but eating cheese on its own has never become a habit in the eastern Mediterranean. There people usually have it for breakfast or as an appetiser – grilled or fried or simply cut up into pieces. In the east cheese-making has traditionally been left to the Greeks and Turks and cheeses are often called *gebna rumi*, which means Greek cheese. Mediterranean cheeses are largely made from goat's, ewe's and buffalo's milk.

For cooking, feta and halumi are used in the Middle East, Parmesan, pecorino, mozzarella and ricotta in Italy, fromage blanc, Parmesan, and Gruyère in France and Tunisia. Spanish cheeses are not yet generally available in the UK. The flavour of freshly grated Parmesan is far superior to that of the packaged, ready-grated type, so buy a piece and grate it as you need it. It keeps in the refrigerator if you wrap it up well. Aged pecorino can be grated like Parmesan but it is very much sharper and is best only used in dishes featuring strong flavours.

Make sure that ricotta is fresh when you buy it and use it as soon as you can. A bland soft cheese, it tastes rancid after two days. In the Middle East there is a similar version simply called 'white cheese', *gebna beyda*, and this is mostly used as a filling for pastries such as pancakes and *konafa*, which are then bathed in sugar syrup. In Spain a similar curd cheese is called *requeson*.

Feta   Halumi   Parmesan   Pecorino

Fromage blanc   Gruyère   Mozzarella   Ricotta

Pulses

Chickpeas and all kinds of beans, lentils and split peas are the peasant and homely foods of the Mediterranean. They go into salads (sometimes as purées), stews and soups. They are a rich source of fibre, fat, minerals and vitamins and are exceptionally healthy foods. It is the combination and interaction in the body with certain other ingredients which releases and completes the proteins contained in the pulses. The traditional Mediterranean dishes which mix pulses with vegetables, rice, wheat and meat provide just this magic combination.

It is easy to deal with pulses. They keep well for at least a year and often for very much longer. (If they do go bad you will be able to tell by the smell when you open the container!) Years ago most pulses needed overnight soaking but these days, with modern ways of processing and because they reach the shops younger, they generally only need an hour of soaking or none at all. But tradition is strong and many people soak them overnight which does have the advantage of cutting the cooking time. The cooking time depends on their age and type. It can vary from 15 minutes for lentils, to 1–3 hours for broad beans. Add salt when the pulses have begun to soften. Thick-skinned beans like kidney or borlotti beans need 10 minutes' rapid boiling at the beginning of cooking to neutralise toxins.

The following are the most commonly used in the Mediterranean:

Broad beans
Broad beans, both small (an Egyptian variety) and large, are brown but look white when sold without their skins. They need soaking for at least an hour (preferably 3–4 hours) and usually need lengthy cooking.

Chickpeas
Chickpeas are popular all over the Mediterranean. They come in large and small varieties and both can be used in numerous dishes from soups and stews to salads and cream dips. Chickpea flour sold here in Indian shops as gram flour or besan is used in Nice and Sicily.

Black-eyed beans
Black-eyed beans are used in salads and casseroles.

Borlotti beans
Borlotti beans are much used in Italy.

Nuts

The Persians, the Arabs and the Ottomans used nuts to thicken sauces and to decorate dishes. Most of their pastries and sweetmeats are either made with nuts, filled with nuts or garnished with nuts. They introduced them throughout the Mediterranean.

Chestnuts
Although mostly used in desserts, chestnuts are also used in a number of savoury dishes. In Italy dried chestnuts and chestnut flour are also used.

Almonds
Almonds are widespread in Mediterranean cooking. They are blanched and used whole, chopped or finely ground. Toasting or frying whole blanched almonds brings out their full flavour.

Coconut
Coconut is used grated in puddings and sweets.

Hazelnuts
Hazelnuts are used mostly in pastries where they make a cheaper alternative to almonds.

Flageolets
Flageolets are used in French and Italian dishes. It is not really necessary to soak them.

Haricot beans
Haricot beans are used throughout the Mediterranean and are especially prominent in French, Italian, Spanish, Turkish and Greek cooking where they are used in casseroles, soups and salads. They need a few hours' soaking.

Red kidney beans
Red kidney beans are used in soups and salads in most countries.

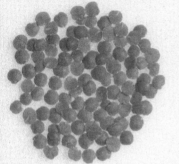

Red lentils

Large green lentils

Brown lentils

Lentils
Lentils are used in soups, salads, stews and mixed with rice. The larger green and brown varieties can be soaked in water for an hour to reduce the cooking time but this is not really necessary.

Yellow split peas

Green split peas

Yellow and green split peas
Yellow and green split peas mostly go into soups and stews.

Pistachio nuts
Pistachio nuts are very expensive but they have an exquisite flavour. They are mostly used in pastries and to decorate puddings. It's easier to buy them already shelled.

Pine-nuts
The kernels of the stone pine cone are very expensive but they are important in Mediterranean cookery. Their unique flavour is brought out if they are very lightly roasted under the grill or gently fried in a dry frying-pan. They are used in both savoury and sweet dishes, are often partnered with fried onions and raisins and go into minced meat fillings.

Walnuts
Chopped, these nuts go into all the usual nutty pastries and into many savoury dishes too. Pounded, they are used to make hot and cold sauces. Walnuts are particularly oily and tend to go stale so you must taste them before you use them. They keep best in their shells. The large, lighter coloured ones have the best flavour.

Grains

Rice and wheat are staples in the Mediterranean and hardly a family meal goes by without one or the other being served. Rice is either served plain, accompanied by a sauce or stew, or with other ingredients mixed in, for example, as a risotto, paella or pilaf. Wheat is eaten in the form of pasta or gnocchi, as cracked wheat or couscous and also whole as ferik when it is young and green. Other grains of the region are barley, millet, rye and maize. Coarse maize flour is used to make the Italian polenta.

Couscous
Couscous is a kind of hard wheat semolina which has been ground, then moistened and rolled in flour. It is the most popular food and the national dish of Morocco, Algeria and Tunisia and it is also an old traditional dish of Sicily. The grain is steamed and served with a stew or broth or with a garnish, and there are also sweet couscous dishes. The couscous found here in packets is precooked. It is very easy to use and the result can be close to the real thing if it is handled properly (see p. 178).

Cracked wheat
This is a staple of the rural parts of Turkey, Syria and Lebanon. Arabs call it burghul, Turks call it bulgur and to Cypriots it is pourgouri. It is whole wheat which has already been boiled until just tender and the husk is about to crack open, then dried (usually spread out on a cloth in the open) and ground. It only needs to soak up water or broth and requires little or no cooking as it has already been cooked. You can buy it coarse or fine ground.

Semolina
Semolina is coarsely ground durum wheat. Italians use it to make gnocchi and in the eastern Mediterranean it is the basis of many pastries which are usually soaked in sugar syrup.

Rice

Rice is one of the distinctive ingredients of Mediterranean cooking. It originally came from India through Iran and was spread by the Arabs all the way to Italy and Spain. In the Arab world and the countries which were once part of the Ottoman Empire, rice is an urban staple but it is not much eaten in North Africa where couscous predominates.

Many different species grow in the marshland areas of the Mediterranean and each has a different character, flavour and texture. While short grained rice is most common, long grain rice is also popular, especially in the eastern Mediterranean. All the rice is milled and white, but varieties differ in terms of the amount of water they absorb, the coating of starchy flour which becomes sticky with cooking, and the hardness of the core which keeps the grain from falling apart. Every region has developed different tastes and likes rice cooked differently.

For Middle Eastern pilafs and French dishes use *patna* rice – a long thin hard grain, or *Carolina* – a long fat grain, both of which remain whole, firm (though tender) and separate when cooked. Use short-grain rice such as Italian *arborio* or *risotto* rice, which is round and starchy, for puddings (where it disintegrates into a jelly), for stuffings (where it needs to be sticky) and in Italian and Spanish dishes where it becomes soft and creamy while keeping a certain wholeness and a slightly resistant core. You will rarely find the very tiny and hard varieties of rice from the region of Valencia which give the paellas of Spain their unique quality. Arborio is the closest you can get to them.

Pudding rice   **Arborio rice**   **Spanish rice**   **Patna rice**

Olives

Throughout the Mediterranean region there are hundreds of different varieties of olives and you can see them in markets in all shapes, sizes and colours. The sight is quite remarkable.

Olives are the most commonly served and simple appetiser, often accompanied by nuts, pieces of cheese, tomatoes and charcuterie. In the eastern Mediterranean olives are eaten for breakfast with bread and cheese. They are used in cooking – in stews, sauces, tarts, salads and breads – though not in Arab and Turkish dishes.

Olives must be cured before you can eat them. They can be picked while still green or yellow or, as they ripen, from red to violet, purple and black. To remove their unpleasant, acrid taste

they are soaked in water for about twelve days, the water being changed daily, or they are rolled in salt, ash or rye and left while their juices drain away. Then they are gently crushed or pricked to bruise their skins and soaked in a brine of 125 g (4 oz) salt to 1.2 litres (2 pints) water.

Traditional embellishments are lemon, vinegar and wine, or bitter orange juice. Other flavourings such as garlic, chillies, coriander seeds, paprika, cayenne and fresh herbs lend a special regional flavour. You can add these to drained ready-cured olives at home, then cover them with oil.

Olives can be pitted, then stuffed with anchovies, blanched almonds or capers.

Green olives

Black olives

Cracked Moroccan olives

Niçois olives

Olives stuffed with almonds

Pastry

Filo dough
Filo *or* phyllo *is paper-thin dough made with flour and water. Used all over the eastern Mediterranean, it is sold in sheets in airtight packets of 500 g (about 1 lb). As the sheets dry out quickly they should only be taken out of the packet when you are ready to use them.*

Kadaif dough
Kadaif *or* konafa *is used to make pastries of the same name in Greece, Turkey and the Middle East. A flour and water batter is poured through a sieve on to a moving hot plate with burners underneath. It sets as soon as it touches the plate and is removed immediately. The resulting soft, white, vermicelli-like strands can be bought ready-made in 500 g (1 lb) bags from Greek and Turkish grocers.*

Oils and vinegars

Olive oil is the natural and traditional cooking oil of the Mediterranean and its flavour and perfume characterise the cooking of the region. In several of the countries it is used almost exclusively.

Lard or pork fat is used in Italy, Provence and Spain for certain dishes, as is goose fat in the Languedoc region of southern France. In several Middle Eastern countries the rule is to use olive oil for dishes to be eaten cold because the oil does not congeal, and butter or clarified butter for hot dishes. Some of the countries are desert lands which have inherited the nomadic custom of using sheep's tail fat. But vegetable oils are now starting to be used because of their cheapness.

My own preference, which accords with the general trend today, is not to use olive oil indiscriminately because it is too rich and strongly flavoured. My advice is to use plenty of it raw in salads, in dishes to be eaten cold, for cooking fish and, if you don't mind the cost, for deep-frying vegetables. Elsewhere, use a light oil with an unobtrusive taste, such as sunflower or safflower. Mixing oil and butter gives you the flavour of butter but you save on butter and the mixture will not burn as easily as butter alone.

Olive oil
Although olive oil is an important and traditional agricultural product of the Mediterranean, its production is shrinking as harvests are irregular and not always even sufficient for the local market. Spain and Italy are the largest exporters but Turkey and Tunisia now export to Italy which re-exports after refining.

The benefits of olive oil are extolled throughout the region. Many health-giving, nutritive and medicinal qualities are attributed to it in its raw state, while for cooking a particular advantage in using it for deep-frying is the high temperatures it can reach without suffering disintegration or deterioration. When the oil is very hot, it effectively seals the food by forming an instant protective coating. This prevents the absorption of excessive oil, and allows food to become crisp and golden on the outside while remaining tender and juicy on the inside.

Many different qualities of olive oil are sold here of which most are blends. It is difficult to say which is the best. The oils from Tuscany and Provence are highly rated but there are equally splendid Spanish, Greek and Tunisian oils. If you ever get a chance to buy oil pressed in a small establishment – perhaps by the grower himself – that may be the best; on the other hand, big processors ensure that their blends have a uniform standard and are cheaper. In any case, the quality really depends on the crop which varies from year to year with the weather. Before you settle on one you must try a few. We all have different tastes and the best one is the one you like best.

For the best possible flavour in an olive oil to be used in salad dressings, look for a fine 'virgin' oil, one which comes from the first cold pressings, has the lowest acidity and is made from good quality olives. The darker, greenish, less refined kind is stronger tasting and makes a wonderful fruity salad dressing. But a light golden oil will be best for cooking and for delicate sauces like mayonnaise. Buy a humbler, cheaper oil for deep-frying. You can re-use olive oil after frying, but purify it by frying a lettuce leaf in it, then filter it to remove any bits before storing it in an air-tight jar. Olive oil is supposed to go rancid if it is kept too long but in my experience it never has.

Other oils
Other oils which are used include groundnut (peanut) and argan oil in Morocco, corn and cottonseed in Egypt, and sunflower, safflower and other light vegetable oils. Nut and seed oils include sesame, walnut and almond. I have also found aromatic oils made from mint, rose and violet which are used in very small quantities in desserts.

Vinegar
Vinegar is one of the most ancient of condiments; it is used in dressings and marinades and as a pickling agent. In the Islamic world it is used instead of wine in sauces and stews. Use wine, sherry or cider vinegar, never malt. The best are matured slowly in barrels. You can flavour your own vinegar at home using fruits and herbs (p. 214).

Light golden olive oil   Virgin olive oil

Sunflower oil

White wine vinegar   Red wine vinegar

Cider vinegar   Sherry vinegar

Pasta

Pasta is the everyday food of Italy where there are reputedly 200 different kinds and shapes. Each type is said to make a difference to the taste as well as to the texture and appearance of the dish because of the amount of sauce each is capable of collecting.

It is best to buy pasta made with durum wheat which preserves the wheatgerm because this is the tastiest as well as the most healthy type. Its size trebles with cooking, it cooks evenly and does not get sticky. It is amber yellow and very slightly speckled. Fresh pasta, such as fettuccine (noodles), ravioli and tortellini (both of which are stuffed), are made with eggs and hard wheat flour, not durum flour which is impossible to work into a dough by hand.

Every country of the eastern Mediterranean also has some kind of pasta, in particular *rishta* (noodles), *lissan al assfour* (birds' tongues) which are added to meat stews, and *itriya* and *shaghria* (spaghetti and vermicelli) which are cooked with rice. Turkish *manti*, a stuffed pasta, is like the Chinese *wonton* and is Mongolian in origin.

Trenette

Ditalini

Tagliatelle

Fettuccine

Tortelloni

Conchigliette

Tubetti

Bucatini

Spaghetti

Vermicelli

Ravioli

Maccheroni

Fusilli

Tortellini

Lasagne

Rigatoni

Flavourings

Mediterranean cooking is very sensual, full of flavours and aromas. From garlic to rose buds, anything which gives taste or perfume is used. The region was part of the spice route from the Far East and everyone has developed a delight in perfumes, spices and aromatics. But the flavours are always moderate and harmonious and there are no extremes. Tunisia is the exception. There they love their food very hot and put a peppery paste called *harissa* into everything – even on bread and butter for breakfast. Generally in the Mediterranean only appetisers are highly spiced or sharp or hot, supposedly to arouse the appetite.

Each country has its favourite aromatics. In Spain and Morocco it is saffron, in Turkey it is cinnamon, allspice and sweet red pepper. Egypt has adopted cumin and coriander. Sumac is much liked in the Lebanon. Cumin is all pervading in Morocco, which is also the only country to use powdered ginger. You will find rose and orange blossom water right through the Mediterranean but in the eastern countries it is used in almost every sweet. Sicilians are alone in using jasmin essence. And in Provence you can detect a breath of anchovy or orange peel. Different herbs are used throughout the region. Mint, coriander, parsley and dill are the herbs of the eastern Mediterranean. The scents of basil, rosemary and sage evoke Italy. Provençal cooking tastes of the mingled wild herbs of the *garrigues* and the *maquis*, the impenetrable wilderness which is thrown on the back of the mountains like a tangled fleece.

A feature of the Mediterranean are the special spice mixtures and bouquets of herbs which are characteristic of each country. People make them at home and keep them in a jar to use with special dishes but you can also buy them at the spice merchant. People used to pound their spices whole with a pestle and mortar but now usually buy them ready ground. When buying spices, buy in small quantities as they go stale quickly.

If you have the opportunity of wandering through a Middle Eastern bazaar go to the spice shops. You will find all kinds of brown, yellow, red and orange powders, strange knotted roots, bits of bark and wood, shrivelled pods, seeds, berries, translucent resins, dried plants, bulbs, buds, petals and enigmatic bottles filled with essences and perfumed oils. Some of these will be your familiar supermarket spices, others will be medicinal herbs, mood-altering plants, aphrodisiac mixtures, incense, magic potions. All these are part of the spice merchants' trade.

Although so many flavourings are used in the Mediterranean they are never allowed to clash. Nor are they ever allowed to dominate a dish or mask the main ingredients – the word used in France to describe this is *assassiner*! Instead they are used in a way that preserves and enhances their natural flavours.

Allspice
These dark brown berries resembling peppercorns are ground and used to flavour meat often together with cinnamon in Arab and Turkish cooking.

Anise
Aniseed is used to flavour both sweets and spirits such as pastis and arak.

Basil
Basil characterises the flavour of southern French and Italian cooking. Sadly the type which grows here is never as fragrant as the one found in the Mediterranean and you cannot substitute dried basil. There is a very large-leafed variety (as large as spinach) and a smaller-leafed type which has a stronger flavour.

Bay leaves
These are used fresh or dry. They are put on the fire with meat and fish (threaded onto skewers for kebabs) and also lend their flavour to sauces, soups and stews.

Bouquet garni
This is a bunch of parsley, thyme and a bay leaf, tied together so that they can be removed from a dish easily before serving. Other herbs such as celery leaves, chervil, tarragon, rosemary and basil can be added for certain dishes.

Capers
Capers are the pickled bud of a bush that grows wild in the Mediterranean. The best are preserved in salt rather than brine or vinegar. Sometimes they are pickled on the branch complete with thorns and leaves. They are good in salads and as a garnish for fish.

Caraway seeds
Caraway seeds are used only in Tunisia and Turkey.

Cardamom
The brown, green or white pods are much used in the Arab world. They need to be cracked open to release their full flavour. You can also buy cardamom in powder form.

Celery

Celery leaves are highly aromatic and used like a herb for their flavour in making pickles, stews, soups and sauces. There is a greener variety with a hard root and no stalk which has a stronger flavour.

Chervil

This mild, fresh-tasting herb goes into French dishes.

Chillies

Chillies are used sparingly except in Tunisia and Algeria. Sometimes they are put whole in a dish to give it a kick and then removed before serving. Otherwise they are chopped up. They do not lose their pungency when they are dried.

Chives

Chives are added to salads and to yogurt dishes.

Chocolate

Chocolate is used in puddings and in some savoury dishes in Sicily and Spain.

Cinnamon

Cinnamon is used most extensively in the eastern Mediterranean. Spice merchants sell the dry brown bark more often in powder form. It gives a delicate perfume to minced meat fillings and to all kinds of meat and chicken stews. It is sprinkled over milk puddings and mixed with nuts in pastries. It is often coupled with allspice.

Cloves

Cloves are mostly used in spiced and preserved fruits and jams.

Cognac

This brandy is used in both sweet and savoury dishes of the Midi region of France.

Coffee

The actual drink spread from the east to the west but it is only in the western Mediterranean that coffee is used as a flavouring for desserts.

Coriander leaves

Mountains of fresh coriander are a common sight in Middle Eastern markets. The leaves are chopped up into salads and give a special flavour to soups, sauces and stews. Put the bunch in a glass of water and keep it in the refrigerator covered loosely by a plastic bag as it spoils very quickly.

Coriander seeds

These little round seeds are a very popular flavouring in the Arab part of the Mediterranean where they are often teamed with cumin. You can buy them ready-ground or you can grind them yourself. The smell of crushed coriander frying in olive oil with garlic is a characteristic smell of Egypt.

Cumin

The thin spindle-shaped yellowish brown seeds are responsible for one of the characteristic flavours of the Arab world. In Morocco ground cumin is all pervading, especially in appetisers since it is supposed to act as a digestive, and also in fish dishes. It is a component of the kind of spice mixture called zahtar, into which you dip bread soaked in oil.

Dibs

Dibs is a kind of molasses made with concentrated date juice which was used in the eastern Mediterranean as a sugar substitute until relatively recently.

Dill
The feathery leaves are a common herb used in Greece and Turkey.

Dried wild mushrooms
In Italy these are used as a flavouring in dishes such as risotto, and with meat and chicken. They must be soaked in water first.

Fennel
The anise-flavoured leaves of the fennel plant are a popular herb in France, Italy and Greece. The wild variety has a strong flavour. It is especially good with fish and snails.

Fenugreek
Both the leaf and the seeds of fenugreek are bitter. They are only used in Greece and Egypt.

Garlic
The Mediterranean is garlic country but it is not used indiscriminately or heavy-handedly as a flavouring except in the dishes where it plays a major role. The worst mistake is to let garlic dominate other flavours. The method of cooking determines the flavour. Raw garlic is the strongest, frying garlic makes it less strong and sweeter, while garlic boiled in a dish gives it a very mild taste.

Cloves and heads vary in size and colour. There is both red or mauve and white garlic. Fresh garlic is preferable to the dried variety and there is also a wild garlic which is little used.

Ginger
Ginger is most often used in a dry powder form, especially in Morocco.

Harissa
This fiery North African paste is a mixture of chillies and garlic with various spices. It is better to buy it in a tube than in a tin because you only need a little at a time.

Grappa
This Italian grape spirit infused with a sprig of rue is also used in nearby Nice to flavour cream cheese and sweets.

Honey
Honey was used as a sweetener in ancient times. Its fragrance depends on the flowers on which the bees have fed. Greeks use honey in their sweets and pastries; usually a spoonful goes into the sugar syrup which is poured over them. In Morocco honey is also used in savoury dishes with delicious results. As it is only used in small quantities it is always worth using a really good honey. The best is made from the nectar of thyme and rosemary flowers, and spring honey is better than autumn honey. Honey from Hymethus in Greece and from Narbonne, Gatenais and Champagne in France are highly esteemed.

Lemon or lime juice
Lemon and lime juice are used to flavour and season a great number of dishes and you can detect their presence in stews and sauces. Lemon or lime wedges are always present to squeeze over an appetiser where their sharp flavour has the effect of whetting the appetite, and over grilled meat or fish. Lemon juice mixed with olive oil is as common a dressing as vinaigrette.

Lemon peel
This gives a wonderful flavour to sauces and stews. Peel it carefully so as to leave the bitter pith behind. Lemon zest is also used in all kinds of dishes.

Mace
Mace is the outer coat of nutmeg. It is used in Italy and France.

Marc
This French eau-de-vie is a spirit distilled from grape skins.

Marjoram
There are many different species of this herb which grow wild. It goes particularly well with tomatoes and is commonly sprinkled on pizzas.

Marsala
This Sicilian dessert wine goes into puddings and pastries.

Mastic
Mastic is the resin which exudes from the lentisc tree. The little white beads are pulverised and used in eastern Mediterranean milk puddings and stews. It is often chewed like chewing gum with a little wax added to soften it.

Mint
Spearmint is much loved and used extensively, both fresh and dried. People dry it themselves and crush it over a dish by rubbing a few leaves between their hands. It is much used in salads and goes well with yogurt and cheese. It also gives a refreshing flavour to cooked vegetables which are to be eaten cold. In Morocco mint tea is the most popular drink.

Mustard
French mustards are sold in the form of a paste. They contain a mixture of the black and white mustard seeds, either powdered or crushed or left whole, usually with added herbs and sometimes with verjuice or wine. You will not find much mustard in the cooking of the eastern Mediterranean.

Onion
So many dishes start with onion frying in olive oil till soft and golden that its flavour and aroma are almost a trade mark of Mediterranean cooking.

Nutmeg
Nutmeg is best grated straight into the dish to preserve its aroma. It is a favourite in Italy and southern France where it is used especially with spinach and cheese.

Orange blossom water
The distilled essence of orange blossom adds a delicate perfume to many Mediterranean dishes and especially to the desserts of the eastern countries. In Morocco it is sometimes sprinkled over salads and also into stews. Use only a little as it can be overpowering.

Oregano
This herb is much used in the northern part of the Mediterranean where it grows wild. The Greek variety – called rigani – has far the best flavour in its dried form. It has a special affinity with tomato and is often used in sauces and stews.

Orange peel
This lends a delightful fragrance to Provençal sauces and stews. The white pith must be scraped off and the rind blanched to remove the bitterness. The zest alone is also used.

Paprika
This sweet red pepper is most common in Turkey and in North Africa and comes in different strengths and shades.

Parsley
It is preferable to use the flat-leafed parsley which has a stronger flavour than the usual curly British kind. Use it very generously.

Pastis
This anis-flavoured drink is used in a variety of dishes in the Midi region of France.

Pekmez
This grape juice reduced to a thick syrup is a traditional Turkish sweetener.

Pepper
There are many different kinds of pepper found in the Mediterranean: the green unripe berries, poivres verts, which are used in France, the unripe ones which turn black in the sun and the milder white ones which are picked late and usually soaked to remove their reddish skin. Black pepper, which is the strongest, is often ground straight onto a dish, or sometimes a recipe calls for it to be pounded coarsely in a pestle and mortar. In large long-cooked dishes such as a daube, whole peppercorns are dropped into the pot. Pepper is not, however, used indiscriminately in Mediterranean dishes.

Pomegranate syrup
This is the boiled-down juice of a type of sour pomegranate. It is used in Syria and Lebanon and lends a most delicious sweet and sour flavour.

Preserved lemons and limes
These preserves give a mellow lemony flavour to many North African dishes. To make them yourself see the recipe on p. 214. It is only the chopped peel that is used as a flavouring. Before using it rinse off the salt.

Ras el hanout
Ras el hanout is a North African spice mixture which may contain a dozen ingredients. Every vendor prides himself on his own special house blend.

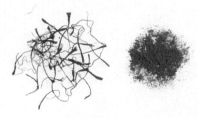

Rose buds
You will find this special kind of highly perfumed rose bud dried in eastern spice mixtures.

Rosemary
This Italian herb is used especially when roasting or grilling chicken and lamb. It is better fresh so try growing it in your garden – it always does well. The powder sold in boxes has an unpleasant taste.

Rose water
The distilled essence of rose petals is used to perfume sweet things in the eastern Mediterranean. The type available here in bottles is much diluted but you should still use it sparingly or it may seem that you are eating perfume. Try adding a few drops to a glass of fresh orange juice or even to water. The flavour is soothing and supposed to put you into a happy mood.

Saffron
This is the thread-like stamen of a violet-coloured crocus; it gives food a faint odour, an unusual, delicate, slightly bitter flavour and an intense yellow colour. The way to extract the best from the stamens is to crush them with a small pestle and mortar or between two spoons and to soak the resulting powder in a little water. You can buy cheaper pre-crushed saffron in a packet. Moroccans and Spaniards make liberal use of saffron in many dishes but they nearly always use a lurid false saffron-coloured powder (not shown) which gives the right colour but no flavour. It can be used where the presence of many other flavourings would make it a waste to use the best-quality stamens.

Sage
This herb is used in southern France and Italy with chicken, pork and veal and in sauces. Use it with a light hand as a little goes a long way.

Sesame seeds
Toast these seeds slightly to bring out their full flavour before adding them to dishes.

Sahlab
The dried ground bulb of a variety of orchid is a thickening agent and also has a delicate flavour. It is used to make an eastern Mediterranean milk drink served sprinkled with cinnamon and chopped pistachios, and an unctuous milk ice-cream where it is combined with mastic. It is so expensive that what you usually get at spice merchants is false sahlab – a mixture of cornflour and shredded coconut.

Spring onions
The Mediterranean variety of this vegetable grows to a much larger size than the English kind. Spring onions are much used in salads instead of ordinary onions.

Sumac
You will encounter this spice in the eastern Mediterranean in Syria and Lebanon. The sour brown seed is ground and sprinkled on salads and on fish. You can also soak the cracked seeds in water for about 20 minutes and then strain the juice which can be used as a substitute for lemon.

Tahina
The oily paste ground from sesame seeds gives a strong nutty flavour to many Middle East salads and sauces. There is also a sweetened, dark variety.

Tamarind
This is a pod with an unusual sharp taste which, combined with a little sugar, gives a very attractive sweet and sour flavour. It is sold as a thick, dark brown, compact, fibrous mass of pods which you must soak in hot water to extract their dark brown juices. However, a commercial paste which is now available has a good flavour and is easy to use.

Tomato purée
Commercial brands vary in flavour – it is better to buy one without added salt.

Thyme
Wild thyme grows mostly in France and Greece. A cultivated variety is easy to grow at home.

Tarragon
This herb is used in Southern France to flavour salads and sauces.

Vanilla
Vanilla came to the western Mediterranean from the Americas in the fifteenth century, but it has only recently been adopted in the eastern part. The long pods can be re-used and are best stored in a sugar jar to flavour the sugar.

Winter savoury
This herb is used in France. It has something of the perfume of thyme with which it is sometimes coupled. It is often used to flavour goat's cheese.

Wine
Both red and white wine are used in cooking in the western Mediterranean.

Turmeric
This spice is the 'poor man's saffron' and in the eastern Mediterranean it is also called 'oriental saffron', though it bears no relation to the cheap powder sold as saffron (see Saffron).

Preserves

The great variety of preserves in the Mediterranean originated as a response to the fear of winter and of scarcity. Peasants used to dry all their own seasonal fruits, including figs, plums, apricots and grapes, and vegetables, such as aubergines, okra, courgettes and peppers, which they threaded into necklaces. They also preserve pork and anchovies in salt and meat in its own fat; they pickle and marinate vegetables, make tomato paste, bottle fruits in syrup and alcohol and crystallise fruits. These preserves play the same important role they did in the past but they have also become delicacies and part of thriving cottage industries.

Anchovies
Anchovies tinned in oil and salted anchovies sold loose are much used in Italy and Spain and also in Provençal and Tunisian cooking where the Italian influence is felt. They are usually rinsed to remove excess salt. Mashed anchovy fillets are used as a flavouring.

Chorizo
This is a peppery garlic-flavoured Spanish sausage which is sliced up and eaten as an appetiser and also cooked in many dishes.

Dried fish roe
Many types of fish roe are soaked, pressed under a weight, washed and left to dry in the sun. Each country has its own variety, e.g. poutargue in France or batarekh in the eastern Mediterranean. Considered a great delicacy and very expensive, it is sliced very thin and served on bread with a squeeze of lemon.

Dried vegetables
Tiny okra, hollowed-out aubergines and red peppers are dried in the sun and sold threaded on a string. They are reconstituted by soaking in water and are used when fresh vegetables are not available.

Crystallised fruits
Crystallised citrus fruit, peaches, apricots, plums, greengages, pears and cherries are chopped up and used in desserts.

Dried fruit

Sun-dried apricots, prunes, figs, cherries, raisins and sultanas are used in savoury dishes with meat and chicken as well as in sweet ones. Several types of fruit are pressed and dried in sheets, notably apricots (which are then called amardine*).*

Marinated vegetables

Many vegetables are sold marinated in oil and are served as an hors d'oeuvre.

Jams

Jams are made with every kind of fruit and even vegetables such as aubergines and with rose and orange blossom petals.

Mergez

These are spicy North African sausages. They are cut up into pieces and used in cooking.

Pâté de foie gras
Pâtés made from the enlarged livers of force-fed geese or ducks are one of the great delicacies of France.

Pickled fruits
Fruits pickled in a vinegar and sugar syrup for a few weeks are served as a condiment.

Pissala
This is a speciality of Nice, an aromatic paste of salted anchovies and sardines.

Pickled vegetables
Many vegetables are pickled in brine or in a salt and vinegar solution.

Preserved meat
In France they make confits of pork, goose and duck in which the meat is cooked and preserved in its own fat. In the Arab world lamb is preserved in the same way while in North Africa the meat is cut into pieces, spiced and hung up to dry.

Rillettes
This is pork cooked in its own fat, pounded to shreds and preserved in the fat.

Salt cod
Dehydrated salt cod is very popular in the Christian Mediterranean because of its early association with Lent. Look for a very white piece. It needs to be soaked for about 36 hours (the time depends on the degree of saltiness), changing the water regularly to remove all the salt before you can cook it. It has a pungent flavour which dilutes with soaking. There are different types of salt cod with different degrees of saltiness and dryness. In the UK you can find it in West Indian and other ethnic shops.

Tarama
Tarama is salted and dried grey mullet roe. However, smoked cod's roe is the usual, but not so strongly flavoured substitute used in the UK.

Spoon sweets
Fruit preserving is one of the important traditional industries in the western Mediterranean. Almost all varieties are sold preserved in sugar syrup and in alcohol. In Greece and Turkey visitors may be offered 'spoon sweets' – fruit preserved in a very sticky syrup – which are usually served with a glass of water.

Tuna fish in oil
Italy has taught Tunisians and Niçois (people from Nice) to put tuna in salads and other dishes. Tuna in brine is equally good and lighter in taste.

Tomatoes, tinned
If the fresh tomatoes available have no flavour then it is best to use good quality peeled tinned tomatoes for cooking.

Traditional Utensils

Mediterranean kitchens are generally simple and austere – dark with small windows to keep them cool in the summer and whitewashed walls which are constantly repainted. Each country has its own traditional utensils but none is essential for the success of a dish. All you really need is a good knife, a wooden spoon, a large heavy frying-pan, a large heavy saucepan and an ovenproof dish, but if you are interested in traditional equipment for the pleasure and charm of using it, the following items are some that you might like to obtain.

Glazed and unglazed earthenware pots and casseroles, which can both go in the oven and on the hob, hold the heat and flavour of food and look beautiful on the table. Unglazed pots are said to impart a special flavour to dishes. Those with a rounded bottom are made to go on a wood fire. Most have no lid and you should use aluminium foil if you want to cover them. A French *marmite* does have a lid and is tall and straight-sided. An Egyptian *tagen* is shorter. A Provençal *tian* is oval. A *cassole* for cassoulet tapers at the bottom. A Spanish *olla* or *cazuela de barra* is round, usually with a curved bottom. A Moroccan *tagine* is shallow, round and has a conical lid like a pointed hat.

All kinds of tinned copper pots in which long-simmered stews will not burn are used. They need to be re-tinned at intervals. You can find copper pots lined with stainless steel but they are very expensive. Heavy-bottomed stainless steel pots or other heavy cookware also give the all-round gentle heat which is important for long and slowly simmered dishes.

A *daubière* is a deep heavy French braising pan made traditionally from earthenware or enamelled cast iron with a lid. It is good for long slow cooking and the food does not stick. A *couscousier* is a North African steamer. You will find them mainly made from aluminium but they can also be enamelled tin or earthenware. A Spanish *paellera* or paella pan is a two-handled frying-pan usually about 38 cm (15 in) across the base and 43 cm (17 in) across the top. Iron ones should be kept oiled when not in use.

The utensils shown on the far right are some of my favourites: a long curved metal blade with a wooden handle for hollowing out vegetables; a large pestle and mortar for crushing nuts and a smaller one for spices (in Spain you find heavy traditional green/yellow earthenware ones useful for making sauces); a garlic press; a *mezza luna* – a sickle-shaped, double-handled chopper for herbs, or its single-handled equivalent; and a Spanish *plancha* or portable cast-iron grill.

Marmite

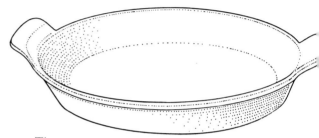

Tian

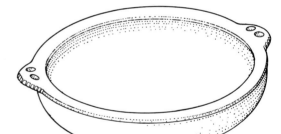

Spanish olla

Moroccan tagine

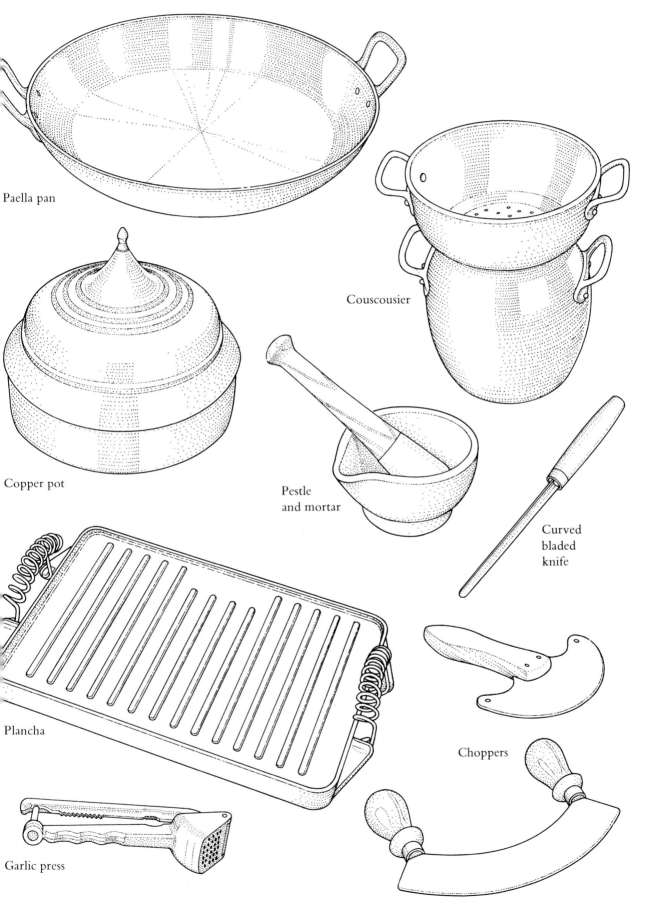

Paella pan

Couscousier

Copper pot

Pestle
and mortar

Curved
bladed
knife

Plancha

Choppers

Garlic press

Appetisers and 'Little Dishes'

Most of the dishes featured in this section, which is necessarily long, can and should also be served as side dishes, vegetables and salads. Some will also make a light meal. Look too in the Fish section for recipes that are suitable for starters.

THE CUSTOM OF serving appetisers, called *mezze* in the Middle East and *tapas* in Spain, with drinks is an important and most delightful feature of Mediterranean life. It is less a part of family life than of entertaining and of the outside world of cafés, tavernas and kebab houses. It signifies leisure, camaraderie and good humour. In the Mediterranean you do not drink very much and you never drink without eating. You have time to enjoy the moment in an unhurried way and to sharpen your conversational skills.

In bars and restaurants, wine, beer, whisky, sherry and arak or flavoured grape spirits, such as raki, ouzo and pastis, are always served with a variety of small dishes. At home the unexpected visitor will be offered a bowl of olives, cubes of white cheese and home-made pickles, a quartered tomato and cucumber sticks, or simply the leftovers from the previous meal or a foretaste of the meal to come, cut up into small pieces. But the array of appetisers placed at the centre of the table or on little tables around the room for a party might be extraordinary, and the time taken over them may stretch to three hours, delaying the main course until very late.

Appetisers are the main trade of eating houses throughout the Mediterranean. The eating houses of Lebanon, Turkey and Spain in particular have established great reputations for them. The custom is to offer a large selection in small quantities and to keep them coming.

Appetisers are triumphs of gastronomy. Because they are meant to whet the appetite, they are usually strongly flavoured and aromatic, either highly spiced, garlicky or sharp with lemon. They are also supposed to be intriguing, amusing, colourful and pleasing in every way. A great deal of effort goes into making them so, and they do bring joy to the heart especially when they are served in the open air on a balcony overlooking the sea, or on a café table in the shade of a giant vine or near a fluttering jasmine.

What kinds of dishes are served as appetisers? All kinds, hot and cold, from little stuffed vegetables or pies to salads and dips. Every country has its own favourites. Choose one or two to serve as a first course and have a large selection for a party.

Right: Athenian olive stall

Pa amb Tomàquet

Bread and Tomato

Bread rubbed with ripe tomatoes to an exquisite pink softness and sprinkled with olive oil is popular in Catalunya in Spain. We had it for breakfast together with pigs' trotters and baby squid in their ink at a bar that caters for the market traders of San Feliú. It was also presented as an appetiser in all the grand restaurants we visited in Barcelona. It is sometimes topped with a slice of ham.

Cut some good crusty white country bread into thick slices. If they are too big cut them again. Cut the tomatoes in half and squeeze out the seeds, then rub both sides of each slice so that the bread is entirely impregnated with juice. Be generous with your tomatoes. Sprinkle lightly with salt and pour a dribble of olive oil on top.

Tapenade

Olive Paste

Tapenade, which takes its name from the French for capers, is the famous aromatic caper and olive spread of Provence. Everyone makes his or her own favourite blend with varying proportions. Frédéric Brun, who has taken over his father's legendary traditional Provençal restaurant, Chez Maurice Brun, in Marseilles, serves this tapenade as an appetiser on fresh or toasted bread. You can keep it for several days in a pot sealed with a thin layer of olive oil.

Serves 8

Pinch of thyme
Small piece of bay leaf
500 g (1 lb) black olives
125 g (4 oz) capers, rinsed
½ garlic clove, crushed
2 tinned anchovy fillets
Pepper or a pinch of mustard (optional)
4 tablespoons rum or to taste
2–3 tablespoons olive oil

Pit the olives. Chop and pound or, more simply, blend the ingredients to a soft smooth paste in a food processor. If the capers are preserved in vinegar they are best soaked in water for 30 minutes first.

Bruschetta

Garlic Bread

Toast slices of white or wholewheat bread under the grill or over a charcoal fire until lightly browned. Put them on a plate and, while they are still hot, rub the top with cut garlic. Pour a little strong green olive oil on each and sprinkle with salt and black pepper. Serve hot.

Variations
* For *bruschetta con salsa verde agrodolce* spread the toast with the sweet and sour green sauce on p. 210.
* Top with a slice of tomato and a small basil leaf.

Anchoïade

Anchovy Paste

The menu of the Chez Maurice Brun restaurant in Marseilles has remained exactly the same since the mid-1930s. The *anchoïade*, like the *tapenade* (left) also given by Frédéric Brun, Maurice's son, is an example of salted preserved food which is particularly popular in the Mediterranean.

100 g (3½ oz) small anchovy fillets tinned in oil, drained
Pepper
3 tablespoons olive oil
1 tablespoon red wine vinegar or to taste
1–2 garlic cloves, crushed (optional)

Soak the drained anchovies in water for a few minutes to remove some of the salt. Drain on kitchen paper, then pound or blend to a paste with all the remaining ingredients.

Variation
For *quichets aux anchois* cut a French loaf in half lengthways, then cut it into pieces. Brush the pieces lightly with olive oil. Spread on a thin layer of *anchoïade*, crushing it in so that it impregnates the bread – this process is called *esquicher*, hence the name. Put the bread under a hot grill until the tantalising aroma, characteristic of Provence, rises and the paste begins to colour and bubble. Serve hot.

Top: Fried aubergine slices (p. 80)
Right: Cipolline in agrodolce (p. 82)
Bottom: Bruschetta

Crudités

Raw Vegetables

A plate of raw vegetables is the most common *hors d'oeuvre* in Provence. It is the most pleasant and refreshing way to celebrate the produce of the land.

Offer one or several of the following:

* Lettuce, endive or chicory leaves or wild salad leaves like the Provençal mixture *mesclun*, dressed with plenty of olive oil, very little or no vinegar, salt and pepper and chopped herbs, such as parsley, chives basil and chervil. *Mesclun*, derived from the Latin *miscellanea*, has become a hallmark of *nouvelle cuisine*. The mixture of salad leaves started with the baskets of mixed young oak leaf, chicory and rocket leaves with dandelion, watercress, borage, purslane and chervil which Franciscan monks grew or picked from the wilderness of the nearby hills.

* A salad of shredded white or red cabbage, dressed as above.

* Radishes served with salt, bread and butter.

* An arrangement of vegetables cut into sticks or pieces just before serving. These may include radishes, celery, fennel, cucumbers, carrots, cauliflower and cooked beetroot. You can serve these with a sauce such as mayonnaise (p. 211) and aïoli (p. 212). A basket bursting with whole, baby vegetables makes a marvellous party piece.

Below : Crudités
Opposite : Prosciutto crudo con fichi e melone

Prosciutto Crudo con Fichi o Melone

Raw Ham with Figs or Canteloupe Melon

Choose a mild, sweet tender ham, preferably the pale-pink prosciutto. Have it sliced paper thin and serve it with very ripe fruit.

Antipasto

In Italy, restaurants offer assortments of cured meats, such as fresh and dry salame, and raw and cooked ham as a first course. They are usually accompanied by vegetables preserved in vinegared brine such as onions, gherkins, green beans, carrots and peppers, artichoke hearts in oil, and also tinned tuna and anchovy fillets. At home antipasto tends to consist only of one or two pork products, but a beautifully presented, interesting selection is an easy option for a buffet party.

Serve with plenty of bread and butter.

Insalata Caprese

Mozzarella and Tomato Salad

The excellence of this popular summer salad depends on the quality of the mozzarella, a bland slightly rubbery cheese which is highly perishable. The type made from a mixture of cow's and buffalo's milk has the best flavour.

Serves 4

175 g (6 oz) mozzarella cheese
300 g (10 oz) firm ripe tomatoes
Salt and pepper
Bunch of basil
4 tablespoons or more olive oil (extra virgin, if possible)
1 teaspoon oregano (optional)

Slice the mozzarella and tomatoes and arrange alternating slices in a serving dish. Season with salt and plenty of pepper, tear the basil leaves into pieces over the salad and sprinkle with olive oil and the oregano, if you like.

Slat Avocado ve pri Hada

Israeli Avocado and Citrus Salad

The blandness of the avocado and sharpness of the citrus fruits combine very refreshingly in this recipe.

Serves 4–6

Juice of 1 lemon
4 tablespoons olive oil
Salt and pepper
2 ripe but firm avocado pears
1 orange
1 grapefruit

Garnish:
Mint leaves

Beat the lemon, oil, salt and pepper in a salad bowl. Peel the avocados, cut them in half and remove the stones, then slice them and turn them in the dressing. Peel the orange and grapefruit, removing all the pith, and cut the flesh into pieces. Toss the fruits in the dressing. Garnish with mint leaves.

Rashe Melon

Israeli Melon Cups

The best part of Israeli food is the exceptional quality of their fruits and vegetables. The delicate contrasting shades of the two types of melon in the shells make a charming presentation.

Serves 6

1 ripe cantaloupe melon
1 ripe honeydew melon
125 ml (4 fl oz) sweet Israeli wine or any other sweet wine

Cut one of the melons in half to use as serving bowls. Remove the seeds. Scoop out the flesh and cut into cubes or use a ball cutter to form balls. Do the same with the flesh of the other melon. Cut a thin slice of skin from the bottom of the reserved shells so that they do not wobble. Put the melon pieces into a bowl, cover with wine and chill.

When you are ready to serve, heap the melon cubes or balls into the reserved shells, putting the odd little bits and scrapings at the bottom.

Cacik

Cucumber and Yogurt Salad

This refreshing salad is popular all over the eastern Mediterranean as a *mezze*. In Turkey it is flavoured with dill and only a touch of garlic. Elsewhere they put mint and often plenty of garlic. The Greek name is *tzatziki*. A splendid summer soup based on this salad was prepared for us by Mrs Neşet Eren of Istanbul (see below).

Serves 6

450 ml (15 fl oz) yogurt, preferably thick ewe's milk or strained yogurt
1 large cucumber, finely chopped or sliced thin
Salt and white pepper
1–4 garlic cloves, crushed
1 tablespoon white wine vinegar
A few sprigs of fresh mint or dill, finely chopped, or 1 tablespoon dried mint

Garnish:
3 tablespoons olive oil

Beat the yogurt and mix in the rest of the ingredients. If you are preparing the salad some time in advance, salt the cucumber first and leave it in a colander for the juices to drain away, otherwise it will be watery. Dribble the olive oil on top.

Variation
Turquoise Soup
For 4 people peel a large cucumber and grate into a bowl. Sprinkle lightly with salt. Beat in 600 ml (1 pint) yogurt. Add only the juice, *not* the pulp, from one garlic clove, and 1 tablespoon of white wine vinegar. Stir in the cucumber with its juice, 2 tablespoons each of finely chopped fresh mint and dill and 3 tablespoons of olive oil. Add a few tablespoons of water to thin the soup, if necessary, though it should be quite thick. Serve very cold.

Israeli Wines

Israel's wine industry has expanded from producing its traditional sweet sacramental kosher wine to include good quality reds, whites and rosés. The major grape varieties are Sauvignon Blanc and Cabernet Sauvignon. Names to look out for include Carmel, Yarden, Gamla and Golan.

Salade Niçoise

Niçoise Salad

Catherine-Hélène Barale, who runs a restaurant in Nice of the same name, is a formidable elderly woman who fiercely upholds Niçois cookery traditions. According to her, the true *salade niçoise* never contains potatoes or any other boiled vegetable. Here, then, is the 'real thing', made with raw vegetables only and including plenty of tomatoes.

Serves 6

10 medium-sized tomatoes, cut in quarters
Salt
1 garlic clove
1 large cucumber, peeled and thinly sliced
200 g (7 oz) very young broad beans or baby
  artichokes, thinly sliced (optional)
2 green peppers, thinly sliced
6 spring onions, thinly sliced
12 anchovy fillets cut into pieces
A 250 g (8 oz) tin of tuna, flaked
125 g (4 oz) black olives
3 hard-boiled eggs, shelled and thinly sliced

For the dressing:
90 ml (3½ fl oz) olive oil
2 tablespoons red wine vinegar
6 basil leaves, finely chopped (optional)
Salt and pepper

Sprinkle the tomatoes lightly with salt and let their juices drain. Cut the garlic clove in half and rub the inside of a bowl or a large serving dish. Arrange all the ingredients decoratively in the dish. Combine the dressing ingredients, pour over the salad, then serve.

Left: Salade niçoise
Right: Panisses (p. 96)

Salata Baladi

Arab Mixed Salad

Serve this popular everyday salad as an appetiser or to accompany a light meal or a grill.

Serves 6

1 small cos lettuce, shredded
3 firm tomatoes, diced
1 green pepper, de-seeded and diced
½ cucumber (peeled or unpeeled), diced
6 spring onions or 1 mild onion, chopped
6 radishes, sliced (optional)
Small bunch of parsley or coriander, coarsely
  chopped
A few sprigs of mint, chopped (optional)
4 tablespoons olive oil
Juice of 1 or more lemons
Salt and pepper

Mix all the ingredients together just before serving.

Variation
Fattoush is a Lebanese bread salad. Open out a pitta bread and put it in the oven or under the grill until it is crisp and brown, then break it into little pieces. The traditional way is to put the pieces of pitta at the bottom of a salad bowl and moisten them with water. Nowadays most people prefer dry croutons to soggy bread and add them to the above salad at the last minute. It is also very good sprinkled with sumac (see p. 53) and pomegranate seeds.

Greek Wines

The Greeks drink ouzo with appetisers and their famous resin-flavoured retsina with most foods. But if you're not a fan – and they are an acquired taste – there are a number of good white wines for drinking with appetisers, fish and seafood. Robola is a lovely light and fruity wine from Cephalonia, in the Ionian Islands. Semeli, produced in Attica, is clean and dry, while Zitza is a naturally sparkling wine from the Epirus region in the north west.

With meat dishes, try Naoussa, a strong and generous red wine from Macedonia in northern Greece, or the full-bodied reds from Nemea, south west of Corinth, in the Pelopponese.

Tabbouleh

Parsley, Mint and Burghul Salad

This fresh-tasting summer salad is served in every Lebanese restaurant. The uniform restaurant menu was born in the region of Zahle as an accompaniment to the local anis-flavoured grape spirit, arak. In 1920 two cafés opened by the river Bardaouni which cascades down the mountain. They gave away assorted nuts, seeds, olives, bits of cheese and raw vegetables with arak. Gradually the entire valley became filled with open-air cafés, each larger and more luxurious than the next, each vying to attract customers who flocked from all over the Middle East (the mountain region was considered the Switzerland of the Middle East) with ever more varied *mezze*. Reputations for dishes such as tabbouleh, kibbeh (p. 85), hummus (p. 73) and moutabal (p. 71) which were local village foods spread far afield and *mezze* became a national institution.

Serves 6 or more

125 g (4 oz) medium-fine burghul (cracked wheat)
Juice of 2 or more lemons
Salt and pepper
75 ml (3 fl oz) olive oil
3 large bunches flat-leaf parsley weighing about
  300 g (10 oz) without stems
Large bunch of fresh mint weighing 75 g (3 oz)
6 spring onions or 1 mild onion, finely chopped
3 tomatoes, diced
Cos lettuce leaves from the heart

Start an hour before you are ready to serve so that the burghul becomes well impregnated with dressing. Soak the burghul in plenty of fresh cold water for about 15 minutes, then rinse and drain, squeezing the excess water out, and put the burghul in a bowl with lemon juice, salt and pepper. When it has absorbed the dressing and become plump and tender, add the oil.

Finely chop the herbs just before serving. It is better to do this by hand but so much easier to use a food processor. If you use a processor make sure that you do not turn the leaves to a mush. Mix the chopped herbs with the spring onions and burghul, taste and adjust the seasoning, adding more lemon juice if necessary. Serve on a large flat dish. Spread the tomatoes over the top and place lettuce leaves, for scooping, around the edge or serve them in a separate bowl.

Horiatiki Salata

Greek Country Salad

This colourful salad, which makes a light lunch in itself, should bring back memories of the gaiety of Greek tavernas and the plaintive notes of the bouzouki.

Serves 4

3 firm ripe tomatoes, cut in wedges
½ cucumber, peeled, split in half, then thinly sliced
1 green pepper, de-seeded and thinly sliced in rings
1 mild onion, thinly sliced in rings
Salt and pepper
4 tablespoons olive oil

Garnish:
150 g (5 oz) feta cheese, cubed
12 or more black olives
Small bunch of parsley, coarsely chopped
1 teaspoon dried oregano or marjoram

Place the salad ingredients in a bowl, sprinkle with salt, pepper and olive oil and toss well. Arrange the feta cheese, olives and herbs on top, then serve.

Ajlouke de Carottes

Carrot and Potato Appetiser

This homely Tunisian appetiser is beautiful, easy to make and full of spicy flavour. Serve it cold with bread.

Serves 6

750 g (1½ lb) carrots
500 g (1 lb) potatoes
Salt
2 garlic cloves, chopped
4 teaspoons cumin
3 tablespoons olive oil
2 tablespoons wine vinegar
Large pinch of cayenne

Peel the carrots and potatoes and cut them into pieces. Put them in a pan with salt, the garlic and water to cover, then boil until soft. Drain and mash, then stir in the rest of the ingredients.

Bottom left: Salade de tomates et poivrons (p. 79)
Bottom right: Ajlouke de carottes
Top: Briouates (p. 91)

Ajlouke de Potiron

Pumpkin Purée

Tunisians like to put harissa (see p. 50) into everything. With it and the other spices in this recipe pumpkin becomes something quite out of the ordinary. Eat it cold with bread.

Serves 6

1 kg (2 lb) piece of pumpkin
Salt
2 garlic cloves, crushed
Juice of 1 lemon or 2 tablespoons wine vinegar
2 tablespoons olive oil
$\frac{1}{2}$–1 teaspoon harissa, or 1 teaspoon paprika and a
  pinch of cayenne
1 teaspoon caraway seeds
1 teaspoon ground coriander

Garnish:
A few black olives (optional)

Peel the pumpkin and scrape away the seeds and fibres. Cut into pieces and boil in salted water for about 10 minutes or until just tender. Drain and mash with a fork or a potato masher, then stir the rest of the ingredients into the stringy purée. Garnish, if you like, with black olives.

Patlıcan Salatası

Aubergine Salad

A favourite Turkish salad, this is a wonderfully fresh-tasting combination of mashed aubergines and yogurt. Mrs Neşet Eren, author of *Classic Turkish Cooking*, adds a colourful garnish.

Serves 6–8

4 large aubergines
75 ml (3 fl oz) lemon juice
75–90 ml (3–3$\frac{1}{2}$ fl oz) olive oil
Salt
4 tablespoons yogurt

Garnish:
6 black olives
1 small onion, cut in half and thinly sliced
1 small green pepper, thinly sliced
1 small tomato, thinly sliced
1 tablespoon parsley, chopped

Pierce the aubergines in a few places with the point of a knife and turn them directly over a flame or under the grill until their skins are black and blistered and the flesh feels soft. Alternatively, roast them in the oven at 200°C (400°F, gas mark 6). Skin them while still hot. Put the flesh in a bowl with the lemon juice, oil, salt and yogurt and mash to a paste with a potato masher, or put everything through a blender. Pour onto a shallow serving dish and garnish with the rest of the ingredients.

Variation
A simple aubergine cream called 'poor man's caviar', popular all over the Mediterranean, is made with 4 grilled mashed aubergines mixed with 75–90 ml (3–3$\frac{1}{2}$ fl oz) olive oil, juice of 1 lemon, salt, pepper and a little crushed garlic.

Spice shop in Cairo's Khan-el-Khalili market

Moutabal

Malak's Aubergine Dip

This aubergine purée, popular all over the Arab Arab world, is also called *baba ghanoush*. There is a mysterious taboo against using tahina with yogurt but Malak Mawaldi, who comes from Syria and lives in Cairo, has broken it with very pleasing results.

Serves 6

3 medium aubergines
1½–2 tablespoons tahina (see p. 53)
2 garlic cloves, crushed
75 g (3 oz) yogurt
Juice of 1 large lemon

Garnish:
A dribble of olive oil
A few sprigs of parsley, finely chopped
A few black olives

Grill or roast the aubergines as described opposite. Peel them and squeeze their juice out in a colander. Mash the flesh with a fork or purée it in a blender, adding the rest of the ingredients gradually and tasting all the time. Pour into a bowl and garnish with the olive oil, parsley and olives.

Ful Midames

The traditional Egyptian breakfast made of dried broad beans is also the national dish. It has recently come into fashion, glamorised with dozens of different garnishes, as a dish to offer tourists.

Simmer 500 g (1 lb) dried broad beans (soaked overnight) with a handful of red lentils in 3 times their volume of water for 1–2 hours or until they are tender, adding salt when they begin to soften. The lentils disintegrate and thicken the sauce.

Put the seasonings on the table – olive oil, salt and pepper, ground cumin, crushed garlic and three lemons cut into wedges – for people to help themselves. The old-style peasant garnishes are: 6 whole hard-boiled eggs, 6 chopped tomatoes, 2 chopped mild onions sprinkled with salt and then rinsed, 3 chopped pickled cucumbers and chopped parsley.

Slata Méchouia Nablia

Pepper Relish

One of the best features of Tunisian food are the many regional *méchouia* (roasted) salads in which the vegetables are grilled or roasted. This bright red one from Nabeul is a fiery appetite-whetter. A popular way of serving it is surrounded by olives and wedges of hard-boiled eggs. I also use it as a relish with cold fish and meat.

Serves 4–6

500 g (1 lb) red peppers
1 or more small, fresh, hot chillies
3 medium tomatoes, peeled
1 tablespoon caraway seeds
2–4 garlic cloves, crushed
2–3 tablespoons olive oil

Cut the peppers in half and put them and the chilli under the grill skin-side up until very brown and blistered. Alternatively roast them in the hottest possible oven for about 30 minutes. Put them in a polythene or plastic bag, close tightly and leave for at least 15 minutes. This helps to loosen the skin.

Peel the peppers and chilli, then remove the seeds and stems, and put the softened flesh in a food processor with the rest of the ingredients. Blend, then transfer to a serving dish.

Slatit Fzill

Radish Salad

This strong-tasting little Tunisian salad goes well with the carrot and potato appetiser on p. 69.

Serves 4

Bunch of radishes, topped, tailed and coarsely
   chopped
Juice of ½ lemon
Salt
Pinch of cayenne
2 tablespoons olive oil
A few sprigs of parsley, finely chopped

Mix all the ingredients together at the last minute, then serve.

Bissara

Egyptian Bean Purée

This garlicky bean dip, with a refreshing herby flavour, is an Egyptian peasant dish. It is made with dried broad beans which you must buy without their skins (see p. 42). Serve it with good fresh bread.

Serves 8

250 g (8 oz) skinned dried broad beans, soaked overnight
1 onion, thinly sliced
5 or more garlic cloves, chopped
1 tablespoon dried mint
Large bunch of dill, chopped
Large bunch of coriander, chopped
Large bunch of parsley, chopped
1 teaspoon ground cumin
Salt
Cayenne (optional)

Garnish:
2 onions, thinly sliced
Olive oil
5 garlic cloves, chopped
Juice of 1 or more lemons

Drain the beans, cover with fresh water and bring to the boil with the sliced onion and chopped garlic. Cook for about an hour until the beans are soft. Add the herbs, salt and spices and cook for another 10 minutes. Drain the beans, reserving the liquid. Put the bean mixture through a blender with enough of the liquid to obtain a smooth cream and turn into a bowl. The mixture should be very moist – it will stiffen as it cools.

Fry the onions for the garnish in 3 tablespoons of the olive oil until the rings are quite brown, almost caramelised, adding the garlic towards the end. Serve the purée hot or cold garnished with the fried onion rings and with plenty of olive oil and lemon juice sprinkled over it.

Variation
There is a fiery Tunisian version which includes a teaspoon of ground cumin, a tablespoon each of tomato paste and harissa (see p. 50) or paprika and a good pinch of cayenne.

Falafel or Ta'Amia

Dried Broad Bean Rissoles

In Israel, Syria and Lebanon this popular street food is made with chickpeas. But in Egypt, where the rissoles originate, they are made with dried broad beans and are by far the best – very green with herbs and strongly flavoured with garlic and spices. They are called *ta'amia* in Cairo and *falafel* in Alexandria and are eaten for breakfast as well as an appetiser. They make good party 'finger food'.

For this recipe buy the skinless, split broad beans which are pale cream.

Serves 10

500 g (1 lb) skinned broad beans, soaked overnight
Salt and pepper
2 teaspoons cumin
Pinch of cayenne (optional)
1 teaspoon baking soda
6–10 garlic cloves
Large bunch of coriander, finely chopped
Large bunch of parsley, finely chopped
1 large onion, very finely chopped
4–5 spring onions, very finely chopped
Sunflower or other light vegetable oil

Drain the beans well and put through a food processor until they form a very soft paste. The secret of success is to have a paste so smooth and soft that it holds together in the frying oil. Add salt and pepper, cumin, cayenne and baking soda and let the mixture rest for an hour.

Add the rest of the ingredients using plenty of herbs, about 50 g (2 oz) or more. If you chop the onion in the food processor make sure that you drain off any juices. Knead the mixture well with your hands.

Take small lumps of paste, roll them into balls and flatten them into cakes about 5 cm (2 in) in diameter and 0.5 cm ($\frac{1}{4}$ in) thick. Fry the cakes in hot oil, turning them over once, until they are crisp and brown. Lift them out with a slotted spoon and drain on kitchen paper. Reheat in the oven before serving.

Serve, if you like, in pitta bread with chopped lettuce and tomatoes, and tahina (see p. 53) diluted with water and lemon juice and seasoned with salt and pepper as a sauce.

Hummus bi Tahina

Chickpea and Sesame Dip

Nothing from the Arab world, except perhaps kebab, is as well known abroad as *hummus*, but the kind you can now find in supermarkets is generally not well flavoured. You can do much better yourself with little effort. The secret is to keep tasting as you add the seasonings. Serve with warmed pitta bread for dipping.

Serves 4–6

125 g (4 oz) chickpeas, soaked for a few hours
Juice of 2 lemons
3 tablespoons tahina (see p. 53)
2 garlic cloves, crushed
Salt

Garnish:
1 tablespoon olive oil
1 teaspoon paprika
A few sprigs of parsley, finely chopped

Drain the chickpeas and simmer in fresh water for about an hour or until tender. Reserve the cooking water.

Process the chickpeas in a blender with the lemon juice, tahina, garlic and salt and enough of the cooking liquid to obtain a soft creamy consistency.

Serve on a flat plate, garnished with a dribble of olive oil, a dusting of paprika (this is usually done in the shape of a cross) and a little parsley.

Variations
* Sprinkle with sumac (see p. 53) and a pinch of cayenne.
* In Egypt 1 teaspoon cumin is added.
* Garnish with cooked chickpeas (boil more than the required quantity and leave some aside for this) or with shining pink pomegranate seeds.

Bottom left: Hummus bi tahina
Bottom right: Tabbouleh (p. 68)
Top: Falafel (opposite)

Torshi Left

Pickled Turnips

You could easily become addicted to this popular Arab pickle. In Egypt they make it in brine alone, without any vinegar. The beetroots colour the turnips a lovely pink. Keep refrigerated and use within 2 weeks.

1 kg (2 lb) turnips
2 beetroots, raw or cooked, sliced
2 garlic cloves, sliced
1.1 litre (2 pints) water
4–5 tablespoons salt

You can use baby turnips or large ones as long as they are very firm and unblemished. Trim and wash them; peel larger ones if necessary. Cut them in two or four depending on their size and leave baby ones whole.

Place the turnips in one or more sterilised preserving jars layered with slices of beetroot and garlic between them. Put the water and salt in a saucepan, bring to the boil and pour over the vegetables. Seal the jars and leave in a warm place for 3–4 days, by which time the pickle will be ready to eat. Keep in the refrigerator.

Salatet Ads

Lentil Salad

This simple Egyptian salad can be made with green or brown lentils, but not the split red ones.

Serves 4

250 g (8 oz) green or brown lentils
Salt
4 tablespoons olive oil
Juice of ½–1 lemon
Pepper
1 teaspoon ground cumin (optional)
3 spring onions, finely chopped
Small bunch of parsley or mint, finely chopped

Soaking the lentils only makes them cook a little faster and is not really necessary. Simmer in enough fresh water to cover for 20–30 minutes or until tender, adding a little salt towards the end. Drain and immediately mix with the remaining ingredients so that the hot lentils absorb the dressing. Serve cold.

Gigantes Plaki

Large White Beans in Tomato Sauce

The most interesting part of a meal in Greek tavernas is the *metze* in which large white beans are standard fare. Butter beans are the closest you can get to them here. The combination of herbs, lemon and sugar makes this dish a little out of the ordinary.

Serves 6 or more

500 g (1 lb) dried butter beans
1 large onion, finely chopped
2–3 tablespoons olive oil
2 garlic cloves, finely chopped (optional)
1 kg (2 lb) ripe tomatoes, peeled and chopped
1 teaspoon thyme or oregano
2 bay leaves
Salt and pepper
2 teaspoons sugar or to taste
Juice of ½ a lemon
1 tablespoon dried mint
Small bunch of parsley, finely chopped

Soak the beans in water to cover for about 4 hours. (The skins will split but do not worry.) Fry the onions in oil till golden. Add the garlic, if using, and when it begins to colour add the tomatoes and the drained beans with a little thyme or oregano and bay leaves. Barely cover with water and simmer gently until the beans begin to soften, then add salt and pepper, sugar, lemon juice and mint, and cook until they are very tender. This can take less than an hour or much longer depending on the quality of the beans. Be careful not to overcook or they fall apart. Add parsley towards the end of the cooking. Serve at room temperature. This dish keeps well for several days.

Fromage de Chèvre Mariné

Marinated Goat's Cheese

Goat's cheeses of all shapes and sizes, made by local farmers, are a lovely sight on Provençal market stalls. They are now widely available in the UK.

Use small, firm, but not dry cheeses for this French preserve.

6 small round goat's cheeses weighing about 65 g
(2½ oz) each
1 tablespoon black peppercorns
2 garlic cloves
2 small chilli peppers
4 bay leaves
3 sprigs of thyme
3 sprigs of rosemary
300 ml (10 fl oz) olive oil

Put the goat's cheeses, whole or cut in half, in a wide-necked jar together with the aromatics and cover with oil. They will be ready to eat after 1 week and may begin to soften after 4 weeks.

Variation
In the eastern Mediterranean cheeses such as feta, and labne, which is made by draining yogurt until it is firm (see p. 213), are marinated in oil with slices of lemon and plenty of mint.

Left: Pain aux olives (p. 99)
Right: Fromage de chèvre mariné

Gibneh Beyda

White Cheese Dip

The recipe for this mainstay of Egyptian peasant fare was given by Nayra Atiya who serves it for lunch with peasant bread (see p. 97). Nayra, who lives in Shabramant, a village outside Cairo, gets her cheese from Upper Egypt and stores it in oil from year to year. The taste is so strong that she dilutes the cheese with a lot of milk but the ewe's milk or feta cheese found here is far less pungent and rarely needs this treatment.

Serves 4–6

250 g (8 oz) ewe's milk or feta cheese
Milk (optional)
300 ml (10 fl oz) thick ewe's milk yogurt or
  strained yogurt
2 tablespoons each of parsley, mint and dill, finely
  chopped
2–3 tablespoons olive oil
Juice of $\frac{1}{2}$ lemon

Feta cheese varies a great deal in saltiness. If you think it is too salty, soak it in milk for an hour, then drain. Mash the drained cheese with a fork. Beat in the yogurt and add the herbs, leaving a little to use as a garnish.

Sprinkle with oil and lemon juice and garnish with the reserved herbs. Accompany with bread.

Polpettine di Spinaci con Ricotta

Spinach and Ricotta Rissoles

This is a speciality of the region of Abruzzi in Italy where cheese is much used in cooking. The mixture of ricotta and spinach is the filling for *ravioli* and *scrippelle*, thin pancakes. When made into rissoles, the mixture is referred to as a naked (*nudo*) version of these.

Serves 6

2 kg (4 lb) spinach
Salt
500 g (1 lb) ricotta
2 large eggs
125 g (4 oz) grated Parmesan
Pepper
Large pinch of nutmeg
Flour
75 g (3 oz) melted butter

Wash the spinach and remove the stems. Blanch the leaves in slightly salted boiling water until they soften, then strain and squeeze out all the water with your hands. There should not be a drop left – this is the secret of success. If you don't do it, the polpettine will fall apart. Finely chop the leaves.

Mash the ricotta with a fork, add the eggs, then stir in the Parmesan, pepper, nutmeg and the spinach. Take a tablespoon of mixture, shape into an oval and roll it in flour. Continue with the rest.

Half-fill a large frying-pan with water, bring to the boil, then reduce the heat. Very carefully drop in the rissoles and keep the water simmering gently until they rise to the surface. (This happens very quickly.) Lift them out very carefully, using a slotted spoon. Serve hot with melted butter poured over.

Note
These polpettine are also very good served with a tomato coulis (p. 217) sauce.

Small cheese factory on the island of Paros, specialising in kefalotiri

Taramasalata

Fish Roe Salad

Tarama is the salted and dried roe of grey mullet. Smoked cod's roe, which is readily available in the UK, is the usual but less strongly flavoured substitute. In Turkey *tarama* is also the name of the salad made by simply pounding the roes with lemon and olive oil. The following Greek recipe is stretched with plenty of bread.

Serves 6

125 g (4 oz) smoked cod's roe
Juice of 1 or more large lemons
2 large slices of white bread, crusts removed and
  soaked in water
75–125 ml (3–4 fl oz) olive oil
½ small onion, grated and the juice drained off

Skin the roe and put in a food processor or blender with the lemon juice. Add the bread, squeezed dry, and blend well. Then very slowly add the oil until the mixture is the consistency of mayonnaise. Stir in the onion at the end and more lemon juice, if you like.

Artichauts à la Vinaigrette

Artichokes Vinaigrette

The artichokes available in the UK are neither large enough to produce a good heart and an edible stalk, nor young enough to be eaten whole. The best way to have them is boiled whole, accompanied by a vinaigrette (see p. 210). They are easy to cook and fun to eat.

Wash the artichokes well and cut off the stalks. Put them in a large pan of salted water, stem-ends down, and simmer for 30–45 minutes depending on their size. To see if they are done, pull away a leaf and chew the flesh at the base. When tender, drain the artichokes well and leave to cool.

Serve generous quantities of vinaigrette in individual bowls. To eat the artichoke, dip the base of the leaves in the dressing and nibble away the fleshy part. Then remove the fibrous central choke with a spoon and soak the fleshy base in the vinaigrette. This is the best part of the artichoke and worth waiting for. Provide a large bowl for discarded leaves.

Artichauts à la vinaigrette

Asperges à la Vinaigrette

Asparagus Vinaigrette

You can use any variety of asparagus for this recipe but make sure that the stalks are not woody.

Serves 4–6

1 kg (2 lb) asparagus
Salt
90 ml (3½ fl oz) olive oil
1 tablespoon vinegar or the juice of ½ lemon
White pepper
Small bunch of parsley, finely chopped

Rinse the asparagus. Peel away any hard skin and cut off the tough ends. Tie them up in bundles and simmer in salted water until you can pierce the stalks with a pointed knife. Depending on their quality and size this can take from a few minutes to more than 30 minutes. Lift out the bundles and drain well.

Beat the olive oil with the vinegar or lemon juice, salt and pepper. Serve the asparagus with this sauce poured over and sprinkled with parsley.

Variation

We were served a colourful *salsa piperrada* with asparagus in Valencia. Put ½ a green pepper and ½ a red pepper under the grill, skin side up for a few minutes until they are soft and their skins are brown and blistered. Peel them and chop the flesh by hand as finely as you can. Chop 1 small firm tomato, ¼ of a cucumber and a small mild red onion or 3 spring onions into tiny little bits. Beat 120 ml (4 fl oz) olive oil with 2 tablespoons wine vinegar, salt and pepper and stir in all the vegetables just before serving.

White Wines of the South of France

The vine has been cultivated since Phoenician times in southern France, where today some lovely white wines are produced. The fresh and elegant Cassis comes from the area around the little fishing port between Marseilles and Toulon. Bellet is an exceptionally light white from a small vineyard in the hills above. Palette comes from near Aix-en-Provence, while from north of Avignon, one of the few white wines of the Côtes-du-Rhône, Condrieu, is also a top wine of the region.

Henri Fontin's Ratatouille

A *ratatouille* can be served hot or cold, as an *hors d'oeuvre*, a side dish or a main dish. In Nice all the vegetables are fried separately so that each can have a different cooking time and different intensity of heat. As this takes time and requires many pans it is worth making a large amount to eat over several days. The proportions of vegetables vary; the following are the preference of Henri Fontin who gives Provençal cookery lessons in the rambling youth hostel he runs in Séguret near Avignon.

Serves 6

750 g (1½ lb) aubergines
500 g (1 lb) courgettes
2 green peppers
1 large Spanish onion, peeled
Olive oil
Salt and pepper
2 large beef tomatoes, peeled and de-seeded
1 teaspoon fresh thyme
2 bay leaves
¼–½ teaspoon cayenne pepper, or 1 small dried chilli

Cut the vegetables into 1–1.5 cm (½–¾ in) pieces. Fry the first 4 vegetables separately. Fry the courgettes, peppers and onion in 2 or more tablespoons of oil each very gently on low heat, until they are cooked *al dente* – tender but still firm. The aubergines will need more oil and it must be hot to begin with to seal them. Cook them until they are very soft. Add salt and pepper to taste.

Combine the cooked vegetables with the tomatoes, herbs and cayenne pepper or chilli for 15 minutes more over medium heat, stirring constantly.

Variations

* Fry 5 finely chopped garlic cloves, add 750 g (1½ lb) of peeled, de-seeded and chopped tomatoes and cook until they are reduced to a thick sauce. Add this to the vegetables instead of the two tomatoes. This version is my favourite.

* *Caponata* is a Sicilian relative of ratatouille. Make it like ratatouille but without peppers and courgettes. Add 3 celery stalks, coarsely chopped, a handful of pitted green olives and 2 tablespoons of capers. Give it a sweet and sour taste with 4 tablespoons wine vinegar, 1 tablespoon sugar and, if you like, 1–2 tablespoons of cocoa powder. Garnish with toasted, chopped almonds and chopped parsley.

Pepper Salad

You will find the same kind of pepper salads all over the Mediterranean. All are marvellous but they are only worth making with large, fleshy peppers. They are usually roasted straight on the fire or under a grill but I find it easier to cook them in the oven.

Serves 6

6 peppers, mixed green, red and yellow
4 tablespoons or more olive oil
Salt and pepper

Pre-heat the oven to 240°C (475°F, gas mark 9).

Put the peppers in the hottest part of the oven for about 20–30 minutes, turning them over once until they are really brown. Put them straight into a polythene or plastic bag, close tightly, then leave them for 10–15 minutes. This loosens their skins so that they come off easily. Peel the peppers, pull off the stems, remove the seeds and cut the flesh into strips. Do not wash them but pour the juices which have collected in the polythene bag over them. Dress simply with olive oil, salt and pepper.

Variations

* For a fiery *à la mode de Tunis* version add a handful of black olives, 1 tablespoon capers and 1 or 2 hard-boiled eggs, cut into wedges. Add to the dressing 3 crushed garlic cloves, 1 teaspoon harissa (see p. 50) or a good pinch of cayenne and a teaspoon paprika, and 1 teaspoon caraway seeds, if you like. Served with 250 g (8 oz) tinned tuna, the salad becomes almost a meal in itself.
* In Egypt the peppers are combined with an equal quantity of sliced tomatoes. Garnish with a handful of thinly sliced spring onions and a bunch of finely chopped parsley.
* Roast 2 small fresh chillis and a few whole garlic cloves in their skins with the peppers. Mince the chillis and squeeze the garlic out of its skin like a paste. Beat this into the dressing.

Salade de Tomates et Poivrons

Moroccan Pepper and Tomato Salad

Moroccan food is mild and delicate; only the appetisers are hot and spicy.

Serves 4–6

4 green peppers
3 tomatoes, peeled, de-seeded and diced
Salt
1 teaspoon cumin
Large pinch of cayenne
Juice of ½ lemon
4 tablespoons olive oil
Small bunch of parsley, finely chopped
½ preserved lemon (see p. 214), cut into thin strips or diced (optional)

Pre-heat the oven to 240°C (475°F, gas mark 9).

Roast the peppers for about 30 minutes until they are brown, turning them over once. Put them in a polythene bag and close it tightly. Leave for 15 minutes. Peel the peppers while still warm and cut into small dice. Mix well with the remaining ingredients and leave to cool. Serve cold.

Escalivada

Roasted Vegetable Salad

Escalivada is a Spanish dish which is eaten hot or cold, sometimes with a sprinkling of salt cod or tuna. I like it as a summer salad.

Serves 6

300 g (10 oz) medium onions
300 g (10 oz) green peppers
300 g (10 oz) red peppers
300 g (10 oz) aubergines
75 ml (3 fl oz) olive oil
Salt

Pre-heat the oven to 180°C (350°F, gas mark 4).

Bake all the vegetables for about 1 hour or until they are very soft and the skins are brown. Put the peppers in a polythene bag and close it tight for 10 minutes to loosen their skins. When the vegetables are cool enough to handle, peel them and cut them into long thin strips. Dress simply with olive oil and a little salt. Serve cold.

Fried Aubergine Slices

The aubergine must be the most popular vegetable in the Mediterranean, with every country in the Eastern part claiming to have 100 ways of cooking it. I have never put that legend to the test but I have found many different recipes for fried aubergine slices, all rich and oily but incredibly good.

Use medium-sized or large aubergines, peeled or not according to your preference, and cut them into slices about 1 cm ($\frac{1}{2}$ in) thick. It makes a more attractive presentation to slice them lengthways if they are not too big. Sprinkle abundantly with salt and leave for about an hour to draw out the bitter juices and make them absorb less oil. Rinse well and gently squeeze out the moisture, a few slices at a time, or pat them dry.

Shallow-fry the slices very quickly in hot oil, turning them over once until lightly browned and soft inside. Olive oil for frying gives the best taste but a mixture of olive oil and sunflower oil is fine. Lay the slices on a few sheets of kitchen paper as they are cooked and cover with more paper to remove as much oil as possible. Serve hot or cold, sprinkled with chopped parsley or with one of the following sauces.

Sauces

* For a traditional Arab sauce, mix lemon juice or wine vinegar with fried crushed garlic.
* For another Arab flavour, pour pomegranate juice over the slices and garnish with chopped mint and pomegranate seeds.
* For a hot and spicy Algerian sauce, fry 4 chopped garlic cloves in 3 tablespoons olive oil with 1 teaspoon cumin, 2 teaspoons paprika and a large pinch of cayenne. Add 3 tablespoons wine vinegar or the juice of 1 lemon and simmer a minute longer.
* For Sicilian sweet and sour *melanzane all'agrodolce*, heat 6 tablespoons wine vinegar with a little of the left-over frying oil, some salt and pepper and $1\frac{1}{2}$ tablespoons sugar, or to taste. Pour over the aubergines – there will be enough for 2 large ones – and sprinkle with 6 chopped and fried garlic cloves and a mixture of chopped basil, mint, oregano and parsley. Leave for an hour before serving for the flavours to develop.

Garnishes

* Spread a thick layer of strained yogurt over hot or cold aubergine slices, Turkish-style.
* Cover the aubergine slices, placed in an ovenproof dish, with a tomato coulis (see p. 217). Add salt and black pepper and 1 teaspoon sugar, if the tomatoes are not sweet enough, together with a bunch of finely chopped fresh herbs such as basil, parsley, mint and chives. Bake in a hot oven for 10 minutes and serve hot or cold. This is Provençal.
* Pierre Hiély, proprietor of the Chez Hiély restaurant in Avignon, gave us his recipe for *gratin d'aubergines*. Cover 750 g ($1\frac{1}{2}$ lb) aubergine slices with a plain tomato coulis and top with 300 ml (10 fl oz) single cream simmered with chopped fresh herbs for 10 minutes until reduced. Put it in the oven to heat through.

Aubergines, Toulon market

Champignons Farcis

Stuffed Mushrooms

Those who are not keen on cooking snails but love the traditional garlic and parsley snail sauce will enjoy this Provençal dish.

Serves 6

500 g (1 lb) large flat mushrooms
Olive oil
Salt and pepper
65–75 g (2½–3 oz) parsley, finely chopped
2 slices of dry white bread, crusts removed
2 or more garlic cloves, crushed
2–3 tablespoons cognac (optional)

Wash the mushrooms briefly and cut off the stalks. Sauté in 2–3 tablespoons of oil for 5 minutes or until just tender, sprinkling with salt and pepper and turning them over once. Arrange, stem-side up, on a flat, heatproof dish.

To make the stuffing, chop the mushroom stalks and parsley and crumble the bread finely, or put them through a blender. Turn into a bowl and add as much garlic as you like and a little salt and pepper. Moisten with cognac, if using, and with 2–3 tablespoons olive oil and mix well. Press a little stuffing into each mushroom and grill for 5 minutes. Serve hot.

Wild mushrooms, Genoa market

Champiñones al Ajillo

Mushrooms in Garlic Sauce

Spaniards have a passion for mushrooms and go out into the woods to look for wild ones in the autumn.

We visited La Boqueria, the market of San José in Barcelona, the day before its 150th anniversary as they were preparing for a display of wild mushrooms. We saw a collection of these which had been brought down from the wooded hills still on the tree trunks on which they grew.

This is the simplest way to cook mushrooms, wild or cultivated, and also the one which best brings out their flavour.

Serves 4

250 g (8 oz) oyster or button mushrooms
3 tablespoons olive oil
3 garlic cloves, finely chopped
Juice of ½ lemon (optional)
Salt and pepper
Small bunch of parsley, finely chopped

Trim and wash the mushrooms briefly. They can be sliced if large but are best left whole. Heat the oil, add the mushrooms and garlic and fry over a high heat for 2 or 3 minutes, then add the lemon juice, if using, salt and pepper. Sprinkle with parsley and serve hot or cold.

Tapas

Tapas are popular all over Spain but are most typical of Andalusia. These little dishes which are produced by bar-tenders to accompany drinks have become an institution. Because it is hot people 'live' at night and they eat late – lunch is at three, dinner at eleven – and *tapas* fill the hunger gap and the need to socialise. Simple *tapas*, like crumbled bread with pork fat and crackling, chickpeas and tripe, pork and lamb stew and the mushrooms in garlic sauce described above, are examples of the kind of dishes also made at home. People only pick at *tapas*. They are supposed to sharpen your appetite for the meal to come, not to fill you up.

Terbiyeli Pirasa

Leeks in Egg and Lemon Sauce

A little sugar and a Turkish egg and lemon sauce give leeks a delicate sweet and sour flavour.

Serves 4

1 kg (2 lb) small leeks
75 ml (3 fl oz) olive oil
1–1½ tablespoons sugar (optional)
Salt
2 eggs
Juice of 1½ lemons

Trim the leeks and wash well. If necessary, slit them half way up the middle with a pointed knife to wash out any earth lodged between the leaves. Put them in a saucepan with the oil, 1 tablespoon sugar, a little salt and just enough water to cover. Bring to the boil and simmer until only just tender. Lift them out with a slotted spoon, reserving the cooking liquid, and arrange them on a serving dish.

To make the sauce, beat the eggs and lemon juice with about 3 tablespoons of the cooking liquid and pour into a small saucepan. Cook over a very low heat, stirring constantly, until the sauce thickens. Be careful not to let it curdle. Add salt and pepper and ½ tablespoon sugar if you want the sauce to be sweeter.

Pour the sauce over the leeks and let them cool before serving.

Cipolline in Agrodolce

Sweet and Sour Onions

In this Sicilian dish the little onions take a long time to peel and a long time to cook but they have such a delicate refreshing flavour that it really is worth trying.

Serves 6

500 g (1 lb) pickling onions or shallots
3 tablespoons olive oil
Salt
2–3 tablespoons wine vinegar
2 teaspoons sugar or to taste

To make the onions easier to peel, plunge them in their skins into boiling water for 1 minute, then drain and peel. Fry the onions whole very gently in oil, shaking the pan occasionally and turning them until they are a rich golden brown. Add salt, vinegar and sugar, cover with water and simmer slowly, uncovered, for about an hour or until they are very soft and the liquid is absorbed. Add more water, if necessary, during the cooking and adjust the balance of sugar and vinegar to your taste.

Cebollitas Rebozadas

Spring Onion Fritters

This recipe comes from Mercè Navarro of the restaurant Roig Robí in Barcelona. Mercè is one of the band of women chefs who have recently made great names for themselves in Spain.

Serves 6

18 fat spring onions
150 g (5 oz) flour
1 tablespoon olive oil
1 egg yolk
200 ml (7 fl oz) water or soda water
1½ teaspoons baking powder
Sunflower oil for deep-frying

Peel off the outer skin of the spring onions and trim the roots and green ends. To make the batter, mix the flour with the oil and egg yolk and gradually beat in the water or soda water to make a smooth cream. Season with salt and let it rest for 30 minutes, then beat in the baking powder.

Dip the spring onions in the batter and deep-fry, a few at a time, in hot oil until golden. Drain on kitchen paper. Keep the fritters hot in a low oven until all are fried. These go well with romesco sauce (p. 211).

Variation

For Turkish pumpkin fritters substitute pumpkin, cut into 1 cm (½ in) slices. Serve with yogurt.

Zucchine Marinate

Marinated Courgettes

This fresh-tasting southern Italian salad makes the best use of raw, young, tender courgettes.

Serves 4

**500 g (1 lb) small young courgettes, finely sliced,
  coarsely chopped or grated**
3 tablespoons olive oil
Juice of ½ lemon or more
2 garlic cloves, cut in ½
Salt and pepper
Small bunch of parsley, finely chopped

Mix all the ingredients except the parsley in a bowl and leave to marinate for a day. Remove the garlic and add the parsley before serving.

Red Wines from Southern Italy

Not many southern Italian red wines are known outside their area of production. There are, however, some notable exceptions, one of them being Lacryma Christi del Vesuvio ('The tears of Christ'). The wine is warm and generous, very much in keeping with the character of the city of Naples.

Another splendid red, probably the best of the region, is Taurasi, produced in Avellino, only a few miles inland. A rich, full-bodied wine, it ages well and provides an excellent accompaniment to the local specialities such as meat soups and stews.

Over on the other side of the Apennines, in the Marches, an exceptionally well made full and velvety red simply called Rosso Piceno, is produced in the foothills near Ascoli Piceno. Further south we come to the region of Puglia, one of the largest wine-producing areas in the country. Traditionally, the heavier wines have been shipped north for blending with the lighter wines of northern Italy, but local winegrowers also produce good-quality wines for drinking with the simple, unpretentious dishes of the region – wines like those of Castel del Monte or the very powerful Primitivo.

Fiori di Zucca o di Zucchine Fritte

Marrow or Courgette Flower Fritters

Large yellow marrow blossoms and smaller courgette flowers have a delicate perfume. Deep-fried, they make enchanting summer delicacies popular in Italy and the South of France.

Serves 6

500 g (1 lb) marrow or courgette blossoms
2 tablespoons olive oil
75 g (3 oz) flour
Salt
1 egg white, stiffly beaten
Oil for frying
2 lemons, cut into wedges

Remove the stems and pistils from the flowers and wash them. Gently press them in a cloth to dry them.

Make a light batter. Mix the oil into the flour and beat in enough water – about 175 ml (6 fl oz) – to obtain a smooth creamy consistency. Add a little salt and let the batter rest for an hour. When you are ready to cook, fold in the stiffly beaten egg white.

Dip each flower in the batter and fry for about a minute until the fritters are crisp and golden, turning them over once. Be careful not to let them brown too much. Test if the oil is hot enough by flicking a drop of batter in and seeing if it sizzles. Lift the flowers out with a slotted spoon and drain on kitchen paper. Serve accompanied by lemon wedges.

Variations
* The flowers can be stuffed with slivers of mozzarella and, if you like, tiny pieces of anchovy fillets, before being dipped into batter and fried.
* For the French version – *beignets de fleurs de courgettes* – mix the egg yolk into the flour and use milk instead of water. Serve the flowers with a fresh tomato coulis (see p. 217) mixed with chopped herbs.
* Sprinkled with sugar, the fritters make a good dessert.

Tortilla de Pimientos

Sweet Pepper and Potato Omelette

One of the most attractive sides to life in Spain is the 'tapas' crawl' which involves visiting several bars and combines drinking and eating, chance meetings and lively conversation. To hurry in this part of the world is a sin. This *tapas* dish was made for us by Alicia Ríos. The easy way to succeed with a Spanish omelette is to use a large, non-stick frying-pan. Be prepared to use plenty of oil and to discard the excess.

Serves 6

5 eggs
Salt
I onion, thinly sliced
I green or red pepper, cut in half, then thinly sliced
I–2 potatoes, thinly sliced
Olive oil

Beat the eggs with a pinch of salt. Fry the vegetables together in olive oil until they are tender but not mushy. Drain well and stir into the eggs.

Wipe the pan with kitchen paper and heat 2 tablespoons of oil in it. When it begins to sizzle, pour in the egg and vegetable mixture, then lower the heat. When the eggs begin to set, run a spatula round the edge to release the omelette. Shake the pan and cook until the bottom is firm. Turn the omelette over using a spatula or turn it upside down onto a plate and then slip it back into the pan, cooked-side up, making sure that there is enough oil. Cook until the omelette is firm but still slightly moist inside. Serve hot or at room temperature, cut into wedges.

Chakchouka

Tunisian Eggs

There are many regional versions of this Tunisian vegetable dish. This one from Nabeul is made with eggs and has become popular all over the Arab world. Serve it hot as an appetiser or as a light meal.

Serves 4

2 green peppers, thinly sliced
3 tablespoons olive oil
3 garlic cloves, crushed
Salt
I teaspoon harissa (see p. 50) or I teaspoon paprika and large pinch of cayenne
I teaspoon ground caraway or cumin (optional)
4 tomatoes, peeled and sliced
4 eggs

Fry the peppers in oil in a large frying-pan until they are soft. Add the garlic and as soon as it begins to colour add the salt, harissa and spices and stir well.

Add the tomatoes and drop the eggs in whole. Cook gently until they set.

Variations
* Fry I chopped onion with the peppers.
* Add 125 g (4 oz) sliced mergez (see p. 55) with the tomatoes.
* Fry I diced aubergine with only I pepper.

Chakchouka

Kibbeh

Stuffed Cracked Wheat Shells

Syrian cooking, and especially the cooking of Aleppo, is considered the pearl of Arab cooking. This famous Syrian dish – a minced meat filling stuffed into shells of cracked wheat – is a bit fiddly to make but well worth the effort. Malak Mawaldi skilfully turns out the shells in a twinkling of an eye. In Egypt, where Malak lives, the dish is called *kobeiba*.

Makes 20

For the shells:
250 g (8 oz) burghul (cracked wheat)
500 g (1 lb) minced beef
1 onion, coarsely chopped
Salt and pepper

For the stuffing:
1 onion, finely chopped
2 tablespoons sunflower oil
2 tablespoons pine-nuts
500 g (1 lb) minced beef
Salt and pepper

Sunflower oil for deep-frying

To make the shells, soak the cracked wheat for about 20 minutes in water, then drain. Blend the meat, onion, salt and pepper in a food processor. Then process again, in batches, with the cracked wheat and continue until the mixture is soft enough to work like a dough. Knead well by hand.

For the stuffing, fry the onion in oil till soft, then add the pine-nuts and fry till golden. Add the meat, salt and pepper and stir until the meat changes colour.

Wet your hands. Take a small egg-sized portion of the shell mixture and roll into a ball. Make a hole in the centre with your finger and shape into a thin-walled pot with a pointed bottom by turning and pressing it in your palm. Place some stuffing into the hole and pinch the top of the pot together to seal it. Shape the top into a point. Repeat with the rest of the mixtures, wetting your hands frequently.

Heat the oil. Deep-fry 4 or 5 kibbeh at a time until golden brown and drain on kitchen paper. Serve hot.

Variations
* For a spicier version, add 1 teaspoon cinnamon and $\frac{1}{2}$ teaspoon allspice to the stuffing.
* *Labaneya*, is kibbeh cooked in yogurt. First stabilise about 900 ml (1$\frac{1}{2}$ pints) yogurt to prevent it curdling while it cooks by beating in an egg white and then bringing the yogurt slowly to the boil, stirring constantly in the same direction. Then add salt and the uncooked kibbeh and cook gently, uncovered, for about 20 minutes. Towards the end of cooking, stir in a bunch of chopped coriander, or some dried mint fried in butter. Serve hot or cold.

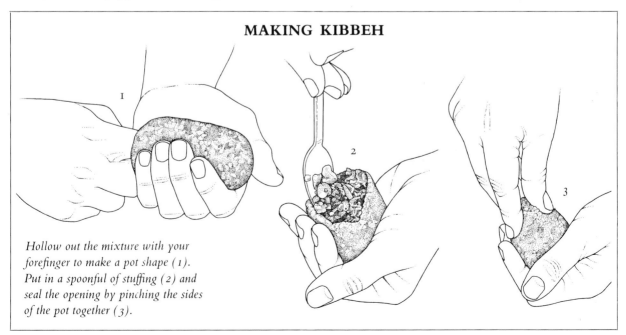

MAKING KIBBEH

Hollow out the mixture with your forefinger to make a pot shape (1). Put in a spoonful of stuffing (2) and seal the opening by pinching the sides of the pot together (3).

Keftedes

Meatballs

Roula Makris of Athens gave this recipe for one of the most popular Greek *metzethes*.

Makes 15–20

2–3 slices of white bread, crusts removed
500 g (1 lb) minced beef or lamb
1 large egg
1 large onion, grated
1–2 garlic cloves, crushed
2 tablespoons olive oil
1 teaspoon ground cumin
Salt and pepper
Small bunch of parsley, finely chopped
1 teaspoon dried oregano
A few sprigs of mint, chopped (optional)

For frying:
Flour
Sunflower oil

Soak the bread in water and squeeze it dry. Mix all the ingredients together and work with your hands for about 5 minutes to achieve a soft, dough-like consistency.

With wet hands, form the mixture into walnut-sized balls, then flatten them slightly. Flour the keftedes twice so as to have a good crust. In a large frying-pan heat the sunflower oil until it sizzles. Fry the keftedes for 5–6 minutes, being careful not to overcrowd the pan. Turn them over once so that they are evenly crisp and brown. Drain on kitchen paper and serve hot.

Hígado y Riñones al Jeréz

Liver and Kidneys in Sherry Sauce

This is a quick and easy Spanish dish made with chicken livers and calves' or lambs' kidneys. Serve as a *tapa* or as a main course with potatoes or rice, or simply with bread.

Serves 6

250 g (8 oz) calves' or lambs' kidneys
250 g (8 oz) chicken livers
Salt and pepper
Pinch of ground nutmeg
Flour
2 large tomatoes, peeled, de-seeded and chopped
1 garlic clove
125 ml (4 fl oz) dry sherry
3 tablespoons olive or sunflower oil

Cut out the tough cores from the kidneys, snip the membranes and rinse very briefly, then cut into bite-sized pieces. Pull off the veins from the livers and separate the pieces. Season the kidneys and livers with salt, pepper and nutmeg, and roll in flour to seal in the juices.

Simmer the tomatoes with the whole garlic clove and sherry for about 10 minutes or until the sauce is reduced and thick. Sauté the kidneys and livers for 1–2 minutes in hot oil, putting the kidneys in first. The livers should remain pink inside. Lift them out of the oil and add them to the sauce. Heat through, stirring gently. Remove the garlic clove before serving.

Tapas

The best thing to drink with Spanish *tapas* is sherry – a dry, well chilled fino makes an excellent aperitif. Amontillado is darker and rounder in flavour while oloroso is darker and richer still. Or you could, if you are lucky enough to find one, treat yourself to a palo cortado, a rare type which is both dry and rich.

These sherries, or fortified wines, are primarily made from the Palomino grape and should be served chilled. Also, once opened, don't leave the bottle standing around on the sideboard. Keep it in the fridge and drink it within a week, if you possibly can, or it will lose its freshness and flavour.

You might, of course, prefer a light red wine or a fresh dry white with your *tapas*. In Spain, ask for *un tinto* or *un blanco de la casa*. Or try *un clarete*, a dark rosé wine. In Spain today it has become fashionable to drink sparkling wine, *espumoso*, with food. There are several good examples to choose from, especially those produced in Catalunya and made by the *méthode champenoise* which are called *cava*. To go with *tapas* choose a Brut Nature.

Spanakopitta

Spinach and Cheese Pie

The recipe for this Greek pie comes from an Athenian cookery writer, June Marinos.

Serves 8

1 kg (2 lb) spinach
1 onion, finely chopped
4 spring onions, finely chopped
2 tablespoons olive oil plus 6 more if using it to brush the pastry
4 tablespoons dill or parsley, finely chopped
4 eggs
250 g (8 oz) feta cheese
2 tablespoons kefalotiri or Parmesan cheese, grated
Large pinch of nutmeg
Pepper
500 g (1 lb) filo pastry (see p. 45)
125 g (4 oz) melted butter (optional)

Pre-heat the oven to 190°C (375°F, gas mark 5).

First make the filling. Cut away the spinach stems and wash the leaves thoroughly. Drain and squeeze out the water, then shred the leaves. In a large saucepan gently fry the onion and spring onions in 2 tablespoons of the oil. Add the spinach, dill or parsley and stir until the spinach is soft and the liquid has evaporated. Allow to cool.

Beat the eggs lightly in a bowl. Add the feta cheese, mashed with a fork, and the kefalotiri or Parmesan cheese, the spinach mixture (drained of its juice), nutmeg and pepper and stir well. Brush a rectangular baking tin with oil or melted butter. The tin should be about 38 × 28 cm (15 × 11 in) or a little smaller than the sheets of filo. Place half the sheets of filo at the bottom, one on top of another. Brush each sheet with oil or melted butter and let the edges come up the sides of the tin. Spread the filling evenly on top, fold over the edges of the filo dough and cover with the remaining filo, tucking the edges down the sides of the tin. Brush each sheet – and the top one generously – with oil or melted butter. Cut the pie into squares or diamonds with a sharp knife, but do not cut through to the bottom or the filling will leak into the pan.

Bake about 1 hour or until the pie is crisp, golden and puffed up. Cut the squares or diamonds right through to the bottom and serve hot.

Above: Spanakopitta

Arancini di Riso

Rice Croquettes

These rice balls flavoured with meat sauce are a southern Italian speciality. They have a crisp golden crust and are soft and moist inside. The recipe is from Il Fagiano at Selva di Fasano, Puglia.

Makes about 16

500 g (1 lb) short grain or pudding rice
Salt
2 eggs
50 g (2 oz) grated Parmesan or caciotta cheese
Breadcrumbs (optional)
Oil for frying

For the meat sauce:
1 medium onion, finely chopped
1 tablespoon sunflower or olive oil
300 g (10 oz) minced beef or veal
3 tablespoons tomato paste
150 ml (5 fl oz) white wine
Salt and pepper
2 bay leaves
A sprig of rosemary or thyme

For the crust:
Flour
1 egg
50 g (2 oz) fine dry breadcrumbs

Cook the rice, covered, in 1.2 litres (2 pints) water with a little salt for about 20 minutes or until the rice is soft. Let it cool, then stir in the eggs and the cheese and mix well. Work with your hands until it sticks together in a soft mass.

To make the sauce, fry the onion in oil till soft, add the meat and fry for 1–2 minutes or until it changes colour. Add the tomato paste and stir well, then add the wine, salt and pepper, the bay leaves, rosemary or thyme, and cook until the liquid is absorbed. Remove the herbs, let it cool and stir into the rice. Add breadcrumbs if necessary to obtain a stiff consistency.

Wet your hands, take a lump of the mixture the size of a small orange and roll into a ball. Continue with the remaining mixture. Roll the balls in flour, then in the lightly beaten egg and lastly in breadcrumbs being careful not to break the balls. Fry a few at a time in hot oil turning them until they are golden all over. Carefully lift them out and drain on kitchen paper. They can be kept hot or re-heated in the oven.

Variation

Franca Colonna Romano's Sicilian version of rice stuffed with meat sauce is quite enchanting but takes longer to make. Add a pinch of saffron powder to the rice cooking water. Instead of mixing the rice with the meat sauce, take a lump of rice mixture the size of a small egg and hollow it like a nest. Fill with a spoonful of sauce, cover with more rice and roll into a ball, then continue as above. Franca garnishes the croquettes with little twigs with leaves on them to make the balls look like oranges.

Parmesan seller, Lerici

Börek

Little Savoury Pies

These pretty and delicious cheese and meat pastries from Turkey are on the menus of Middle Eastern restaurants all over the world. In Turkey the pastries are often made with a yeast dough, but it is easier to use filo. Cigars and triangles are the traditional shapes and it is considered elegant to make tiny ones for parties.

Filo is sold by the half kilo. Use half the sheets for one filling and half for the other.

Makes about 60–70

250 g (8oz) filo pastry (see p. 45)
3–4 tablespoons melted butter or oil

Cheese filling for peynirli börek:
350 g (12 oz) feta cheese
Pepper
Pinch of nutmeg
Large bunch of mint, parsley or dill, finely chopped

Pre-heat the oven to 180°C (350°F, gas mark 4). Make the filling first. Mash the cheese with a fork and mix in the pepper, nutmeg and herbs.

Take about half the sheets of filo and return the rest to the polythene bag at once, pressing out the air

before closing. To make the pastries cut the sheets with scissors into rectangular strips about 7.5 cm (3 in) wide and put them in a pile so that those underneath do not dry out. They can do so very quickly if they are not kept covered.

Brush the top one very lightly with melted butter or oil. Make cigarette- or triangle-shaped pastries as shown on p. 90 using 1 heaped teaspoonful of filling for each. Place all the little pies on a greased baking sheet. Brush the tops very lightly with butter or oil. Bake for about 25 minutes or until golden.

**Meat filling for kiymela börek as made at the
    Konyali Restaurant in Istanbul**
1 onion, finely chopped
2 tablespoons olive oil
250 g (8 oz) minced beef
1 tomato, peeled and chopped
Salt and pepper
1 egg
Large bunch of parsley, finely chopped
A few sprigs of mint or dill, finely chopped

To make the filling, fry the onion in oil until soft. Add the meat and stir until it changes colour, then add the tomato, salt and pepper and cook gently for 5 minutes. Stir in the egg and the herbs, remove from the heat and let the mixture cool a little. Proceed as for the main recipe. This filling is usually made into triangular pies.

Preparation of börek

89

MAKING FILO PASTRIES

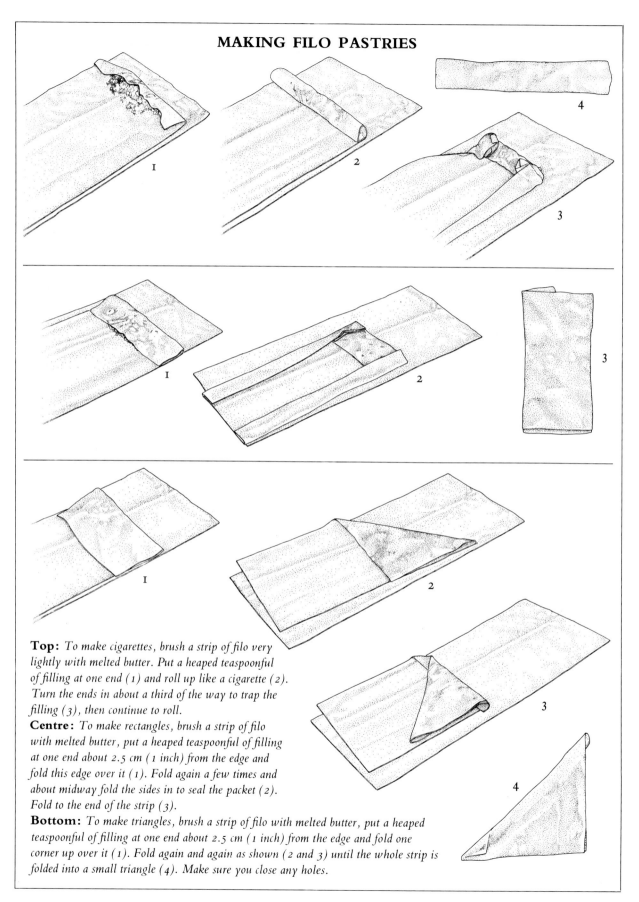

Top: *To make cigarettes, brush a strip of filo very lightly with melted butter. Put a heaped teaspoonful of filling at one end (1) and roll up like a cigarette (2). Turn the ends in about a third of the way to trap the filling (3), then continue to roll.*

Centre: *To make rectangles, brush a strip of filo with melted butter, put a heaped teaspoonful of filling at one end about 2.5 cm (1 inch) from the edge and fold this edge over it (1). Fold again a few times and about midway fold the sides in to seal the packet (2). Fold to the end of the strip (3).*

Bottom: *To make triangles, brush a strip of filo with melted butter, put a heaped teaspoonful of filling at one end about 2.5 cm (1 inch) from the edge and fold one corner up over it (1). Fold again and again as shown (2 and 3) until the whole strip is folded into a small triangle (4). Make sure you close any holes.*

Briouates

Deep-fried Pastry Parcels

Moroccan *briouates* are little stuffed parcels of paper-thin pastry deep-fried in oil. Favourite fillings are minced meat, prawn and chicken. If you do not like frying you can bake them in the oven for 30 minutes at 180°C (350°F, gas mark 4). The pastry leaves, *ouarka*, described on p. 154, are so difficult and take so much time to make that I substitute filo instead. The traditional shapes are triangles, rectangles and cigarettes.

Makes about 25

250 g (8oz) filo pastry (see p. 45)
1 egg yolk
Sunflower oil for deep-frying
Icing sugar (optional)
Cinnamon (optional)

Filling for briouates de kefta (minced meat pastries):
350 (12 oz) lean minced beef
½ large onion, finely chopped
Small bunch of coriander, finely chopped
Small bunch of parsley, finely chopped
1 teaspoon cinnamon
Pinch of ginger
Salt
Pinch of cayenne (optional)
3 tablespoons sunflower oil
4 eggs, lightly beaten

Mix all the filling ingredients together except the eggs, then transfer the mixture to a frying-pan. Cook gently for a few minutes, stirring until the moisture evaporates and the meat separates. Drain off the fat, then add the eggs and stir until they set to a lightly scrambled consistency.

Cut the filo sheets into rectangles about 13 cm (5 in) wide and stack them on top of each other. Take a sheet of dough and put a heaped teaspoon of filling at one end and fold into a triangle as shown opposite. Stick the loose edge down with a little egg yolk. Fry in hot oil until crisp and golden. Drain on kitchen paper and serve sprinkled with icing sugar and cinnamon if wished.

Filling for briouates aux crevettes (prawn pastries):
1 tablespoon butter
1½ tablespoons flour
300 ml (10 fl oz) milk

Salt
White pepper
500 g (1 lb) peeled cooked prawns
Lemon wedges

Melt the butter in a saucepan, add the flour and stir until the flour is absorbed. Add the milk, a little at a time, stirring constantly. Sprinkle with salt and pepper and cook on a low heat, still stirring, until the mixture thickens. Add the prawns and mix well. The mixture should be quite thick. Cut the sheets of filo into 13 cm (5 in) wide rectangles. Put a heaped teaspoon of filling at one end of a strip in the shape of a sausage and roll up the filo like a cigarette, as shown opposite. Stick the loose edge down with a little egg yolk. Fry in hot oil until crisp and golden and drain on kitchen paper. Serve accompanied by lemon wedges.

Variation
The El Minzah Hotel in Tangiers makes a spicier version of this filling by adding ½ teaspoon cumin, 3 crushed garlic cloves, a large pinch of cayenne and a bunch of finely chopped coriander.

Filling for briouates de poulet (chicken pastries):
½ chicken, weighing about 1 kg (2 lb)
2 large onions, grated
4 tablespoons sunflower oil
Salt and pepper
1 teaspoon cinnamon
Large bunch of coriander, finely chopped

Put all the filling ingredients except the coriander in a saucepan and cook very gently with the lid on, stirring from time to time, for about 30 minutes or until the chicken is so soft that it comes away from the bone. The onion should stew and become soft and transparent – if it looks as though it will begin to colour, moisten with a little water. Take out the chicken, discard the skin and bones, and chop the flesh.

Continue to cook the onions, uncovered, until any liquid has disappeared and the sauce is really thick. Add the coriander for approximately the last 3 minutes of cooking, then stir in the chicken pieces.

Cut the filo pastry into rectangles and proceed to wrap up the filling into little triangles as for the briouates de kefta, or in rectangles (see opposite), sticking the loose edge down with egg yolk. Fry in not too hot oil, turning over once, until crisp and golden.

Pizza

Pizza, like tomatoes, is associated with Naples. There is a *pizza casalinga* (home pizza) made with pastry dough, but the classic pizza is made with rough bread dough. It is a large round tart with a variety of fillings on top. A *calzone* is a pizza folded over the filling like a pie. Pizza is served in wedge-shaped portions as a starter and a whole one constitutes a meal in itself. It must be eaten hot straight from the oven as it soon hardens in an unappetising way. Prepare the filling in advance so that it is ready for spreading as soon as the dough is rolled out.

Makes 4 × 23 cm (9 in) pizzas and 6 calzoni

500 g (1 lb) plain flour, plus extra for flouring
¼ teaspoon salt
25 g (1 oz) fresh or 15 g (½ oz) dried yeast
About 250 ml (8 fl oz) warm water
Pinch of sugar
4 tablespoons olive oil

Sift the flour into a bowl together with the salt.

Dissolve the yeast in ½ a glass of the measured water, together with a pinch of sugar to activate the yeast. When it begins to froth pour into the flour. If you use vitamin C-added dry yeast add it directly to the flour. Add 3 tablespoons of the oil and just enough water to make a firm dough. Pour in the water gradually, mixing first with a wooden spoon, then working the flour into the liquid with your hands. Add a little more flour if it is too sticky. Knead well for at least 10 minutes or until the dough is smooth and elastic. Pour a drop of oil in the bowl and roll the dough in it to prevent a dry crust forming. Cover the bowl with a damp cloth and leave the dough to rise in a warm place for about an hour or until it has doubled in bulk. Punch it down and knead for a few minutes, then roll in the remaining oil and let it rise again for 30 minutes.

Pre-heat the oven to 240°C (475°F, gas mark 9).

Divide the dough into 4 balls and roll them out thinly on a floured board, using a lightly floured rolling pin, to a thickness of about 0.5 cm (¼ in). Push the dough with your hands to stretch it. Lift the rounds carefully and transfer them to an oiled baking sheet. Spread the filling evenly on top and bake in the hottest part of the oven for about 25 minutes or until the edges and bottom are crisp. In the very high temperature of a baker's oven, the dough, which can be rolled much thinner, is cooked within 15 minutes.

Serve pizzas fresh and hot straight from the oven.

Pizza alla Marinara

Tomato Pizza

This is also called *pizza aglio, olio e pomodoro* which means 'garlic, oil and tomato' because these are the traditional Neapolitan ingredients.

Pizza dough (see left)

Filling for 4 × 23 cm (9 inch) pizzas:
1 kg (2 lb) ripe tomatoes, peeled, or 1 × 820 g
(1 lb 12 oz) tin of peeled tomatoes, drained
Salt and pepper
1½ tablespoons dried oregano
4–6 garlic cloves, finely chopped
Olive oil

Make the pizza dough and leave to rise twice.

Pre-heat the oven to 240°C (475°F, gas mark 9). To make the filling, drain the tomatoes in a colander, squeeze out the excess juice and chop them. Divide the dough into 4 balls and roll them out to a thickness of less than 0.5 cm (¼ in). Spread the tomato evenly on top, season with salt and pepper, sprinkle with oregano and garlic. Dribble a little olive oil over the top and bake as described in the main pizza recipe.

Variations
* For *pizza alla Siciliana*, add 12 black olives and 4 large or 8 small anchovy fillets, split in half or chopped.
* For *pizza alle vongole o cozze*, sprinkle the filling with 1 kg (2 lb) clams or mussels, cooked and shelled (see p. 138).

Pizza Margherita

Mozzarella and Tomato Pizza

Naples boasts dozens of different fillings but the most popular ones are the very simplest. Pizza is the best of poor man's food.

Pizza dough (opposite)

Filling for 4 ×23 cm (9 in) pizzas:
1 kg (2 lb) ripe tomatoes, peeled, or an 820 g (1 lb 12 oz) tin of peeled tomatoes, drained
Salt and pepper
350 g (12 oz) mozzarella, diced, coarsely shredded or thinly sliced
4 tablespoons grated Parmesan (optional)
Large bunch of basil, chopped
3 tablespoons olive oil

Make the pizza dough and leave to rise twice.

Pre-heat the oven to 240°C (475°F, gas mark 9). Chop the tomatoes, drain them in a colander and squeeze out the excess juices thoroughly or the pizza will be soggy. Divide the dough into 4 balls and roll them out to a thickness of less than 0.5 cm ($\frac{1}{4}$ in) and spread the pulp evenly over them. Cover each one with mozzarella and a tablespoon of Parmesan, if using. Season with very little salt and plenty of pepper, sprinkle with basil and a little olive oil and bake as described in the main pizza recipe opposite.

Pizza margherita on sale in Nice

Lahmacun

Turkish Meat 'Pizza'

A kind of meat pizza is made in Turkey by bakers and in restaurants. There are many regional versions in different shapes and sizes and with different toppings. This recipe is for one we made at home in Egypt years ago. I am not sure if it came originally from Turkey or from Syria but it is very good.

Serves 12 or more

Pizza dough (opposite)

For the topping:
500 g (1 lb) onions, finely chopped
4 tablespoons sunflower oil
750 g (1$\frac{1}{2}$ lb) ripe tomatoes, peeled and chopped, or a 400 g (14 oz) tin of peeled tomatoes
750 g (1$\frac{1}{2}$ lb) lean minced lamb or beef
4 tablespoons tomato purée
Salt and pepper
Juice of $\frac{1}{2}$ lemon
Bunch of parsley, finely chopped
Good pinch of cayenne, or 1 small chilli, finely chopped
50 g (2 oz) pine-nuts, toasted (optional)

Make the pizza dough and leave to rise twice.

Meanwhile fry the onions in 3 tablespoons of oil until soft but not golden. Add the tomatoes and cook until the sauce is thick and the liquid has disappeared.

Pre-heat the oven to 230°C (450°F, gas mark 8).

Put the raw meat in a bowl with all the topping ingredients including the tomato mixture and work well into a paste with your hands. Knead the dough again for a few minutes and divide into 3. Roll each one out as thinly as possible on a floured surface with a floured rolling pin and ease onto 3 oiled baking sheets about 35 cm (14 in) by 40 cm (16 in).

Spread a thick layer of meat mixture on each sheet of dough. Let them rest for 10 minutes and bake for 10–15 minutes or until the mixture has cooked and the dough is brown around the edges. Cut into squares.

Note
A quick and easy lahmacun can be made with the same filling on bought, opened-out pitta bread.

Variation
Adding 1 tablespoon of tamarind paste and 1 teaspoon of sugar to the fried onion lends a delicious sweet and sour flavour.

Calzone

Italian Filled Pizza

Calzone – a type of closed pizza made with bread dough – is a speciality of Naples where they call it *cazune*. It provides a very filling meal. Like pizza it varies from one region to another. There are different fillings as well as different shapes and it can be deep-fried or baked.

Makes 6 calzoni

Pizza dough (see p. 92)
2 ripe tomatoes, peeled and finely chopped

For the filling:
750 g (1½ lb) ricotta, crumbled
500 g (1 lb) mozzarella, shredded or diced
Salt and pepper
175 g (6 oz) ham, cut into strips

Below: Calzone
Opposite: Pissaladière

Pre-heat the oven to 240°C (475°F, gas mark 9).

Make the pizza dough and leave to rise twice. Mix the filling ingredients together. Divide the risen dough into 6 balls and roll them out as thin as you can. They should be about 23 cm (9 in) in diameter. Place on large flat oiled baking sheets. Spread the filling on half of each round leaving a 2 cm (¾ in) margin on the edge. Moisten this margin with water and fold the other half of the dough over the filling so that the edges meet, making a half moon turnover. Press the edges firmly together. Twist and pinch them to seal them if you like. Repeat with the remaining rounds.

Moisten the top of each calzone with a little of the chopped tomato. Bake in the hottest part of your oven for about 20 minutes or until crisp and brown round the edges. Serve immediately hot and fresh.

Variation

You can stuff calzone with the usual pizza filling ingredients such as tomatoes, salame and raw ham cut into pieces, anchovy fillets, capers, pitted black olives, and currants. Another filling used is grated pecorino mixed with enough beaten egg to bind it.

Pissaladière

Onion Tart

This famous onion tart of Nice derives its name from the anchovy paste, *pissala*, which used to be brushed on it. Now the traditional anchovy garnish is more often absent while the thick onion filling has become even thicker. You may find the larger quantity of onion given in the recipe excessive but that is the way the Niçois (and I) prefer it.

Serves 6

For the dough:
250 g (8 oz) plain flour
1 egg, beaten
¾ teaspoon salt
15 g (½ oz) fresh yeast, or 1½ teaspoons dried yeast
¼ teaspoon sugar
75 ml (3 fl oz) warm water
A few drops of olive oil

For the filling:
1–2 kg (2–4 lb) onions, thinly sliced
3–4 tablespoons olive oil
Salt and pepper
2 teaspoons mixed fresh herbs such as basil, thyme and rosemary, chopped
12 or more anchovy fillets
A few black olives, stoned and halved

To make the bread dough, sift the flour into a bowl and make a well in the centre. Put the beaten egg and salt in the well. Put the yeast, sugar and water in a bowl and leave it until it froths. Then gradually stir the yeast mixture into the flour, mixing it in with your fingers to form a ball of soft dough. Add a little flour if it is too sticky and knead well with your hands for 10 minutes or until the dough is smooth and elastic. Pour a drop or two of olive oil on the dough and turn it in your hands so that it becomes lightly oiled all over. Cover with a damp cloth and leave to rise in a warm place for an hour or until it doubles in bulk.

While the dough is rising make the filling. Cook the onions in the olive oil in a covered pan on a very low flame, stirring occasionally, for 40 minutes or until they are very soft. Add the salt, pepper and herbs and continue to cook for a few minutes longer. Cut the anchovy fillets in half lengthways.

Pre-heat the oven to 190°C (375°F, gas mark 5). Grease a pie plate or flan dish about 35 cm (14 in) in diameter with oil. Punch the dough down, knead it lightly and press it into the pie pan with the palms of your hands. Spread the onion mixture over the dough and make a lattice pattern of anchovy fillets on top. Put half an olive in the middle of each square. Let the dough rise again for 10–15 minutes, then bake for 25–30 minutes or until the bread base is cooked. Serve hot.

White Wines from Naples

There are a number of interesting wines to choose from in the Naples area, the white wines being mostly light and delicate, which is how Neapolitans like them.

One of the best is Greco di Tufo, produced in Avellino. Made from indigenous grapes, it is also good for drinking on its own as an aperitif. Another lovely soft white is Bianco d'Ischia, from the island of that name. The delicate Biancolella also comes from Ischia, and there is little to beat it with a dish of gently steamed sea bass or spaghetti con cozze (see p. 188).

Avellino is also the home of the Fiano di Avellino, a very special, if rather expensive white wine. Taurasi white and the dry and delicate Lacryma Christi are also available.

Panisses

Chickpea Fritters

Niçois dishes such as pasta, gnocchi and these *panisses* testify to a very strong Italian influence. For 500 years until 1860 Nice was part of the House of Savoy which included Sardinia and Piedmont. As a result the Niçois dialect is often more Italian than French. Panisses, fritters made with chickpea flour, can be savoury or sweet. They are intriguing, with a soft texture and subtle flavour. They can be eaten on their own or as an accompaniment to meat and vegetables. The recipe comes from Ravioli Croese, a fresh pasta shop in Vieux Nice. *Panelle*, found in Sicily, are similar to panisses but include chopped parsley.

Makes about 30

250 g (8 oz) chickpea flour, sifted flour
Salt
1 litre (1¾ pints) water
Sunflower oil for deep frying
Pepper

Put the chickpea flour in a large saucepan with a pinch of salt and beat in the water gradually. Bring to the boil and cook, stirring continually, for about 5–10 minutes until the mixture is thick and smooth. You will have to keep stirring vigorously to avoid lumps forming, so cover your hand with a cloth as the bubbling mixture spatters.

Pour the mixture into a shallow baking tray. It should be no more than 0.5–1 cm (¼–½ in) deep. The mixture will not stick and you do not need to oil the tray. When cooled to a firm and slightly rubbery mass, turn out onto a board and cut into 7.5 cm (3 in) long and 2 cm (¾ in) wide strips.

Deep-fry the fritters in hot oil until golden. Lift out with a slotted spoon and lay them on kitchen paper to drain. Serve hot, sprinkled with salt and plenty of black pepper.

Variation
For a dessert version serve cold with icing sugar. Only use a tiny pinch of salt in the boiling water for this version.

Bread

The importance of bread in Mediterranean life cannot be overstated. It is present at every meal and it is usual to go out twice a day to buy it fresh from the oven. So much is eaten with appetisers that you often have no room for the main course. The most common breads of the Mediterranean – the long French *baguette*, the crusty round bread of Italy, the sesame rings of Turkey and the flat pouched *pitta* of the Arab world – are all available in the UK.

People use bread to soak up sauces and to pick up morsels of food. It goes at the bottom of a juicy salad and in a bowl of soup; it is pounded into sauces with olive oil and crumbs are sprinkled over a *gratin*. The simplest appetisers in the western Mediterranean are a slice of bread smeared with olive oil and rubbed with garlic or tomatoes (see p. 62) or spread with an olive and anchovy paste (see p. 62). Catalans even soak day-old bread in red wine mixed with sugar. You must try it – it is really good.

Socca

Socca – a thin layer of chickpea flour and olive oil batter baked in a tray in a very hot bread oven – is the favourite morning snack for workers in Nice. The sheets are light brown and crisp round the edges but meltingly soft inside. Wrapped up in newspaper and eaten with the fingers, *socca* is sold in the streets and markets.

Eish Baladi

Egyptian Bread

Eish means life in Egypt and *baladi* means local, hence the name of this soft round bread which is used to scoop up food and to soak up juices. The bread is smaller and thicker than pitta and is made with wholemeal flour.

In Egypt the bread is baked in very hot, wood-burning ovens. To achieve a similar result at home the bread should be cooked under the grill. As domestic grills differ, you will have to experiment to find out what position under your grill works best. The most important thing is that the grill should be allowed to become as hot as possible before the bread goes under it.

The instructions for making the bread are long but the work is very easy. Small quantities are given as the bread does not keep very well but you can easily double and triple them.

Makes 12

250 g (8 oz) strong wholemeal plain flour
250 g (8 oz) strong white flour
½–1 teaspoon salt
2 tablespoons sunflower oil
1½ teaspoons dried yeast, or 15 g (½ oz) fresh yeast
Pinch of sugar (optional)
About 250 ml (8 fl oz) water

Put the flour into a warmed mixing bowl with a little salt and 1 tablespoon of oil and make a well in the centre. If you are using fresh or ordinary dried yeast, dissolve it in some of the water with a pinch of sugar and leave it in a warm place for a few minutes until it froths. Then add it, with the rest of the water, to the flour. If you are using vitamin C-added dried yeast, which is particularly effective, simply stir it into the dry flour and add enough water, mixing it in gradually with a spoon and then working it in with your hands to make a firm soft dough. The amount of water needed varies depending on the quality of the flour.

Knead the dough vigorously in the bowl or on a floured board for about 15 minutes or until it is smooth and elastic and no longer sticks to your hands. Sprinkle the bottom of the bowl with the remaining tablespoon of oil and roll the ball of dough in it to prevent the surface becoming dry and crusty. Cover with a damp cloth and leave in a warm, draught-free place for at least 2 hours or until nearly doubled in bulk.

Punch the dough down and knead again for a few minutes, then divide it into 12 equal-sized portions. Flatten them on a lightly floured board with a floured rolling pin until they are about 0.5 cm (¼ in) thick and about 10 cm (4 in) in diameter. Oil them and lay them on baking sheets a good distance apart, as they spread. Cover with a lightly floured cloth and allow them to rise again in a warm place for about 20 minutes.

Pre-heat the grill to its highest setting. Wet your hand with cold water and dampen the top of each bread to prevent it browning. Put the breads under the grill, allowing room for the dough to rise. As soon as the breads puff up – in about 2 minutes – turn them over and leave under the grill a minute longer. If you are not going to eat them right away, put them in a polythene bag and seal it to keep them soft.

Variation
Use ⅓ rye flour mixed with ⅔ wholemeal flour.

Eish baladi seller in downtown Cairo

Pain aux Olives

Olive Bread

Greek olive bread is made with whole black olives but in this recipe from Provence, given by Niçois baker André Espuno, they are chopped. The bread is delicious straight out of the oven and is best eaten within a day.

Makes 4 small loaves

500 g (1 lb) plain flour
½ teaspoon salt
4 tablespoons olive oil
25 g (1 oz) fresh yeast, or 1 tablespoon dried yeast
1 teaspoon sugar
200 ml (7 fl oz) warm water
150 g (5 oz) black olives, pitted and chopped

Put the flour and salt in a bowl together with 3 table-spoons of the olive oil. Mix the yeast with the sugar and 60 ml (2½ fl oz) of the water. Leave it to froth for about 15 minutes. Pour this mixture into the flour and, with the remaining water, work it into a stiff, sticky dough.

Knead for about 10 minutes or until the dough is smooth and elastic, adding a little more flour if necessary. Add the olives and knead them into the dough. Put the remaining oil into the bowl and turn the dough in it to grease the surface and prevent a dry crust forming. Cover the bowl with a damp cloth and leave the dough to rise in a warm place for about 1½ hours or until it doubles in bulk.

Knead the dough again and divide it into 4 balls. Place the balls on an oiled baking tray. Press them down gently or shape them in any way you like. Let the dough rise again, covered with a damp cloth, for about 1 hour.

Pre-heat the oven to 240°C (475°F, gas mark 9). Brush the loaves with water to soften the crust and bake for about 30 minutes, or until they sound hollow when tapped on the bottom. Cool on a wire rack.

Pan Bagnat

Salad Rolls

Nice has not always been the playground of the rich and the character of the cuisine is simple and earthy. Because of the fresh, light, warm weather there is a good deal of outdoor picnic food. The origin of *pan bagnat*, which in Provençal means 'moist bread', is the pieces of country bread which peasants mixed into a salade niçoise (p. 67) to soak up the juices and so make a more substantial meal. Pan bagnat now refers to a sandwich filled with a kind of salade niçoise. All kinds of breads, including a *baguette* and a large round loaf, can be used. In Nice soft round rolls about 20 cm (8 in) in diameter are baked especially for it. Smaller rolls, soft or crusty, are more elegant to serve and easier to eat. They make wonderful summer snacks for a morning or afternoon break and ideal picnic fare. Prepare them at least one hour before serving.

Per person

1 soft or crusty roll
1 garlic clove
1½ small tomatoes, thinly sliced
2–3 slices hard-boiled egg
4–5 black olives
2–3 anchovy fillets or a few pieces of crumbled tuna
A few cucumber slices
2–3 thin ribbons of green pepper
A sprinkling of chopped spring onion
A few drops of vinegar (optional)
1 tablespoon olive oil
Salt and pepper
A sprig of parsley, coarsely chopped

Slice off the top of the roll and remove some of the soft centre. Cut the garlic clove in half and rub the inside of the roll with the cut sides. Fill with the salad ingredients and sprinkle with vinegar, if using, oil, salt, pepper and parsley. Press the cut slice of the roll on top like a lid and keep in a cool place while the juices are absorbed by the roll.

Variation
Add thinly sliced celery or fennel and radish.

Turkish country bread

Mahshi Filfil

Stuffed Peppers

Stuffed peppers of one kind or another are a culinary
feature of every country in the Mediterranean. This
particular eastern version is meant to be eaten cold
as a first course. A combination of tamarind and
sugar gives it an unusual, delicate, sweet and sour
flavour. Normally the dish is made with green
peppers but I think it is especially attractive to mix
them with red and yellow ones.

Serves 6

6 medium peppers
250 g (8 oz) short-grain rice
1 large onion, finely chopped
4 tablespoons olive oil
2 tablespoons pine-nuts
2 tablespoons currants
Salt and pepper
1½ tablespoons tamarind paste (see p. 53)
2 teaspoons sugar
Large bunch of mixed parsley, mint and dill,
    finely chopped
2 medium tomatoes, peeled and chopped
5 spring onions, chopped

Pre-heat the oven to 190°C (375°F, gas mark 5).
   Cut a small slice off the stem end of each pepper and
reserve. Remove the cores and seeds. Wash the rice
and drain well. Fry the onion in oil in a large saucepan
until soft and golden. Add the pine-nuts and when
they begin to colour add the rice and stir well. Add
the currants, salt and pepper.
   Dissolve the tamarind in 600 ml (1 pint) boiling
water, stir in the sugar and pour over the rice mixture.
Add the herbs, tomatoes and spring onions, stir well
and cook, covered, for 10 minutes. The rice should
still be slightly hard and underdone and also very
moist.
   Pack the filling loosely into the peppers and cover
with the reserved tops. Place upright in an ovenproof
dish. Pour 150 ml (5 fl oz) water around the peppers.
Cover with a lid or with foil and bake for 40 minutes,
then uncover and bake for a further 20 minutes or
until the vegetables are soft.

Sheikh el Mahshi Tamatem

Stuffed Tomatoes

This dish is popular in Egypt. The filling is given the
revential title *sheikh* because the meat and pine-nuts
are prestigious ingredients. Eat the tomatoes hot as
an entrée or as a light main course. They are also an
excellent idea for a buffet.

Serves 4

4 large tomatoes
1 onion, chopped
2 tablespoons sunflower oil
1½ tablespoons pine-nuts
250 g (8 oz) ground lamb, beef or veal
1 tablespoon raisins or currants
1½ teaspoons cinnamon
½ teaspoon allspice
Salt and pepper
Small bunch of parsley, finely chopped

Pre-heat the oven to 180°C (350°F, gas mark 4).
   Slice off the tops of the tomatoes and reserve. Discard the seeds and some of the pulp.
   To make the stuffing, fry the onion in oil until it is
golden. Add the pine-nuts and let them colour. Add
the meat, stirring well until it changes colour. Stir in
the raisins or currants and add the cinnamon, allspice,
salt, pepper and parsley.
   Stuff the tomatoes and cover with the reserved tops.
Pack tightly in a small ovenproof dish with a little
water at the bottom. Bake for 30 minutes, or until the
tomatoes are just soft.

Stuffing for Vegetables

Assam al Mougi, who gave us several Egyptian
recipes, makes a filling for vine leaves and
other vegetables such as aubergines, courgettes
and peppers which he stuffs and cooks all
together in a great big pot. To make this
filling, fry a chopped onion in oil till golden,
add 125 g (4 oz) minced lamb or beef and
when the meat changes colour, add 125 g
(4 oz) tinned, peeled tomatoes, salt, pepper and
1 teaspoon of ground cumin. Cook until the
liquid is reduced, then stir in 50 g (2 oz) short-
grain rice and lots of chopped mint and parsley.

Mahshi Bassal

Stuffed Onion Rolls

This Arab speciality is exceptionally good with its slightly sweet and sour caramel taste.

Serves 6–8

3 very large Spanish onions
1–2 tablespoons pomegranate syrup (p. 52) or tamarind paste (p. 53)
2–3 tablespoons sugar
3 tablespoons sunflower oil

For the stuffing:
750 g (1½ lb) minced beef or veal
Salt and pepper
2 teaspoons cinnamon
1 teaspoon allspice
Large bunch of parsley, finely chopped

Peel the onions and cut off the ends. Using a sharp knife, cut from top to bottom on one side of each onion through to the centre only and no further. Boil for about 15 minutes or until the onions soften and start to open so that each layer can be detached. Drain and separate each layer carefully.

Knead the ingredients for the stuffing. Put a walnut-sized lump into each onion layer and roll up tightly. Line the bottom of a large, heavy saucepan with the unused small bits of onion and pack the rolls tightly over them in layers. Dissolve the pomegranate syrup or the tamarind concentrate in 300 ml (10 fl oz) boiling water. Add 1 tablespoon of sugar and the oil and pour over the onions. Add more water to cover and place a plate on top to hold them down.

Simmer gently for about 30 minutes, or until the onions are very tender and the water mainly absorbed, adding a little water to cover, if necessary, during the cooking. Turn out the onion rolls and place them in circles in a large, flat ovenproof dish. Sprinkle with the remaining sugar and place them under the grill for a few minutes to give them an attractive brown colour and a caramelised flavour. Serve hot or cold.

Mahshi Cousa Bil Laban

Stuffed Courgettes with Yogurt

The hot yogurt sauce gives this Syrian and Lebanese speciality a delicious tart flavour and an appealing presentation.

Serves 6

12 medium courgettes (about 1 kg/2 lb)
Salt
A few lettuce leaves

For the stuffing:
250 g (8 oz) minced beef or lamb
75 g (3 oz) short-grain rice
Salt and pepper
1 teaspoon cinnamon
½ teaspoon allspice
Pinch of nutmeg
3 tomatoes, chopped

For the sauce:
1.4 litres (2½ pints) yogurt
2 tablespoons cornflour
1 garlic clove, crushed
1 tablespoon dried mint

Wash the courgettes, slice off the stem end and trim the other end. Using an apple corer, scoop out the pulp via the stem end, being careful not to break through the skin, so that you end up with hollow courgettes.

Mix the stuffing ingredients together and stuff the courgettes but only ¾ full so that they do not tear when the rice expands.

Arrange the lettuce leaves at the bottom of a large heavy saucepan (this is to protect the vegetables from burning) and pack the courgettes in layers on top. Add salted water to cover and simmer gently with the lid on for about 30 minutes or until the rice is tender and the water absorbed. (Uncover towards the end, if necessary, to let any remaining water evaporate.)

In the meantime prepare the sauce. Pour the yogurt into a saucepan and put it over a low heat. Mix the cornflour with a little water and add this paste to the yogurt to prevent it from curdling. Stir constantly until the yogurt boils, then stir in the garlic and mint. Pour the sauce over the courgettes and cook for another 10 minutes. Lift the courgettes out of the pan and arrange in a serving dish. Strain the sauce and discard the lettuce leaves. Pour the sauce over the courgettes and serve hot or cold.

Oturtma

Stuffed Aubergines

There are many methods of stuffing aubergines and as many different fillings. This classic Turkish method is easy, delicious and presentable. If you mind the frying, try the variation below and poach the aubergines in tomato juice.

Serves 6

3 medium aubergines
Salt
Sunflower oil for frying

For the stuffing:
1 large onion, coarsely chopped
2 tablespoons sunflower oil
350 g (12 oz) ground beef or lamb
500 g (1 lb) tomatoes, peeled and chopped
Salt and pepper
1 teaspoon cinnamon
1 teaspoon allspice
1 tablespoon raisins or currants
Large bunch of parsley, finely chopped

Cut the aubergines in half lengthways. Sprinkle them with salt and leave them in a colander to drain for an hour. (This makes them absorb less oil.)

Pre-heat the oven to 200°C (400°F, gas mark 6). To make the stuffing, fry the onions in oil till soft, add the meat and fry, stirring and crushing it with a spoon until it changes colour. Add the tomatoes, salt and pepper, cinnamon, allspice and raisins or currants and cook gently until most of the liquid is absorbed, then add the parsley.

Rinse the aubergines and squeeze them gently a few at a time to get rid of the juices. Fry in hot oil, beginning with the skin-side down and turning over once until lightly browned and soft inside. Drain on kitchen paper. Place the aubergine halves, cut-side up, in a flat ovenproof dish. Cover with the stuffing and press down well. Bake for about 15 minutes or until the aubergines are very tender. Serve hot.

Variation,

Instead of frying the aubergines, rinse them and put them in a large saucepan with 600 ml (1 pint) good tomato juice and enough water to cover. Add two sliced garlic cloves and 1 tablespoon dried mint. Simmer for about 20 minutes until tender but not too soft. Lift out carefully and proceed as above.

Imam Bayıldı

The Imam Fainted

This stuffed aubergine recipe is one of Turkey's legendary dishes. It is eaten cold as a first course.

Serves 6

6 small or 3 medium, long, slim aubergines
  weighing about 750 g (1½ lb)
Salt

For the stuffing:
500 g (1 lb) onions, thinly sliced
5 garlic cloves, finely chopped
Olive or sunflower oil
1 green pepper, thinly sliced (optional)
250 g (8 oz) tomatoes, peeled and chopped
Pepper
1 teaspoon sugar
Large bunch of parsley, finely chopped

1 large tomato, cut into slices
Good-quality tomato juice

Peel the aubergines lengthways, leaving a thin ring of skin around both ends. Cut medium aubergines in half lengthways. Sprinkle with salt and leave for 30 minutes while the juices are drawn out, then rinse and dry them.

Pre-heat the oven to 200°C (400°F, gas mark 6). To make the stuffing, gently fry the onions and garlic in 3 tablespoons of oil until soft. Add the green pepper and tomatoes, season with salt and pepper and a little sugar. Cook gently for about 15 minutes or until the liquid is reduced, then stir in the parsley. Quickly shallow-fry the aubergines in oil hot enough to seal them, turning them to brown them slightly all over. Drain on kitchen paper.

Using a sharp knife, make a deep slit along the length of the whole or half aubergines but do not cut them right through. Open the slit, sprinkle, if you like, with a little salt and spoon in as much of the stuffing as the slit will hold. Lay the aubergines close to each other, open-side up, in a baking dish and garnish with tomato slices. Pour in enough tomato juice so that the aubergines are almost covered and bake for 45 minutes or until tender. Serve at room temperature.

Variation

Instead of baking the aubergines, you can stew them in tomato juice on top of the stove with a few sprigs of mint or thyme for about 45 minutes.

Dolmathes Avgolemono

Stuffed Vine Leaves with Egg and Lemon Sauce

This Greek delicacy is at its best in spring, made with tender young vine leaves and spring lamb. But the leaves preserved in brine which you can buy are perfectly good and can be found all year round. The dish takes a little time but it is fun to prepare.

Serves 6–10

250 g (8 oz) vine leaves
Extra vine leaves or lettuce leaves for lining the
  pan
3 tablespoons olive oil
600 ml (1 pint) water

For the stuffing:
750 g (1½ lb) lean minced lamb
Salt and pepper
1 large onion, grated or finely chopped
1 teaspoon dried thyme
Large bunch of parsley, finely chopped
Large bunch of dill or mint, finely chopped

For the sauce:
1 tablespoon cornflour
3 eggs
Juice of 1 large lemon
300 ml (10 fl oz) stock
Salt and white pepper

If you are using fresh vine leaves, remove the stems and plunge the leaves in boiling water for a few seconds. As soon as they change colour and go limp, remove carefully and let them drain. If you are using preserved leaves, pour boiling water over them and soak for an hour, changing the water (use cold water) twice to get rid of the salt.

Put all the stuffing ingredients in a bowl and knead well. Line a saucepan with vine leaves or lettuce leaves to prevent the stuffed leaves from sticking.

To stuff a leaf, place it vein-side up on a plate. Put up to a heaped tablespoon of stuffing in a sausage shape near the stem end. Fold this end over the stuffing, then fold the two sides in and roll the leaf up like a small cigar, tucking in the edges to make a neat package (see right). Squeeze gently and place in the saucepan.

Stuff all the leaves in the same way and place them tightly together, so that they don't unfold, in circles in the pan starting close to the sides and continuing into the centre. Repeat with further layers until they

are all used up. Sprinkle with oil and cover with about 600 ml (1 pint) water. Place a small plate on top to hold the parcels down, cover the pan and simmer over a low heat for about 30 minutes or until the leaves are done. Test by tasting one.

To make the sauce, beat the cornflour with the eggs and lemon juice until the cornflour has dissolved. Heat the stock in a pan adding salt and pepper if it is not already seasoned. Add a few tablespoons to the egg and lemon mixture, then pour this into the pan, stirring vigorously. Continue to stir vigorously over a very low heat until the sauce thickens and the taste of uncooked starch has gone. Do not let the sauce boil (a few bubbles do not mean that it is at risk of curdling) and let it thicken to a firm jelly-like cream.

Serve the dolmathes hot or cold with the sauce poured over, or serve the sauce separately.

STUFFING VINE LEAVES

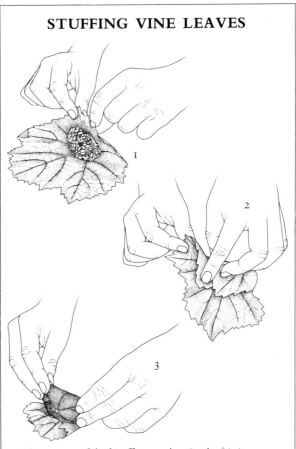

Place a spoonful of stuffing on the vine leaf (1).
Fold the stem end over and fold the two sides in (2).
Continue to roll, tucking the edges in as you go (3).

Soups

THE old traditional Mediterranean soups of peasant origin are so rich and substantial they are more like a stew. Thick with vegetables, pulses, grain and also sometimes with offal such as feet, heads and tripe, or little pieces of meat, chicken or sausage, they are so rich that they often constitute a main meal. They were once so important in the South of France that the evening meal is called *le souper*. The pot was hung over the hearth and left to 'murmur' for hours as little bits of something were dropped in and great whiffs of vapour escaped whenever the lid was lifted. I could have collected hundreds of different recipes for this section from the *potajes* of Spain and *minestrones* of Italy to the *hariras* of Morocco. They are the most individual kind of cooking that you will find and everyone has their own different recipe. A French saying: *Chacun sait ce qui bout dans sa marmite* ('everyone knows what is boiling in his pot') reflects the very private nature of the soup. Because it is not meant for entertaining, it has not become standardised in the way dishes offered to guests which are scrutinised and compared often do.

In the eastern Mediterranean rich soup has always been part of the bazaar trade. Merchants who start work very early buy it for breakfast to keep themselves going through the day of haggling. By tradition in the Muslim world it is also the ritual food of the month-long fast of Ramadan, served when the cannon booms at sunset to mark the end of the fast each day. Despite my admiration for these soups I have preferred to include more of the lighter kinds here: vegetable creams and refreshing summer soups, such as the cold soups of Andalusia.

The fish soups which are the heart and soul of the Mediterranean and a legacy of ancient Greece are in the chapter on fish.

Right: Street market in Tetouan

Soupe de Tomates

Tomato Soup

This fresh light Provençal soup consists entirely of delicately flavoured tomato pulp. It summons up for me the diaphanous fawn-coloured mountains and the tender climate of Provence.

Serves 4–6

1 onion, finely chopped
2 tablespoons olive oil
1 garlic clove, crushed
2 kg (4 lb) tomatoes, peeled and de-seeded
Salt and pepper
2 teaspoons sugar (optional)
1 bay leaf
Sprig of fresh thyme, or ½ teaspoon dried
A few fresh mint leaves, finely chopped
A few fresh basil leaves, finely chopped
3–4 cloves
Pinch of cayenne (optional)

Fry the onion in the oil until soft, add the garlic and when the aroma rises, add the remaining ingredients. Cook, uncovered, over a low heat for about 20 minutes or until the tomatoes have softened and the liquid has reduced. Remove the bay leaf and put the soup through a blender, then return to the pan and cook to a creamy consistency. Serve hot.

Gazpacho Andaluz

Andalusian Cold Soup

There is nothing more refreshing in the summer than a Spanish cold soup made from a mixture of tomatoes, cucumbers, peppers and onions blended to a light cream with olive oil and vinegar. *Gazpacho* has become popular far beyond the borders of Andalusia where it originates. There is not one gazpacho recipe but hundreds, the varying proportions of ingredients resulting in endless versions in delicate shades of white, green, red and salmon. The secret lies in the harmonious merging of the ingredients with no one element dominating the others. Traditionally the soup was eaten between courses, sometimes as an accompaniment to the main dish, and also as a meal in itself. It was brought to the fields by the *caseras* who cooked for the gangs of casual farm workers at harvest time. I have included three versions. This one, which comes from El Molino near Granada, is greener than the more familiar tomatoey version.

Serves 4–6

2 small green peppers, de-seeded
1 kg (2 lb) ripe tomatoes, peeled and de-seeded
2 small or 1 large cucumber, peeled
2 garlic cloves, crushed
1 slice of day-old white bread, crusts removed
125 ml (4 fl oz) olive oil or to taste
6 tablespoons wine vinegar or to taste
Salt
Garnishes from gazpacho recipe opposite
  (optional)
Bread croutons, fried in olive oil or toasted

Cut up the vegetables and put them through a blender with the garlic and bread. Add the olive oil to taste, vinegar, salt and blend to a light creamy consistency, adding a few tablespoons of iced water if necessary. Serve very cold, accompanied by the garnishes and croutons if desired.

Left: Gazpacho andaluz
Right: Ajo blanco (opposite)

Gazpacho de Tomates

Andalusian Cold Tomato Soup

This is a popular version of *gazpacho* with a good tomato flavour and lovely red colour.

Serves 6

1 green pepper, cut into pieces
1–3 garlic cloves, crushed
3 slices of white bread, crusts removed and broken into pieces
1.5 kg (3 lb) ripe tomatoes, peeled
6 tablespoons wine vinegar
5 tablespoons olive oil
Salt
1 teaspoon sugar

Garnish:
1 cucumber, diced finely
1 onion, peeled and diced finely
1 red pepper, diced finely
1 green pepper, diced finely
1 tomato, diced finely
2 hard-boiled eggs, diced finely

Put all the soup ingredients through a food processor and blend, starting with the pepper, adding a little cold water, if necessary, to dilute it to a light smooth cream. Chill and add ice cubes just before serving. Accompany with the garnish ingredients in separate little dishes.

Ajo Blanco

White Soup with Garlic and Grapes

We were stunned by this soup at the El Molino restaurant in an old country mill in Durcal near Granada. The restaurant is part of the Andalusian Centre of Gastronomic Investigation which includes a museum of traditional Andalusian cooking. The menu is made up of old recipes. Most, such as stuffed vine leaves, mashed chickpeas and pigeon pie, were of Arab and Moorish origin and gave us an extraordinary feeling of *déjà vu*.

This soup, which is called 'white garlic', has always been popular. It is intriguing, refreshing and most subtle in flavour. The ingredients are traditionally pounded with a pestle and mortar, a method which really does improve the flavour, but you can use a food processor.

Serves 6

200 g (7 oz) shelled fresh almonds or ground almonds
200 g (7 oz) day-old good white bread, crusts removed
Milk for soaking (optional)
4 garlic cloves, crushed
125 ml (4 fl oz) olive oil
600 ml (1 pint) or more iced water
Salt
4 tablespoons white wine vinegar or to taste
250 g–500 g (8 oz–1 lb) muscatel or other good grapes, peeled and de-seeded

If you are using fresh almonds, boil them for 2–3 minutes. Drain and peel when they are cool enough, then grind them in the processor. If you are using ground almonds, put them straight in the processor with the bread, soaked in milk or water and squeezed dry, and the garlic. Blend to a smooth paste. While the blender is going add the olive oil, drop by drop, then in a slow stream, as with mayonnaise (p. 211). Then add very cold water until the soup has a thick creamy consistency. Season with salt and vinegar, add the grapes and serve chilled.

Three varieties of Italian tomatoes

Potaje de Garbanzos y Espinacas

Chickpea and Spinach Soup

This soup from La Mancha, north west of Valencia, is rich enough to make a meal in itself.

Serves 8

500 g (1 lb) chickpeas, soaked overnight
1 medium potato, chopped
500 g (1 lb) cooked ham, diced
Salt
Pinch of saffron-coloured powder (see p. 52)
1 slice bread
1 large garlic clove
4 tablespoons olive oil
1 kg (2 lb) spinach, shredded

Drain the chickpeas and cover with fresh water. Simmer for about 1 hour or until tender. Add the potatoes, ham and a little salt and cook for about 30–60 minutes longer. Add the saffron, and extra water if necessary.

Fry the bread and garlic together in the oil, turning them to brown them all over. Remove with a slotted spoon, then pound or blend to a smooth paste and stir into the chickpeas; it serves to thicken and flavour the broth.

Heat the spinach, covered, in the oil left in the pan and turn it over until it crumples to a soft mass. Add to the soup and simmer for a few minutes before serving.

Zuppa di Peperoni alla Solferino

Pepper Soup

This colourful, delicately flavoured Tuscan soup, which is substantial enough to be a main course, comes from the Ristorante Solferino at San Macario in Piano near Lucca.

Serves 4

4 chicken wings
Salt and pepper
6 large peppers (red, green and yellow)
Small bunch of basil, coarsely chopped
1 sprig of mint, finely chopped
2 sprigs of marjoram, finely chopped

Pre-heat the oven to 240°C (475°F, gas mark 9).

Make 1.5 litres (2½ pints) stock using the chicken wings (see p. 214 for method). Meanwhile roast the peppers for about 30 minutes or until they are soft and browned all over, turning them over once. Put them in a closed polythene bag for 10 minutes to make peeling easier. While the peppers are still warm, cut out the stalks, core and de-seed them, then peel them over a bowl to collect the juices. Cut the flesh into thin strips.

Strain the chicken stock, add the peppers and their juices and simmer, covered, for about 20 minutes. Skin, bone and shred the chicken wings, then add the chicken flesh to the soup, together with the herbs, and cook a few minutes longer. Serve hot.

Wines from Tuscany

Chianti Classico and Brunello di Montalcino reign supreme in Tuscany, but if you want to try something different go for a wine called Rosso delle Colline Lucchesi, a fine red from the hills behind Lucca, or Rosso di Cercatoia, a beautifully made wine from a very special little vineyard at Montecarlo. A small town not far from Lucca, this is also where the fragrant Chablis-type Montecarlo Bianco comes from. These wines are not produced in any quantity, but they can be found in the UK. And if you are in Tuscany, look for an *enoteca*, a shop specialising in the best wines of this and other regions.

Soupe de Potiron

Pumpkin Soup

This bright orange Provençal soup is very delicate in flavour.

Serves 4

1 kg (2 lb) pumpkin flesh
1 onion, coarsely chopped
Salt and pepper
1 teaspoon cinnamon
½ teaspoon thyme
1 bay leaf
300 ml (10 fl oz) milk
60 g (2½ oz) long-grain rice

Cut the pumpkin into cubes and put them with the onion in a pot. Cover with water, add salt, pepper, cinnamon, thyme and the bay leaf and simmer for 15–20 minutes or until the pumpkin is soft.

Remove the bay leaf and put through the blender, then return to the pan. Add the milk and enough water for a light creamy consistency. Boil the rice separately in salted water for 15 minutes or until tender. Drain, then stir into the soup and serve.

Shorbat ads

Shorbat Ads

Lentil Soup

Lentil soup is eaten all over the Mediterranean, and there are consequently many versions, all of which are worth trying. It is a very homely soup and an easy one. The following Egyptian recipe is pleasantly spicy and lavishly garnished.

Serves 6 or more

500 g (1 lb) red lentils
1.8 litres (3 pints) meat or chicken stock (see p. 214)
Salt and pepper
1 teaspoon ground cumin (optional)
Pinch of cayenne (optional)

Garnish:
1½ large onions, coarsely chopped
4 tablespoons sunflower oil
3 garlic cloves, crushed
1 teaspoon ground coriander
Small bunch of parsley or dill, finely chopped
2 pitta breads, cut in triangles and opened out
1–2 lemons, cut in wedges

Put the lentils in a large pan with the stock and bring to the boil. Remove any scum and simmer for about 30 minutes, or until the lentils disintegrate. Add salt, pepper, cumin and cayenne, if wished, when the lentils begin to soften. Add water, if necessary, to thin the soup to a light, creamy consistency.

To make the garnish fry the onion in oil till it is very brown – almost caramelised. Add the garlic and coriander and fry until the aroma rises.

Toast the pitta bread in the oven until it is crisp and and brown, then crumble into pieces. Serve the soup, garnishing each serving with the spiced fried onion. Sprinkle with parsley or dill and accompany with lemon wedges and the toasted bread.

Variations
* Add 125 g (4 oz) rice or vermicelli, 20 minutes before the end.
* Add 2 tomatoes, peeled and chopped, or 2 table-spoons tomato purée.
* Add 500 g (1 lb) chard or spinach. Wash the leaves, remove the stems, cut the leaves into shreds and add 20 minutes before the end.
* Add the juice of 1 lemon or 3 tablespoons wine vinegar.
* Add meat to the stock to make the soup a meal in itself.

Yayla Çorbasi

Yogurt Soup

This Turkish soup, called 'mountain pastures', has a slightly tart and minty flavour.

Serves 6

5 tablespoons rice
1.8 litres (3 pints) chicken stock
Salt and pepper
600 ml (1 pint) yogurt
2 egg yolks
2 tablespoons dried mint
50 g (2 oz) butter
2 teaspoons paprika

Boil the rice in the stock until soft. Add salt and pepper. Beat the yogurt with the egg yolks, add a little stock and beat well, then pour the mixture into the soup, stirring. Add 1 tablespoon mint and cook, stirring all the time, for a few minutes or until the soup thickens. The yolks prevent the yogurt curdling and also thicken the soup. Before serving, melt the butter, stir in the paprika and the rest of the mint. Let the mixture sizzle and dribble over the top of the soup.

Soupa Avgolemono

Egg and Lemon Soup

You must have good flavourful home-made stock for this famous Greek soup.

Serves 6

1.8 litres (3 pints) chicken stock
125 g (4 oz) vermicelli or rice
Salt and pepper
Large bunch of parsley, finely chopped
2 eggs
Juice of 1–2 lemons

Bring the stock to the boil and add the vermicelli or rice. Add salt and pepper, and simmer for about 15 minutes. Add the parsley. Just before you are ready to serve, beat the eggs with lemon juice and a ladleful of hot broth and pour this mixture into the pan, stirring vigorously until the soup thickens. Turn off the heat quickly before the yolks curdle. Serve immediately.

Soupe au Pistou

Vegetable Soup with *Pistou*

The most popular soup of Nice is a type of minestrone with a paste of garlic, basil and Parmesan added at the end. This magic 'pommade' is called *pistou* – the word comes from the Niçois *pista*, 'to pound'. The smell of garlic and basil fills the entire house when the ingredients are crushed with a pestle and mortar. You should not let the food processor rob you of that pleasure.

The soup can be made with many different vegetables and with macaroni or rice, but this particular recipe is based mainly on green beans and fresh white haricot beans called *coco*. Dried ones can be used instead. A large amount of fresh basil is needed to make the pistou, so try growing it at home. It is a nourishing summer soup often eaten in the evening as the principal *plat de résistance*.

Serves 8–10

250 g (8 oz) fresh white haricot beans, or 175 g
  (6 oz) dried ones, soaked overnight
350 g (12 oz) small French green beans
2 leeks, diced
2 small turnips, diced
3 large carrots, diced
3 large courgettes, diced
1 celery stalk, diced
2 medium potatoes, peeled and diced
2 tomatoes, peeled and chopped
2 tablespoons olive oil
2 garlic cloves, finely chopped
Salt and pepper

For the pistou:
2–4 garlic cloves
Large bunch of basil leaves
50 g (2 oz) grated fresh Parmesan
4 tablespoons olive oil

Boil the drained haricot beans until tender. Bring 2 litres (3½ pints) water to the boil in a large saucepan. Add all the ingredients and simmer, uncovered, for about 1 hour, adding more water if necessary.

Meanwhile, make the pistou. Pound the garlic in a mortar, then add the basil and pound to a paste. Stir in the grated Parmesan with a fork and beat in the oil. You can use a blender but the result will not be as good.

Pour the pistou into the soup 15 minutes before serving or pass it round at the table, together with a dish of grated Parmesan and a flask of fruity olive oil.

Harira

Moroccan Ramadan Soup

I have been given many different recipes for *harira*, a dish made especially during Ramadan, the Muslim month of fasting. This recipe, with its large quantity of herbs, comes from Sadir Daghmoumi, a chef at the El Minzah Hotel in Tangier. Unlike Turkey, where women never set foot in a professional kitchen, the best cooks in Moroccan restaurants are always women.

Serves 10

250 g (8 oz) beef or lamb cut into cubes
250 g (8 oz) chickpeas, soaked for 1 hour
2 onions, finely chopped
500 g (1 lb) tomatoes, peeled and chopped
A few celery leaves
Pepper
$\frac{1}{2}$ teaspoon saffron-coloured powder (see p. 52)
2 mastic grains (see p. 51), pulverised (optional)
$\frac{1}{2}$ teaspoon ground ginger
Salt
2 tablespoons tomato paste
125 g (4 oz) vermicelli
50 g (2 oz) flour
Large bunch of parsley, finely chopped
Large bunch of coriander, finely chopped

Garnish:
3 lemons, cut in wedges

Put the meat in a large pan with 3 litres (5 pints) of water. Bring to the boil and remove the froth, then add the drained chickpeas, onions and tomatoes. Stir in the celery leaves, pepper, saffron powder, mastic and ginger. Simmer, covered, for at least an hour or until the chickpeas and meat are very tender. Add the salt when the chickpeas begin to soften. Add the tomato paste and vermicelli.

Mix the flour with enough water to make a smooth paste. Pour in a ladle of hot soup, beat well and pour back into the pan. Bring back to the boil, stirring vigorously, until the soup thickens. Add the parsley and coriander and cook for 15 minutes longer until the taste of flour has disappeared. Serve hot, garnished with lemon wedges.

Above: Soupe au pistou (opposite)

Vegetables

Vegetables can be served as a separate course before or after the main dish as well as a side dish. They can even be a meal in themselves. You will also find many vegetable recipes in the section on appetisers.

THE MEDITERRANEAN lives by agriculture and vegetables are cherished like miracles through summer droughts and winter winds and rains. The plants have two periods of activity: a quick burst of life in the spring which is an explosion of sizzling nature as early as January and February, and then again in October when the first autumn rains appear and there is a sensation of rebirth. At both these times the sun brings the vegetables to an exceptionally high quality of flavour, fragrance and texture, and that is how they arrive at the market.

Covered and open-air street markets, from Arab souks to the weekly events in leafy squares in the South of France, are dazzling and luxurious affairs, full of noise and bustle, with a spectacular profusion of multi-coloured sights and smells beckoning from every stall and basket. Never miss an opportunity to visit one and, if you can, go early in the morning when the market comes to life.

You may wonder where all the vegetables on sale at these stalls go. For although the Mediterranean has a passion for vegetables they are not considered prestige foods – meat, which is not eaten very much, has this honoured position – and, except in Provence, you will not often see them on restaurant menus, nor will they always be offered to you as a guest. Vegetables are what people eat at home, and for those who cannot afford meat they are the main part of the diet. This means that they are treated with special affection and imagination and that a great deal of attention is lavished on them. They are crunched raw, marinated, grilled, sautéed in oil, deep-fried, or simply boiled or steamed. They are made into fritters and put into omelets, tarts or pies and they are given a pine-nut and raisin garnish or a breadcrumb and Parmesan crust. Spaniards put in bits of cured ham and Turks mix in yogurt. In Sicily vegetable dishes may have a sweet and sour flavour but the traditional southern Italian inclination towards sobriety discourages any but the simplest treatment which best retains their full natural flavour. The enormous variety of stuffed vegetables is perhaps the greatest triumph of Mediterranean gastronomy. Every vegetable which can be hollowed and every leaf which can be wrapped is stuffed. *Les petits farcis* of Provence are the prettiest but the *dolmas* of the east have the best flavour.

Right: Yellow peppers, Toulon market.

Garniture de Légumes à la Jardinière

Vegetable Garnish

An array of well shaped little vegetables left whole or larger ones cut into pieces makes an ideal accompaniment tó a meal and can also be served as a dish in itself. In France the mixture is called a *jardinière*. Restaurants dice or shape the vegetables with ball scoops or cut them with fluted cutters.

Choose a selection of three or more vegetables, such as carrots, turnips, Brussels sprouts, green beans, peas, asparagus, artichoke hearts, cauliflower, small broad beans, courgettes or potatoes. Peel or wash and trim them, and cut them if you like. Steam or boil each vegetable separately with a pinch of salt until it is tender but still crisp. Sprinkle with olive oil, pepper and chopped fresh herbs. A pinch of sugar or ground nutmeg adds a delicate touch. Arrange them around the main dish or serve them on their own. Accompany, if you like, with mayonnaise (p. 211), aïoli (p. 212), all–i–oli (p. 213), romesco (p. 211) or tarator sauce (p. 214).

Variation

In Spain they like to boil vegetables together to a tenderness which melts in the mouth and call the dish *hervido*. Three or more vegetables in season, such as onions, leeks, potatoes, carrots, celery, cauliflower, green beans and courgettes, are dropped whole into boiling salted water at different times according to the length of cooking they require. They are served straight from the pan, and a flask of olive oil and one of vinegar are passed around with lemon wedges so that they can be dressed to taste on the plate.

Artichauts à la Barigoule

Braised Artichokes

Pierre Hiély, of Chez Hiély in Avignon, gave us this traditional Provençal recipe. The dish can only really be made with the tiny artichokes which have no chokes and which are so tender that you can eat them whole. They are starting to become available here.

Serves 4

8 small, violet artichokes about 5 cm (2 in) long
1 onion, chopped
1 carrot, chopped
3 tablespoons olive oil
300 ml (10 fl oz) white wine
Salt and pepper
1 lettuce, shredded
A handful of sorrel, shredded
1 garlic clove, crushed
½ teaspoon dried thyme, or a sprig of fresh thyme

Using a sharp knife, trim the stalks and leaf points and remove the outer leaves of the artichokes. Cut them into quarters.

Fry the onion and carrot gently in the oil. Put the artichokes in and fry over a high heat for a minute or so. Then lower the heat, pour in the wine and add the rest of the ingredients with enough water to half-cover the artichokes. Cook gently, covered, for about an hour, or until tender, turning them occasionally.

Garniture de légumes

Anginares me Koukia

Artichokes with Broad Beans

Artichokes are always married to broad beans in the eastern Mediterranean. In this Greek dish, which can be served cold as a starter, they are presented with their long stems pointing towards the sky surrounded by broad beans. For a brief period during our own summer the broad beans are so young and tender that you can eat them in their pods. Otherwise shell them and, if necessary, skin them.

Serves 4

4 large globe artichokes
1½ lemons
1 kg (2 lb) broad beans in the pod
5 spring onions, finely chopped
75 ml (3 fl oz) olive oil
3 tablespoons dill or parsley, finely chopped
Salt and pepper

You can use the artichoke bottoms alone (see the illustration below). If the stem is tender enough, trim it, leaving about 3.5 cm (1½ in), and peel it. Alternatively, with smaller artichokes, remove all the tough outer leaves with a sharp knife and trim the base, slice across the tender inner leaves about halfway down and cut out the prickly purple leaves and the hairy chokes from the centre. Rub each artichoke over with a cut lemon and drop it in a bowl of water acidulated with the juice of ½ a lemon to prevent it discolouring. Cut around the pods of the broad beans to remove the strings or shell them.

Soften the spring onions in the oil for 2–3 minutes in a large saucepan, then add the remaining lemon juice and the rest of the ingredients. Cover with water and simmer gently with the lid on for about 30 minutes or until the artichokes and beans are tender. Serve the artichokes hot or cold, surrounded by the broad beans and sauce.

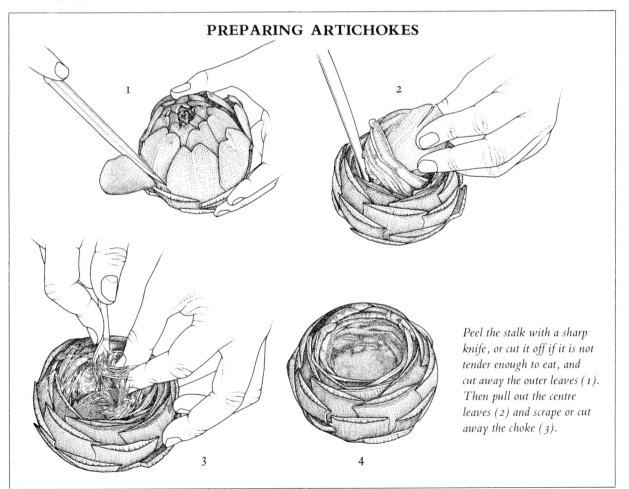

PREPARING ARTICHOKES

Peel the stalk with a sharp knife, or cut it off if it is not tender enough to eat, and cut away the outer leaves (1). Then pull out the centre leaves (2) and scrape or cut away the choke (3).

Taze Bakla Basti

Young Broad Beans in the Pod

In the oriental Mediterranean broad beans are eaten in their pods when they are just beginning to grow and the pods are still very tender. This simple Turkish way of cooking them preserves their delicate flavour. They have a short season so keep your eyes out for them. When the pods are too tough, shell the beans (use twice the weight) and cook them in the same way.

Serves 4

500 g (1 lb) young tender broad beans in their pods
Bunch of spring onions
3 tablespoons olive oil
½–1 teaspoon sugar
Salt and pepper
Small bunch of dill or mint, finely chopped (optional)
Strained yogurt (optional)

Wash, top and tail and cut around the pods to remove the string. Leave the pods whole or cut into two or three pieces. Put them in a pan with the spring onions, oil, sugar and seasoning and 300 ml (10 fl oz) water. Cook, covered, for 15–20 minutes or until the beans are tender. Stir in the mint or dill and keep the lid on for a few minutes so that the beans absorb the flavours. Serve hot or cold with the yogurt poured over the top if you like.

Variation

Broad beans are one of the most common vegetables in Egypt. For an Egyptian touch, cook 1 kg (2 lb) shelled beans with 2 tablespoons sunflower oil, 2 small crushed garlic cloves, ½–1 teaspoon sugar, salt and just enough water to cover for 10–20 minutes or until tender. Add a small bunch of finely chopped fresh coriander towards the end.

Horta

Boiled green leaves, served cold with a dressing of olive oil and lemon juice, are typical of Greece. Wild ones treated in this way include dandelion, charlock, mustard, various endives, rock samphire and poppy leaves. They are brought to the markets in baskets by villagers who have picked them in the fields and on the hillsides. Beetroot leaves, which we discard in Britain, are considered delicacies. A touch of bitterness, however, makes many of these an acquired taste.

Courge à la Persillade

Provençal Pumpkin

For people who like pumpkin, this garlicky parsleyed treatment suits it very well. In the Vaucluse region of Provence the pumpkin is left in the oven for over an hour until it becomes almost a cream.

Serves 6–8

1.5 kg (3 lb) pumpkin
4–5 garlic cloves, finely chopped
Salt and pepper
4 tablespoons olive oil
Large bunch of parsley, finely chopped

Pre-heat the oven to 200°C (400°F, gas mark 6).

Peel the hard rind off the pumpkin and remove the seeds and stringy bits. Cut the flesh into 2.5 cm (1 in) cubes, mix with the remaining ingredients and bake for 20–30 minutes or until just tender.

Tian de Courgettes

Baked Courgettes

Many Provençal dishes take their name from the local earthenware casserole, the *tian*, in which they are cooked. This particular one provided by Martine Bourdon-Williams of Nice is a pleasant mixture of many different textures and flavours.

Serves 8

1.5 kg (3 lb) courgettes
Salt
8–10 chard leaves or 125 g (4 oz) spinach, shredded
2 large onions, chopped
1 garlic clove, finely chopped
3 tablespoons olive oil
250 g (8 oz) short-grain rice
3 eggs
Small bunch of basil, finely chopped
Large bunch of parsley, finely chopped
3 rashers lean bacon, finely chopped
50 g (2 oz) grated Parmesan
Pepper

Trim the courgettes but leave them whole and un-peeled. Boil in salted water for about 20 minutes, or steam until tender. Mash with a potato masher in a colander and let the juices drain away. Fry the onions and garlic in 2 tablespoons of the olive oil till golden. Cook the rice in boiling salted water for 10 minutes or until it is still not quite done, then drain.

Pre-heat the oven to 200°C (400°F, gas mark 6). Beat the eggs lightly in a bowl. Add the basil and parsley, the bacon, Parmesan and pepper, then add the mashed courgettes, the fried onion and garlic and the rice. Mix well and taste before adding any salt because the Parmesan is salty.

Oil a large earthenware dish with the remaining tablespoon of oil and pour the mixture in. Bake for about 40 minutes or until it is firm and browned on top. Serve hot.

Tian d'Epinards

Baked Spinach

Yvette Brieunne of Lacoste gave this recipe for spinach with rice bound by an egg and milk custard which she bakes in a *tian*.

Serves 6

750 g (1½ lb) spinach
Salt
125 g (4 oz) long-grain rice
4 eggs
300 ml (10 fl oz) milk
White pepper
A pinch of ground nutmeg

Pre-heat the oven to 190°C (375°F, gas mark 5).

Wash the spinach well and cut off the stems. Blanch the leaves in salted water. Drain as soon as they soften, then cut them into strips. Put the rice in a pan of boiling salted water and simmer for 15 minutes or until tender, then drain.

Beat the eggs and gradually stir in the milk. Season with salt, pepper and nutmeg. Mix all the ingredients together and pour into a shallow ovenproof dish. Bake for 30 minutes or until set.

Variation

Substitute Swiss chard leaves for the spinach. Cook the chard leaves as above.

Côtes-du-Rhône

A number of excellent red wines are produced in the Rhône valley, south of Burgundy. Less expensive than their illustrious neighbours, they are mostly a blend of different grapes, Syrah being a consistent component. The exception is Hermitage, one of the great wines of the area, which is produced from Syrah alone. It is this variety of grapes which gives Rhône wines their characteristic deep red colour.

Another marvellous red with a powerful, generous texture is Gigondas. But the most famous has to be Châteauneuf-du-Pape, from near Avignon. Made from no less than 13 different grape varieties, it is just right with red meat or a good strong cheese.

Melokhia

Egyptians would die for the taste of *melokhia* and so would I, but it is definitely an acquired taste. It looks a bit like spinach and is part of the mallow family. It is chopped, or dried and crushed, and put in stews and sauces. The most popular dish is a soup simply called *melokhia*. It is made with chicken or rabbit stock and the leaves give it a glutinous texture. A fried mixture of crushed garlic and coriander called *ta'lia* added to the soup marks Egyptian food by its distinctive smell. One day friends of mine in London were making *melokhia* soup. A stranger knocked on the door asking if they were Egyptian as he recognised the aroma wafting out of the window!

Sabanekh bil Zeit

Spinach in Oil

Pink pomegranate seeds look especially beautiful sprinkled over the spinach in this Syrian dish made for us by Malak Mawaldi of Cairo.

Serves 4

750 g (1½ lb) spinach
2 onions
4 tablespoons olive oil
1 garlic clove, crushed
Large bunch of coriander, chopped
Salt and pepper
Juice of ½ lemon
Seeds from ½ pomegranate

Wash the spinach well and remove the stems. Squeeze the water out of the leaves. Chop 1 onion and fry it in 2 tablespoons of the oil in a large pan until soft. Add the garlic and fry until golden, then add the spinach, coriander, salt, pepper and lemon juice. Cook, turning the spinach over until it crumples into a soft mass.

Slice the remaining onion, then fry in the remaining oil until it is crisp and very brown. Serve the spinach cold, garnished with the fried onion and the pomegranate seeds.

Opposite: Bamia Marsousa

Bamia Marsousa

Okra in a Mould

Cairo has been colonised by the countryside – village life with mud brick houses sheltering hens and sheep and goats has sprouted in the streets and on roof tops. This pretty dish is one of many from Upper Egypt which have come to the city. It makes the best use of an unusual vegetable with a unique flavour and gelatinous quality.

Serves 6

1 kg (2 lb) okra
500 g (1 lb) tomatoes, peeled and sliced
2–3 garlic cloves, crushed
Juice of 1 lemon
75 ml (3 fl oz) olive oil
1 tablespoon sugar (optional)
Salt and pepper

Pre-heat the oven to 170°C (325°F, gas mark 3).

Wash the okra and trim off the stem ends. Pack the okra in 1 or 2 layers in a round, shallow mould or baking dish with their pointed ends converging like rays towards the centre. If you pack them tightly they should stay in place. Put a layer of tomatoes in between or on top of the okra, sprinkling a little garlic here and there. Beat the rest of the ingredients with about 150 ml (5 fl oz) water and pour over the top, adding a little more water, if necessary, to cover the vegetables.

Bake for 45 minutes or until the okra are tender. Cool, then carefully turn out onto a large flat plate, letting any excess juices run out and being careful not to upset the okra pattern. Serve hot or cold.

Egyptian and Lebanese Wines

Only small quantities of wine are produced in Egypt, mostly around Alexandria where grapes are also distilled to make the anis-flavoured spirit arak.

Arak is the Lebanese national drink and Lebanon also produces some beautiful wines. Ksara, the biggest winery in the Middle East, which was founded by the Jesuits in the Bekaa valley, makes excellent reds. Château Kefraya is a pleasant rosé from the same region while Château Musar from Mount Lebanon is an outstanding big, full-bodied red.

Judias Verdes Barcena

Green Beans with Ham

Jamón serrano, raw cured ham which has been salted (sometimes only slightly) and dried in the warm air, is a typical Spanish product which lends a distinctive flavour to many a Spanish dish. In this recipe, which combines tomatoes, garlic and a slight sweet and sour flavour, it turns green beans into something out of the ordinary.

Serves 4

500 g (1 lb) green beans
Salt
1 small onion, chopped
2 tablespoons olive oil
2 garlic cloves, crushed
50 g (2 oz) cured raw ham or unsmoked bacon, cut into small pieces
2 tomatoes, peeled and chopped
1 tablespoon wine vinegar
½ teaspoon sugar
Pepper

Top and tail the beans and string them, if necessary. Cut into pieces. Boil them in salted water for 10 minutes until slightly tender and drain. Fry the onion in oil till soft. Add the garlic and, when it begins to colour, add the ham, tomatoes and beans. Half-cover with water, add the wine vinegar, sugar and pepper and simmer, covered, for about 10 minutes or until the beans are tender. Serve hot.

Gratin de Tomates Provençal

Baked Tomatoes

In the Provençal dialect, which is the language of the troubadours, tomatoes are called *pommes d'amour* – apples of love. This is a simple and lovely way of preparing them as a starter or a side dish.

Serves 8

4 large beef tomatoes
Salt
40 g (1½ oz) breadcrumbs
4 garlic cloves, crushed
Large bunch of parsley, finely chopped
Pepper
75 ml (3 fl oz) olive oil

Pre-heat the oven to 190°C (375°F, gas mark 5).

Cut the tomatoes in half and sprinkle lightly with salt. Put them cut-side up in a greased, shallow, oven-proof dish. Mix the rest of the ingredients together, adding a little salt and press some of the mixture on each tomato half.

Bake for 30 minutes or until the tomatoes are soft, but still hold their shape.

Ail au Four

In Provence they are very partial to baked garlic which they serve as a vegetable to accompany meat and all kinds of dishes. It is mellow and creamy and has nothing in common with raw garlic.

Have one head per person or half a head if they are very large. Fresh garlic is particularly good to use. The old Provençal way of cooking them was to blanch them before baking them and to take them out of the oven 2 or 3 times during cooking to douse them with water so that the skins did not burn. It is easier though to bake them in foil in a hot oven – 230°C (450°F, gas mark 8) – for 20–30 minutes or in a mild oven – 160°C (325°F, gas mark 3) for an hour until they are very soft. Open the foil to brown them a little while before the end of the cooking time. Eat the garlic by cutting a slice off the root end of each clove and squeezing the cream out.

Topinambours à la Daube

Stewed Jerusalem Artichokes

These Jerusalem artichokes cooked in wine come from a part of Provence which is blanketed in vineyards.

Serves 4

625 g (1¼ lb) Jerusalem artichokes, peeled
1 small onion, finely chopped
2 tablespoons olive or sunflower oil
3 garlic cloves, crushed
Salt and pepper
Pinch of ground nutmeg
150 ml (5 fl oz) white wine

Cut the Jerusalem artichokes into pieces or leave them whole if they are very small. Fry the onion in oil until golden. Add the Jerusalem artichokes, garlic, salt, pepper and nutmeg and stir for a minute or so. Pour the wine in, add enough water to cover and simmer with the lid on for about 15 minutes, or until the artichokes are just tender.

Fenouils à la Tomate

Fennel with Tomatoes

The gentle aniseed taste of fennel goes well with the traditional garlic, onion and tomato flavours of Provence.

Serves 6

3 small fennel bulbs
1 large onion, chopped
3 tablespoons olive oil
2 garlic cloves, crushed
250 g (8 oz) tomatoes, peeled
125 ml (4 fl oz) dry white wine
2 bay leaves
Salt and pepper

Trim the fennel and cut in half lengthways. Fry the onion in oil till soft. Add the fennel and garlic and cook a few minutes. Then add the tomatoes and wine, water to cover, bay leaves, salt and pepper and simmer gently for 1 hour or until very soft. Serve hot.

Daube d'Aubergines

Aubergine Stew

This Provençal *daube* is one of the most sumptuous aubergine dishes I know.

Serves 6

750 g (1½ lb) aubergines
Salt
750 g (1½ lb) tomatoes, peeled and chopped
35 cl (½ bottle) red wine
Pepper
2–3 teaspoons sugar
1 garlic clove, crushed
1 teaspoon dried thyme
1 bay leaf
Sunflower or olive oil for frying
Small bunch of parsley, finely chopped

Peel the aubergines, cut them in half lengthways and then into thick slices. Sprinkle with salt and leave to drain in a colander for 30 minutes. Meanwhile, place the tomatoes, wine, a very little salt, pepper, the sugar, garlic, thyme and bay leaf in a large pot and simmer over a low heat for about 20 minutes.

Rinse the salt off the aubergines, dry them with a cloth and shallow-fry them in hot oil. Turn them over once to brown them all over, then remove with a slotted spoon and squeeze gently on kitchen paper.

Add the aubergines to the tomato sauce and simmer very gently, covered, adding a little water if necessary, for about 30 minutes. Add the parsley towards the end of cooking. It is as good cold as it is hot.

Batingan bi Jibn

Baked Aubergines and Cheese

Different kinds of cheese can be used for this uncommon Egyptian dish but goat's cheese is particularly delicious. It can be served as an appetiser or as a light main course.

Serves 6

2 large aubergines
2 garlic cloves, crushed
Pepper
Salt (optional)
2 large tomatoes, peeled and diced
1 tablespoon dried mint
500 g (1 lb) goat's cheese, grated or crumbled

Pre-heat the oven to 200°C (400°F, gas mark 6).

Roast or grill the aubergines and peel them as described on p. 70. Peel while still warm and squeeze out the juices. Chop up the flesh, then place in a baking dish, and add pepper and salt. You may not need any salt because of the saltiness of the cheese. Add the tomatoes and mint and mix well.

Sprinkle with the cheese and bake for about 25 minutes or until the cheese melts and is slightly brown. Serve hot.

Turkish Wines

There is hardly a corner of Turkey where grapes are not grown. Although most are for use as table grapes or sultanas, a variety of wines are also produced in all parts of the country made from both indigenous and imported stock. Some of the best wines come from Thrace, Marmara and the Aegean coastal areas, but there are some delightful whites from Central Anatolia such as Narince and a good red wine, Buzbağ, from the south.

Few Turkish wines are available generally outside the country other than in Turkish restaurants and shops, though you might find raki, which many Turks like to drink at the beginning of a meal, in particular with *mezes*. Made from the distilled remains of the grapes after wine-making and flavoured with aniseed, it is usually served diluted with water.

If you want something non-alcoholic to go with your meal, a glass of ayran (see p. 207) might be just the thing.

Kıs Türlüsü

Winter Vegetables in Olive Oil

Root vegetables cooked in oil and served cold make a very pleasant dish, as those who travel to Turkey in winter discover.

Serves 6

1 celeriac
250 g (8 oz) Jerusalem artichokes
3 large carrots
1 medium potato or sweet potato
4 tablespoons olive oil
Juice of $\frac{1}{2}$ lemon
2 teaspoons sugar
Salt and pepper
Small bunch of dill or parsley, finely chopped

Peel the vegetables and cut into small cubes. Put them in a large saucepan with the oil, lemon juice and seasoning. Half cover with water and cook gently with the lid on, stirring occasionally, for about 20 minutes or until they are cooked but still a little crisp.

Serve cold, sprinkled with herbs, with the small amount of remaining liquid as a sauce.

Variation

Egyptians make *torli*, an everyday dish of vegetables and meat cooked in oil with whatever is in season. For a vegetarian summer version use onions, garlic, potatoes, green beans, tomatoes and courgettes. Add them, in that order, to a large pan with a few tablespoons of oil. Moisten with a little water, season with salt, pepper and lemon juice and cook, covered, over a low heat until tender. Add a bunch of mixed herbs towards the end and serve hot or cold.

Tbikha

Turnip Stew

A marriage of turnips, spinach and tomatoes turns up everywhere in the eastern Mediterranean. The following recipe, which can be served hot or cold, relies on the natural flavours of the vegetables, but there is also a spicy version in the variations.

Serves 4

1 large onion, coarsely chopped
3 tablespoons olive or sunflower oil
500 g (1 lb) turnips, peeled and grated
500 g (1 lb) tomatoes, peeled and cut into pieces
Salt and pepper
2 teaspoons sugar (optional)
Juice of $\frac{1}{2}$ lemon (optional)
500 g (1 lb) spinach
Large bunch of parsley, finely chopped

Fry the onion in oil in a saucepan. When the onion is soft, add the turnips and tomatoes. Season with salt and pepper, half cover with water and simmer, uncovered, until the turnips are cooked but still a little crisp. Turn the turnips over once so that they cook evenly, adding sugar and lemon juice if the dish is to be eaten cold. Wash the spinach, cut off the thick stems and cut the leaves into ribbons. Put them in the saucepan and cook, stirring, until they crumple. Garnish with parsley.

Variations

* If you want a spicy Tunisian dish, add $1\frac{1}{2}$ teaspoons paprika, 1 teaspoon powdered coriander, and a large pinch of cayenne.
* Other vegetables, such as petits pois, pumpkin cut into pieces, or sliced courgettes, can be added at the same time as the turnips.
* Cooked chickpeas are often added to this stew. Their firmness adds a welcome texture.

Navets au Sucre

Caramelised Turnips

These are usually finished in a pan with duck or mutton, but they are also very good cooked and served on their own. Choose tender crisp turnips. Soft or fibrous ones will not do.

Serves 6

1 kg (2 lb) small young turnips
3 tablespoons sunflower oil
2–3 tablespoons caster sugar
A little stock or water
Large pinch of ground nutmeg
Salt and pepper

Wash and trim the turnips. Put them in a pan with the oil, sprinkle with sugar and cook, turning the turnips so that they colour evenly, over a very low heat until the sugar caramelises. Cover with stock or water, add the nutmeg, salt and pepper and simmer uncovered for 20–40 minutes or until the turnips are tender and the liquid is reduced. Serve hot.

Left: Kış türlüsü

Patatas Bravas

Peppery Potatoes

Alicia Riós gave the recipe for this simple Spanish peasant dish which is also served as a *tapa*. Use the smaller quantities of vinegar and paprika if you are serving it as a side dish.

Serves 4

1 kg (2 lb) new potatoes
Salt
Olive oil for frying

For the sauce:
5 tablespoons olive oil
1 tablespoon tomato paste
1–2 tablespoons wine vinegar
1–2 teaspoons paprika
Pinch of cayenne or a few drops of Tabasco sauce

Boil the potatoes in their skins in salted water until they are almost tender. Drain, and when they are cool enough to handle, peel and cut them into quarters or into bite-sized pieces. Shallow-fry them in hot oil until crisp and golden, turning them over once. Drain on kitchen paper and transfer to a serving dish.

Mix all the sauce ingredients together, pour over the potatoes and mix well. Serve hot or warm.

Fish and Seafood

A variety of different fish can be used for most of the recipes in this chapter. In the Mediterranean when you ask what kind of fish to use a likely answer is 'any fish you like' so do not feel restricted.

A MEDITERRANEAN fish market is an extraordinary sight. Although the yield of the sea has never been great except for around southern Italy and the coasts of Tunisia and Andalousia, such a wide variety of fish is rarely seen outside the region.

For me, two of the most memorable markets are at opposite ends of the Mediterranean – Turkey and Spain. Wandering around the stalls in Istanbul is like being at a nautical carnival, with paintings in the background, net curtains and coloured lights. The fish are displayed in artistic arrangements, standing on their tails or curved in an arc, their brilliant red gills opened out for exhibition as a testament to their freshness. I saw live ones swimming in plastic buckets, others on slabs being splashed flamboyantly with jets of water.

The Valencia fish market is in the main covered market with shafts of sunlight spotlighting the fish through the stained glass windows. The Spanish fishmongers, in contrast to the hefty, mustachioed Turkish men, are all extraordinarily elegant women in starched, lacy pinafores, their hands flashing with diamond rings. The names of these magnificent women are displayed over their stalls: Maria José, Miranda, Lola, Carmen. I had never seen such a range of crustaceans and molluscs before – tiny baby octopus and cuttlefish, piles of prickly sea urchins, blood-red prawns and a host of creatures I couldn't put a name to. The sight simply made me want to buy it all up and rush into the nearest kitchen.

The bustling activity, the exuberance, the double-entendre humour, and the respect, if not tenderness, with which the fish is eyed and handled in these two markets is an indication of just how highly fish is prized in the Mediterranean.

Alan Davidson's *Mediterranean Seafood* (Penguin Books) is the major source of information for anyone wishing to learn about fish or the Mediterranean. I travelled with his book in my hand and found that everyone there was also raving about it. You cannot do better than to buy a copy of his handbook which, among its many virtues, gives the names of fish and other marine creatures in seven languages.

Right: A Turkish fisherman displaying his wares on the Golden Horn

Soupe de Poisson

Cream of Fish Soup

This speciality of Marseilles is subtle and delicate – a great soup for a grand occasion. It is a creamy broth where the fish is present only as a liquid purée. In restaurants along the coast it is served with toast and a sauce called *rouille*. I have heard some local complaints about this practice because the garlicky rouille is so fiercely hot that it drowns the delicate flavours. But I confess that I love the two together. You may, as I do, prefer the mayonnaise-like rouille on p. 211 to the one given below.

The soup is made in France with whatever is at hand such as small soft-shell crabs, conger eel and a collection of small rockfish such as *wrasse*, *rascasse* and *girella*. Conger eel gives the soup an attractive unctuous texture but cod or whiting can be used instead to give it body. It may sound difficult but it is not if you follow the unorthodox procedure I describe.

Serves 8

750 g (1½ lb) small shrimps
1 large Spanish onion, chopped
300 ml (10 fl oz) dry white wine
1 bay leaf
2 sprigs of thyme
Bunch of parsley
Bunch of fennel leaves (optional)
7.5 cm (3 in) piece of dried orange peel
Salt
500 g (1 lb) conger eel, cod or whiting
5 tablespoons olive oil
3 garlic cloves, crushed
1 kg (2 lb) tomatoes, peeled and chopped
1 teaspoon sugar
125 ml (4 fl oz) cognac
2 packets of real ground saffron (p. 52)
Pinch of cayenne

For the traditional rouille of Provence
3–4 slices of white bread, crusts removed
4 garlic cloves, crushed
½–1 red chilli pepper, de-seeded and chopped, or
  1 teaspoon paprika and a good pinch of cayenne
¼ teaspoon saffron-coloured powder (p. 52)
  (optional)
5 tablespoons olive oil
1–2 tablespoons tomato paste (optional)

Garnishes:
Grated Gruyère or Parmesan
About 24 slices of French bread, toasted in the oven

Kakavia

The making of fish soup, so much part of Mediterranean life, is generally believed to be a legacy of ancient Greece and *kakavia*, the fishermen's standby in the Greek islands, to be the descendant of the original soup. It is usual for fishermen out at sea to bring supplies of onions, potatoes, tomatoes, lemons and olive oil on board and to cook them up in a large pot. They throw in the smaller fish caught in their nets and make a substantial meal of the soup with bread. This is *kakavia* and you will find versions of it, sometimes with all kinds of embellishments such as saffron and paprika, garlic and orange peel, in nearly every port around the sea.

Wash the shrimps. Put them in a large pan with the onion and pour in 3 litres (5 pints) water. Bring to the boil and remove the scum. Then add the wine, the bay leaf, thyme, parsley and fennel leaves, the orange peel and a pinch of salt and simmer for 1 hour.

Fry the conger eel, cod or whiting in the oil. Turn the fish over and when the flesh begins to flake remove it from the pan. Now fry the garlic in the same oil and, when the aroma rises, add the tomatoes, sugar, cognac, saffron and cayenne and cook for 15 minutes or until the tomatoes are soft and the sauce reduced.

Skin and bone the fish and blend to a purée with the tomato sauce in a food processor. Do it in batches and transfer to a very large pan. Then blend the shrimps and their broth, also in batches – this may seem strange but it is how it is done in France to extract the maximum from the shrimps. Strain the broth into the pan containing the fish purée and mix well.

To make the rouille, blend the bread with the rest of the ingredients and add enough of the reserved fish stock to make a light cream.

A few minutes before serving gradually re-heat the soup. Adjust the seasoning – it should be strongly flavoured and peppery – and serve very hot. It is usual in France to place 2 pieces of toast broken into small pieces, with a good blob of rouille and a tablespoon of grated cheese in each soup plate before ladling in the soup. Some prefer to spread the rouille on the toast and to eat this with the soup.

Brodetto

Italian Fish Soup or Stew

Brodetto, which means 'little broth', is the king of Italian fish dishes. Many towns on the Adriatic boast brodetto as a speciality and each insists its version is the best. Those of Rimini, Porto Recanati and San Benedetto del Tronto have become famous. Brodetto is also called *caciucco* on the Tuscan coast, *ciuppin* or *buridda* in Liguria, *ghiotto* in Sicily and *cassola* or *ziminu* in Sardinia.

The excellence of the dish is measured by the type and especially the number of different fish which are used. The general rule is the greater the variety, the finer the soup, but there are also some wonderful variations made with only one fish such as sole or bass.

Brodetto is never the same twice. Its beauty lies in the simplicity of execution and of flavouring. The secret is not to mask the flavour of the fish and to give each just the right amount of cooking that it needs.

All kinds of fish and shellfish are used depending on what is available, and every town and hamlet has a favourite list. The following may be included: sole, flounder, turbot or brill, red and grey mullet, bass, bream, monkfish, skate, cod, John Dory, hake, sardines, mackerel, anchovy, eel, cuttlefish, squid, mussels and clams. The *cigale* (mantis shrimp) and *scorfano* or scorpion fish are often, but not always, included for their special flavour. The list can be very much longer and fish not found in the Mediterranean can also be used. Brodetto makes a splendid meal in itself for a large party. Here is a basic recipe with which to improvise.

Serves 10

2 kg (4 lb) assorted fish, cleaned and scaled
750 g (1½ lb) squid or cuttlefish
1 kg (2 lb) mussels or clams
3 onions, finely chopped
75 ml (3 fl oz) olive oil
2 small chillies, de-seeded and finely chopped
(optional)
750 g (1½ lb) tomatoes, peeled, de-seeded and
chopped
250 ml (8 fl oz) white wine
Salt and pepper
Pinch of real saffron or saffron-coloured powder
(p. 52) (optional)
2 tablespoons wine vinegar (optional)
Large bunch of parsley, finely chopped
10 slices of toasted bread

Clean and wash the fish and cut off their heads. Use the fish heads to make 2.5 litres (4½ pints) of stock (see p. 216). Cut larger fish into pieces and leave smaller ones whole. Clean the squid or cuttlefish (see p. 145), cut the bodies into rings and divide the tentacles into small clusters. Prepare and shell the mussels and clams (see p. 138).

In a large casserole, fry the onions in oil till golden, add the chillies and then the tomatoes. Cook gently for 10 minutes, then add the wine and stock, salt, pepper, saffron and vinegar, if using, and cook for 15 minutes more.

Start adding the fish in layers to the simmering stock, according to the length of cooking time each needs. First cook the squid and cuttlefish, though small ones take hardly any time; the firmer-fleshed fish, such as monkfish, next; and then the delicate-fleshed fish such as the mullet and John Dory, which require only a few minutes. Put the mussels and clams in last. It should take about 15 minutes. Test the fish to see if it is done then sprinkle with the chopped parsley.

Serve in bowls, accompanied by toasted bread. In Italy it is usual to put the bread in the bowl and to serve the fish and broth on top.

Soupe de poisson with rouille (opposite)

Bourride

Fish Stew

Bourride is a fish stew or soup of the French Riviera which is made with either one type or a mixture of white fish. The strained stock is blended with aïoli (see p. 212) and extra egg yolks into a delicate, pale yellow cream. The dish is something of an event and worth making, especially since it can be made with any white fish you like and is also much easier than it seems.

Serves 8

For the stock:
Fresh fish bones and heads
1 onion, chopped
2 leeks, chopped
1 carrot, chopped
2 garlic cloves, chopped
35 cl ($\frac{1}{2}$ bottle) dry white wine
1 large piece of orange peel
A few sprigs of fresh thyme, or 1 teaspoon dried thyme
A few parsley stalks
2 bay leaves
A few fennel leaves
Salt and pepper

Aïoli sauce (p. 212) made with 300–600 ml (10 fl oz–1 pint) olive oil
2 kg (4 lb) fillets or steaks of any white fish, such as bass, bream, monkfish, whiting, gurnard, grey mullet, halibut, John Dory, turbot or cod
3 egg yolks
$\frac{1}{2}$ French loaf, sliced and fried in olive oil or lightly toasted in the oven

Put all the ingredients for the stock in a large pan with about 3 litres (5 pints) of water. Simmer for about 30 minutes, then strain and let it cool a little.

Make the aïoli. (If you make a large quantity and have some left over, it will keep for several days.) Put the fish in the stock, slowly bring to a simmer and poach just until the flesh is translucent and just begins to flake. (This will take 6–20 minutes, depending on the type and thickness of the fish.) Transfer the fish carefully into an ovenproof terrine and cover with a little stock. Keep warm in a low oven. Remove the remaining stock from the heat and allow to cool for a few minutes, then gradually blend in the aïoli so that it does not curdle.

Beat half the aïoli into the egg yolks. Put this in a bowl or pan placed in boiling water, then beat in the fish stock – by the ladleful to begin with – until it thickens into a light creamy consistency. You can then pour it all back into the pan to heat it through but do not bring to the boil. Place the toasted or fried bread in individual bowls and pour the creamy stock over it; this is eaten like a soup. Serve the fish separately with the remaining aïoli.

Cuscus con Brodo di Pesce

Many people are surprised to find couscous dishes in Sicily. Although these are distinctively Italian, they are closest to the Tunisian dishes of North Africa. There is less than a hundred miles of sea between Sicily and Tunisia and their relationship is ancient. When the Arabs ruled Sicily they recruited their soldiers in Tunisia. When France colonised Tunisia many of the immigrants who came to farm the land for the French were Sicilian. Workers and fishermen have been travelling between the two places for centuries, so what is surprising is not that couscous dishes can be found in Sicily, but that they should be confined to three towns, Trapani, Marsala and Mazara del Vallo. There are all kinds but the fish one is perhaps the best.

Franco Cusenza makes fish couscous at the Antica Trattoria in S. Vito lo Capo, Sicily. He prepares the grain in a *couscousier* in the same way that it is made in Morocco (see p. 178), but flavours it before steaming with a little olive oil, chopped onion, garlic and parsley, some fresh bay leaves and chilli powder. For the fish soup Franco fries an onion and adds tomato and plenty of water, then the fish – grouper, *San Pietro* (John Dory), *scorfano* (scorpion fish), prawns, *cocciu* (stargazer fish), *cipolla* (onion fish) and *martello* (hammer fish) – putting the large ones in first, in order of cooking time. (You could use the recipe for brodetto on p. 127.) Strain the broth and reduce it to make it strong. Skin and bone the fish and cut it into pieces. Moisten the couscous with broth, pile it onto a serving dish and arrange the fish on top.

Bourride de l'Algue Bleue

A Special Bourride

Rene Théveniot, *chef de cuisine* at L'Algue Bleue, the restaurant at L'Auberge de la Calanque in Le Lavandou, gave us his personal and grand version of *bourride* which constitutes a sumptuous meal. He makes it with fillets of sole, sea bream and sea bass – these last two left whole – and with mussels in their shells. Everything, including the vegetables, is cooked at the same time. The broth is served separately, thickened to a delicious creaminess at the end with an aïoli (see p. 212) and with egg yolks and cream. The aïoli sauce is served in a sauce boat, and garlic toast arrives on a separate plate. The serving of the bourride is something of a ritual.

Making the aïoli and the 'liaison' sounds complicated and perhaps confusing but if you follow the steps it will all work out beautifully.

Serves 6

150 ml (5 fl oz) olive oil
2 large onions, cut into slices
Whole head of garlic, cut in $\frac{1}{2}$
1 tomato, cut in $\frac{1}{2}$
$\frac{1}{2}$ red pepper
2 sticks celery, chopped roughly
6 large potatoes, weighing about 1.5 kg (3 lb), sliced
2 branches of wild fennel, or the feathery leaves from fennel bulbs
A sprig of thyme
1–2 sprigs of savory
1 kg (2 lb) mussels, scrubbed and cleaned (see p. 138)
1 sea bream, weighing about 750 g ($1\frac{1}{2}$ lb)
1 sea bass, weighing about 750 g ($1\frac{1}{2}$ lb)
1 sole, weighing about 500 g (1 lb), filleted
250 ml (8 fl oz) dry white wine
Salt and pepper

For the aïoli sauce:
6 garlic cloves
4 egg yolks
500 ml (17 fl oz) olive oil

For the aïoli 'liaison':
4 egg yolks
250 ml (8 fl oz) single cream
Salt and pepper

Garnish:
Sliced French bread, rubbed with a little olive oil and garlic and toasted

First make the aïoli as described on p. 212. To make the 'liaison' or thickening, take half the quantity of aïoli and gradually beat it into 4 egg yolks, then beat in the cream and add salt and pepper. Keep the remaining aïoli aside.

Put the oil in a very large casserole or saucepan with the vegetables, herbs and mussels. If the mussels are sandy, you should steam them open separately (see p. 138) and strain their liquid into the pan through a very fine sieve. Lay the fish on top and cover with about 2 litres ($3\frac{1}{2}$ pints) of water. Bring to the boil, add the wine, salt and pepper and simmer, uncovered, for about 10 minutes or until the fish is only just done. If you test the flesh near the head with the point of a knife it should just come away.

Lift the fish out very carefully without breaking them and place on a large serving platter with enough broth to keep them moist. Take out the mussels and vegetables with a slotted spoon and keep aside, leaving a few potato slices in the broth to give it body. Crush these potato slices, then strain the broth into another pan.

Pour the *aïoli* 'liaison' into the broth, stirring well, and heat to just below boiling point. As soon as the surface begins to tremble, strain into a soup terrine.

In large soup bowls, serve pieces of fish and mussels (you can reheat them just before serving) with some potato slices and other bits of vegetables. Drop a few slices of toasted bread into the soup tureen, ladle them out again along with a little broth and pour over the vegetables. Pass the remaining aïoli around for people to spread on the remaining bread.

Fishermen in the Vieux Port, Marseilles

Zarzuela de Pescado

Catalan Seafood Stew

The name of this most sensational Spanish seafood stew, *zarzuela*, means operetta or musical comedy, and the fried mixture is truly a feast for the eyes and for all the senses. This recipe is from Carles Camós, the flamboyant owner of the Hotel Big Rock in Platja d'Aro. The ingredients can vary depending on what is available. Usually two or more white fish are used – halibut, grouper, turbot, monkfish or hake – but Carles uses only monkfish. Scorpion fish is usually included to flavour the broth but there is no broth in this recipe. Instead a larger quantity of monkfish is called for. In Spain lobsters and prawns as well as shellfish are sold live and that, of course, is the best way to use them. Here you can buy shellfish live and frozen uncooked prawns but with the rest you must do what you can.

Serves 6

For the sofrito sauce:
3 onions, grated
2 tablespoons olive oil
2 large ripe tomatoes, peeled, de-seeded and finely chopped
Salt

For the picada sauce:
3 thin slices of white bread, crusts removed, fried in oil
6 blanched almonds, toasted
3 garlic cloves

1 large or 2 small monkfish tails, cut into 6 pieces
Flour
Olive oil for frying
300 g (10 oz) squid, cleaned (see p. 145) and cut into rings
3 small lobsters weighing 400 g (14 oz) each
6 prawns
6 king prawns
24 mussels, cleaned (see p. 138)
12 large clams, cleaned (see p. 138)
2 garlic cloves, finely chopped
Large bunch of parsley, finely chopped
200 ml (7 fl oz) brandy

Start by making the two sauces – they are the hallmarks of Catalan cooking. To make the *sofrito* gently fry the onions in the oil till soft and just beginning to colour. Add the tomatoes and salt and cook for 10 minutes, stirring constantly. Add 125 ml (4 fl oz) water, stir and continue to cook until the sauce is thick but still quite liquid. Keep aside. To make the *picada* pound the bread to a paste with the almonds and garlic or blend them in a food processor. Keep aside.

Coat the monkfish pieces with flour and fry in shallow oil in a large frying-pan until they are brown. Transfer to a large, shallow, preferably earthenware casserole. Very quickly, fry the squid. Fry the fresh lobster and prawns until they turn pink. (Cooked lobsters and prawns do not need frying.) Fry the mussels and clams until they open. Transfer the seafood, as they are cooked, to the casserole.

Sprinkle in the chopped garlic and the parsley. Pour the brandy into the casserole and flame. When the flames die down pour in the sofrito sauce and add 125 ml (4 fl oz) water, then put the casserole over a gentle heat for 4 minutes. Stir in the picada, check the seasoning and cook for another 5 minutes.

Variations
* If you are using live lobsters, you can boil them separately.
* You can steam open the mussels and clams (p. 138) instead of frying them.
* Add a small, finely chopped chilli pepper with the onion or a pinch of saffron powder and a glass of white wine to the tomato sauce and serve the stew with lemon wedges.

Spanish Rosé and White Wines

Catalan wines are really worth noting. Try Rosado del Ámpurdan, a lovely rosé, with a dish like *zarzuela*. The fine and elegant Penedés wines have great quality, the whites especially, and the Chardonnay white from the same region has a beautiful scent and distinctive flavour.

A delightful white wine from the Valencia area is Alto Turia. It goes well with fish, as would a well chilled montilla or a rosé from around Denia or Alicante.

Opposite: Zarzuela de pescado

Bouillabaisse

The people of Marseilles do not accept that it is possible to make a real *bouillabaisse* outside of the Riviera, and they consider it presumptuous that anybody should even try. One reason given is that the spiny scorpion fish *rascasse*, which gives a unique aroma to the broth and is said to be the soul of bouillabaisse, is not available. But there are so many other flavours which come into play and with the Mediterranean fish now obtainable at many fishmongers you should be able to do very well even without *rascasse*. Anyway, as it is often difficult to find *rascasse* on the Riviera now and as there are so many versions of what real bouillabaisse should be, it is not right that the Marseillais should keep the monopoly.

Bouillabaisse is a meal in itself, or rather two courses – a soup and a separate fish dish. It is worth making for a large number because you need a good variety of fish. Make a selection from the following which are available here, many from British waters: moray or conger eel, red mullet, gurnard, a small monkfish tail, small bream, small bass, John Dory. If you are near the Mediterranean, get *rascasse* and other small rockfish. You can also choose to make a sumptuous bouillabaisse with spiny lobsters and king prawns.

Once the fish is cleaned, gutted and scaled and the ingredients are assembled, it is quick and easy to make.

Serves 10–12

125 ml (4 fl oz) olive oil
2 large onions, chopped
2 leeks, finely chopped
5 garlic cloves, crushed
500 g (1 lb) ripe tomatoes, peeled and chopped
A sprig of thyme
2 bay leaves
Sprig of fennel
A 5 cm (2 in) piece of dried orange peel
3 litres (5 pints) boiling water or fish stock (see p. 216)
Salt and pepper
$\frac{1}{4}$ teaspoon saffron
2.75 kg (6 lb) fish

To serve:
10–12 slices of French bread, toasted and (optional) rubbed with garlic
Bunch of parsley, finely chopped
A bowl of aïolli (see p. 212)
A bowl of rouille (see p. 126)
1.5 kg (3 lb) boiled potatoes

Heat 4 tablespoons of oil in a large pan. Fry the onions and leeks till golden, then add the garlic and when the aroma rises add the tomatoes and cook 5 minutes. Add the thyme, bay, fennel and orange peel. Pour in the boiling water or stock, beating vigorously, and raise the heat to high. Season with salt and pepper, add the rest of the oil and continue to boil vigorously for a few minutes so that the oil is properly mixed and does not float, then add the saffron. Reduce the heat and put in the fish and simmer for 5–8 minutes.

Lift each fish out carefully as soon as it becomes cooked and arrange on a serving dish. Leave one or two of the softer-fleshed fish in for a longer time so that they disintegrate, giving body to the soup. The total cooking time should be 15 minutes maximum. Keep the fish warm. Pour or strain the broth straight into a serving bowl or over pieces of toasted garlic bread placed in individual plates. Sprinkle with chopped parsley. Serve accompanied by aïoli and rouille and hot boiled potatoes.

Variation
Add a tablespoon of tomato paste and a tablespoon of pastis to the broth.

Small Provençal rockfish used locally to make bouillabaisse

Midye Çorbasi

Mussel Soup

In Turkey, where this recipe comes from, mussels are particularly large but any size will do.

Serves 6

2 kg (4 lb) mussels
1 large potato, peeled and cubed
1 leek, chopped
3 celery stalks and leaves, chopped
4 spring onions, finely chopped
750 g (1½ lb) tomatoes, peeled and diced
Juice of ½ lemon
Large bunch of parsley, finely chopped

Clean and cook the mussels as described on p. 138. Sieve the mussel liquor into another pan and add enough water to make about 1.25 litres (2 pints). Add the potato, leek and celery, salt and pepper and simmer for about 20 minutes. In the meantime, remove the mussels from their shells and reserve. Add the spring onions to the soup and cook for 5 minutes, adding water if necessary. Just before serving, add the tomatoes, lemon juice, parsley and mussels and heat through.

Variation

For a spicy Tunisian version add 1 teaspoon cinnamon, 1 teaspoon cumin and 1 teaspoon harissa or a good pinch of cayenne.

Pescado Frito

Fried Fish

Frying is the most common way of cooking fish in Spain, and Andalusia has turned it into an art as anyone lucky enough to eat fried fish there knows. Whether it is small fish like whitebait, anchovy, sprats, smelts and small sardines, or larger fish like red mullet, young hake and sole or squid, the dish is invariably pure magic.

You can make a great feast with a medley of different fried fish. The bigger the variety, the more interesting the dish. Sprinkle with chopped parsley and serve with lemon wedges and bread.

Maria José Sevilla Taylor, who took me around the coastal eating places, revealed the secret of perfection. The fish must be very fresh, preferably just out of the water, and the oil must be very hot. Olive oil, though expensive, can reach higher temperatures than other oils without deteriorating and gives the very best results. It can be used 4 or 5 times but it should be filtered to get rid of impurities each time. The first time, of course, will be the best.

Choose fish of roughly the same size. Different sizes must be fried separately as they take different times and need different temperatures. They must be cleaned, gutted and scaled, washed and dried. Heads can either stay on or be removed. The fish should be seasoned with salt, then covered entirely but lightly with flour which acts as a shield, preventing the absorption of too much oil. Use a large, high-sided pan so that the fish are not crowded and the oil does not boil over as it expands. There must be enough oil to cover the fish and its temperature should remain constant.

Small fish must be fried quickly at a very high temperature, a few at a time, and turned over once so that they are crisp and deep golden all over. Then drain them on kitchen paper and serve on a warmed plate.

Larger fish – hake is a favourite – take longer and need a lower temperature so that they have time to cook inside before the skin gets burnt. Alternatively they can be cooked in slices. It is usual to roll them in flour and then dip them in beaten egg for extra protection.

Squid, shellfish and prawns out of their shells are fried *en gabardina* – in a batter. For an extra light batter enough for 250 g (8 oz) prawns, shelled but with the tails left on so that they can be picked up, mix 50 g (2 oz) flour, 1 teaspoon baking powder, 1 tablespoon olive oil and 125 ml (4 fl oz) beer. Beat well and let it rest for 30 minutes.

Serve fried fish with aïoli, mayonnaise, all-i-oli or romesco sauce (pp. 211–213).

For a delicious Moroccan flavour marinate before frying in the following *chermoula* marinade and sauce.

For 1.5 kg (3 lb) fish, blend in a food processor or blender: 1 large bunch of fresh coriander, 2 crushed garlic cloves, 3 tablespoons water, 1 tablespoon paprika, 1½ teaspoons cumin, ¼ teaspoon cayenne (or to taste), 3 tablespoons wine vinegar, juice of 1½ lemons, 5 tablespoons of oil. Marinate the fish in this mixture for a few hours. Just before you are ready to fry, dip each fish in flour and fry.

Levrek en Papillote

Sea Bass in Paper Parcels

This is often restaurant fare in Turkey but it is also a delightful way of cooking fish at home. Alya Halici, who gave this recipe, lives in the port of Izmir, where the selection of fish available is enormous. Sea bass is one of her favourite fish, though you can substitute cod, haddock, hake, turbot or halibut.

Per person

1 fish steak up to 2.5 cm (1 in) thick
Salt
Olive oil
A few sprigs of parsley, chopped
1 tablespoon chopped onion, or 1 spring onion,
  chopped
½ small tomato, peeled and chopped

Garnish:
A lemon wedge

Pre-heat the oven to 190°C (375°F, gas mark 5).
   Sprinkle the fish with salt and dab with oil. Brush a large square of greaseproof paper or foil with oil. Mix the parsley and onion together, put half in the centre of the sheet and place the fish on top. Then cover with the rest of the parsley and onion, and top with the tomato. Season lightly with salt and wrap the fish loosely, folding in the ends of the paper to seal the parcel.
   Do the same with the required number of fish steaks and place on an oiled baking tray. If using greaseproof paper, brush the top of each parcel with a little water to prevent scorching. Bake for 20 minutes or until the flesh is translucent and flakes away from the bone. Serve the fish steaks still in their parcels, garnished with lemon wedges.

Top: Gratin de tomates provençal (p. 120)
Bottom: Sardines farcies à la niçoise (opposite)

Sardinas en Vino Blanco

Sardines Granada-style

In Spain sardines are cooked in a shallow earthenware pot which goes straight on the fire. Alicia Ríos Ivars made this dish for us in an outdoor country kitchen near Denia. I first met Alicia at the Oxford Symposium on Food and Cookery where she delivered a paper on garlic and sang an incantation in Spanish to exorcise devils. She is an extraordinarily lovely woman, a university lecturer in psychology and ex-restaurateur who is now researching the history of food in Spain and Spanish regional cooking.

Serves 6

1 kg (2 lb) sardines
Salt
Juice of ½–1 lemon
2 tablespoons olive oil
150 ml (5 fl oz) dry white wine
2–3 garlic cloves, crushed
Small bunch of parsley, finely chopped

Clean and scale the sardines but leave the heads on. Put them in a large frying-pan. Sprinkle with salt and add the lemon juice, olive oil, wine, garlic and parsley. Simmer for 5 minutes until just cooked. Serve hot or cold.

Sardines Farcies à la Niçoise

Stuffed Sardines

In this recipe, a stuffing of prawns and mussels is pressed between two opened-out boned sardines. It was provided by Yolande Bona of the Bagna Caouda restaurant in Nice.

Serves 6

1 kg (2 lb) fresh sardines
300 g (10 oz) mussels
500 g (1 lb) cooked shelled prawns
50 g (2 oz) short-grain rice
3 eggs
2 slices white bread, crusts removed, soaked in
  water
4 garlic cloves, crushed
Small bunch of parsley, finely chopped
Salt and pepper
2 tablespoons grated Parmesan (optional)
Olive oil
Fine breadcrumbs (optional)

Garnish:
Lemon wedges

Pre-heat the oven to 200°C (400°F, gas mark 6).

Scale the sardines and take off the heads and tails. Cut the fish open through the belly and gut them, then lay them flat, skin-side up, and press with your fingers down the spine. This loosens the backbone so that you can pull it out easily. Remove the bones and wash and drain the fish. Keep 12 sardines whole; chop up any that are left over for the stuffing.

To prepare the stuffing, clean the mussels, steam them open as described on p. 138 and shell them. Boil the rice in plenty of salted water for 15 minutes or until tender, then drain. Coarsely chop the mussels and prawns. Place them in a bowl with any chopped sardines, the eggs, rice, the bread squeezed dry, garlic, parsley, salt, pepper and Parmesan. Mix well. Brush a large, round, ovenproof dish with oil. Place 6 opened-out sardines, skin-side down, on the bottom in a circle. Spread a generous layer of stuffing over each and lay a second sardine, skin-side up, on top. Sprinkle lightly with olive oil and breadcrumbs, if you like. Cover the dish with foil and bake for about 15 minutes. Take off the foil and bake for a further 10 minutes.

Serve hot, garnished with lemon wedges.

Tagen Samak

Baked Fish

Assam al Mougi, the flamboyant chef of the Meridien Hotel in Cairo, trained in the kitchen of King Farouk. His fish *tagen*, though easy to make, looks spectacular.

Serves 4

1.5 kg (2–3 lb) any firm white fish fillets
Salt and pepper
Olive or sunflower oil
Juice of ½ lemon
2–4 garlic cloves, finely chopped
1 kg (2 lb) tomatoes, peeled and chopped
2 teaspoons sugar (optional)
250 g (8 oz) onions, finely sliced
2 tablespoons blanched almonds, coarsely chopped
  or sliced
1½ tablespoons raisins

Garnish:
Large bunch of parsley
1 lemon, sliced

Pre-heat the oven to 200°C (400°F, gas mark 6).

Put the fillets in a baking dish in a single layer. Rub with salt, pepper, 2 tablespoons of oil and the lemon juice and cover with foil. Bake for 10–20 minutes or until the flesh becomes translucent and just begins to flake. Keep the fish warm.

Meanwhile, fry the garlic in 2 tablespoons of oil and, as it begins to colour, add the tomatoes with a little sugar if they are not very sweet. Cook gently for 20 minutes or until the tomatoes are reduced to a thick paste. In another pan fry the onions in 3 tablespoons of oil until golden. Add the almonds and raisins and fry until the almonds colour and the raisins puff up.

To serve, lay the fish on a large plate, pour the tomato sauce over and cover with the fried onion mixture. Garnish with parsley, deep-fried in oil if you like, and lemon slices placed around the edge of the dish.

Tagine bel Hout

Fish Tagine with Tomatoes

It is usual in Morocco to cook fish in an earthenware *tagine* (see p. 58). Every city has its favourite flavourings – ginger, saffron powder, sweet and hot red peppers – and its favourite vegetable garnishes. When the *tagine* is put on a charcoal fire, a few reeds or celery stalks are put at the bottom of the dish to stop the fish sticking. This recipe was prepared for us in Tétouan by Anisa Khnous and sent to the public oven to be cooked.

Serves 4

1–1.5 kg (2–3 lb) white fish, such as sea bass, red
  snapper, grouper, hake, whiting, grey mullet or
  small cod
Salt
2½ teaspoons ground cumin
Large pinch of cayenne (optional)
4 tablespoons olive or vegetable oil
3 tablespoons coriander or parsley, finely chopped
2–3 garlic cloves, crushed
5 tomatoes, peeled and sliced
½–1 preserved lemon (see p. 214), washed and cut
  into slices

Ask the fishmonger to clean and scale the fish but leave the head and tail on. (You can, of course, have it filleted if you prefer.)

Pre-heat the oven to 200°C (400°F, gas mark 6). Wash and dry the fish and score the skin in a few places. Rub with salt, most of the cumin, cayenne, if using, and some of the oil inside and out. Stuff with the coriander or parsley and garlic. (If you are using fillets, sandwich them together with this mixture.) Lay the fish in a shallow earthenware dish and surround with the tomatoes and preserved lemon. Sprinkle the remaining oil, a little salt and the remaining cumin on the tomatoes.

Cover with foil and bake for 30 minutes, then remove the foil and bake for another 10–20 minutes or until the flesh becomes translucent and just begins to flake when you test it with the point of a knife. Serve hot.

Pesce alla Marinara

Fish in Tomato Sauce

This is a beautifully simple way of stewing fish in a very light tomato sauce. Small whole sea bream were used in Bari at the Ristorante da Tommaso where this recipe comes from, but other delicately fleshed white fish such as monkfish, hake, halibut, skate and cod can be cooked in the same way, whole or cut into steaks.

Serves 4

2 garlic cloves, chopped
4 tablespoons olive oil
4 medium tomatoes, peeled, de-seeded and
  chopped
Salt and pepper
1 kg (2 lb) white fish
Small bunch of parsley, finely chopped

Gently fry the garlic in the oil in a large pan. Add the tomatoes, salt and pepper and cook for 3 minutes or until the tomatoes have softened. Put the fish in, sprinkle with the parsley and moisten with a little water. Add salt and pepper and simmer gently with a lid on until the fish is done – from 4 minutes for fish steak to about 15 minutes for monkfish tails. The flesh should just begin to flake from the bone. Serve with triangles of toasted bread.

Variations
* At Don Salvatore in Naples they stew fish in much the same way but use the sauce to dress spaghetti or linguine, adding just a touch of grated Parmesan. The fish is served afterwards as the main course.
* La Lucerna restaurant at Bocca di Magra near La Spezia serves a variety of fish cooked together with the addition of a few green grapes, fresh herbs – bay leaf, thyme, fennel, rosemary, oregano, marjoram could be used – and a sprinkle of vinegar.

Right: Samak mahshi bi roz (opposite)

Samak Mahshi bi Roz

Sweet and Sour Fish Stuffed with Rice

This Syrian dish is a favourite of mine. The tamarind sauce gives a most wonderful flavour. You can use bream, bass, John Dory, shad – indeed any large fish. I have made it very successfully with salmon trout. You can use a much larger fish for a party and increase the quantities and cooking time accordingly.

Serves 4

1.25 kg (2½ lb) fish
Salt and pepper
Sunflower oil

For the stuffing:
1½ large onions, chopped
3 tablespoons sunflower oil
4 tablespoons pine-nuts or slivered almonds
250 g (8 oz) patna or other long-grain rice
Salt and pepper

For the tamarind sauce:
3 garlic cloves, crushed
1 tablespoon sunflower oil
2 tablespoons tamarind paste (p. 53)
A 5 cm (2 inch) piece of fresh ginger (optional)
2–3 teaspoons sugar

Pre-heat the oven to 200°C (400°F, gas mark 6).

Ask the fishmonger to gut and scale the fish and trim the tail and fins but to leave the head on. Also ask him to remove the backbone without breaking the skin, or do this yourself through the belly. Slide a sharp, pointed knife behind the ribs to detach them from the flesh on both sides, sever the bone at the head and pull to detach from the body, then sever at the tail. Wash in cold water and season inside and out.

To make the stuffing, fry the onions in oil until golden. Add pine-nuts or almonds and stir until lightly coloured. Add the rice and 450 ml (15 fl oz) water. Season with salt and pepper. Stir well and simmer, covered, for about 15 minutes, or until the rice is tender, adding more water if necessary.

To prepare the sauce, fry the garlic in oil. When it begins to colour add the tamarind concentrate, stir well and add about 300 ml (10 fl oz) water. Peel the ginger and cut it into small pieces, then squeeze the juice out in a garlic press. Add the ginger juice and the sugar, then simmer and stir for a few minutes.

Place the fish on a large piece of strong aluminium foil. Brush the fish and the foil with oil and brush a little of the tamarind sauce inside the fish. Loosely fill with some of the stuffing and pour half the sauce over the fish. Bring the edges of the foil together over the fish and fold them over twice so as to seal the fish loosely and keep the stuffing secure. Bake for 30 minutes or until the flesh flakes with the point of a knife. Unwrap the foil for the last few minutes and re-heat the remaining stuffing and sauce. Cut the fish into slices. Serve with the rest of the stuffing and with the sauce poured over the fish.

Italian Rosé and White Wines of the Adriatic

The wines of Castel del Monte, in Puglia, are fresh and dry, the rosés being particularly fine. Locorotondo is dry but rounder, good with soups and local cheeses as well as with fish. Martina Franca is another very fine wine and Torre Quarto, from around Cerignola, is exceptionally soft and fragrant.

Further north, from the Marches, comes the pale, dry Verdicchio, a perfect accompaniment to the huge variety of fish and seafood to be found along the Adriatic coast.

Balık ve Deniz Urünleri Pilakisi

Fish and Seafood Pilaki

A Greek *plaki* is usually fish and vegetables baked together in the oven. This Turkish version is eaten cold. It is usually made with only one kind of fish or seafood but a combination of several kinds makes a more interesting array for a dinner party. Serve it as a first or a main course or for a summer buffet.

Serves 6

1 monkfish tail
3 small red mullet
2 medium or 3 small squid
1 dozen mussels
4 tablespoons olive oil
2 medium onions, coarsely chopped
2 carrots, thinly sliced
2 garlic cloves, crushed
Small bunch of celery leaves
500 g (1 lb) tomatoes, peeled and chopped
Salt and pepper
1–2 teaspoons sugar
Juice of 1 lemon
Large bunch of parsley, finely chopped (optional)

Wash all the fish. Scale and gut the mullet, but leave the heads on. To clean and prepare the squid, see page 145. Cut the body into rounds and the tentacles into small pieces. To prepare and cook the mussels, see right.

Heat the oil in a large saucepan and fry the onion, stirring occasionally, until it is soft and transparent. Add the carrots and garlic and fry until the aroma rises, then add the celery leaves and tomatoes. Season with salt and pepper, sugar and lemon juice and simmer for a few minutes.

Add the monkfish first and simmer for 10 minutes. Then add the red mullet and squid and simmer for about 4–5 minutes until only just done. Cut the monkfish into pieces when it begins to soften. Add the mussels at the last minute so that they are just heated through, then stir in the finely chopped parsley. Serve cold.

Note
If you want to use only one kind of fish or seafood, which is obviously less trouble, use 1.25 kg (2½ lb) fish or squid or 2 kg (4 lb) mussels for 6.

Salt Cod

I have tried without success to understand the popularity of salt cod. It is a great favourite everywhere in the Mediterranean except in the Muslim countries. The worst aspect is the preparation which consists of long soaking with several changes of water, pulling out the bones, removing the gluey skin and boiling the fish with the release of a most horrible smell. The general belief is that you either love it or hate it. I tolerate it as long as I do not have to cook it, which explains the dearth of salt cod recipes in this book.

Salted and dried cod is a legacy from the time when fresh fish was expensive and there was not enough of it to go round during Lent and when transport and refrigeration were difficult. It was exchanged for Mediterranean wheat with Northern countries and is an example of poor food which has now become a delicacy. There are several kinds of salt cod ranging from a mild, slightly salted but not dried type which keeps for only a few weeks to a heavily salted, hard-dried one which will keep for a year.

Cleaning and cooking live mussels

Scrub the mussels, pull off their 'beards' (the hairy bits that hang out of the shell) and wash in several changes of water. Discard any which are broken and those which feel very heavy or very light or which do not close when they are tapped or dipped in cold water. You can keep live mussels for a day in the refrigerator or longer in a bucket of cold salted water.

To steam mussels open, put them in a saucepan with about 0.5 cm (¼ in) water – enough to produce steam. Put the lid on and bring to the boil. The shells will open in 3–10 minutes. Take them off the heat immediately and discard any which remain closed. Clams can also be prepared in the same way.

Mussels with Lemon Dressing

Mussels with lemon dressing

The simplest way of dealing with mussels is also one of the most attractive. Serve it as a starter.

Serves 4–6

2 kg (4 lb) mussels
300 ml (10 fl oz) olive oil
Juice of 2–3 lemons
Salt and pepper
2 garlic cloves, crushed (optional)
Large bunch of parsley, finely chopped

Clean the mussels and steam them open as described opposite. Let them cool or serve them at once.

To make the sauce, beat the oil and lemon juice with the rest of the ingredients. It is usual to pour some over each serving but I think it is easier and less wasteful to provide little bowls of sauce on each plate for people to dip their mussels in.

Variation

For a spicy Algerian flavouring, beat into the same amount of oil 3 tablespoons wine vinegar, 1 teaspoon paprika, 1 teaspoon ground cumin, a large pinch of cayenne, salt and pepper and 2 crushed garlic cloves.

Granchio all'Olio e Limone

Top right : Arancini di riso (p. 88)
Bottom right : Granchio all' olio e limone
Left : Spinaci in polpettine con ricotta (p. 76)

Fresh Crab Salad

Dressed fresh crab is a popular starter. In Sicily it is served in a bowl on ice or presented in the shell.

A crab weighing about 750 g (1½ lb) will serve 4 people as a starter or 1 person as a main course. Larger ones weighing about 1.5 kg (3 lb) are enough for 6. In this country crabs are nearly always sold ready-cooked. When you buy one make sure that it has been freshly boiled. The fishmonger will usually open it for you and remove the inedible parts. If you acquire a live crab, plunge it into boiling salted water and boil hard for 3 minutes, then simmer for 15–30 minutes, depending on the size. Let it cool.

Twist off the claws and legs and crack them with a nutcracker or hammer. Remove the meat. Hold the crab firmly upside down and carefully pull the shell away from the body with the help of a rounded knife. Break away the inner rim marked with a natural line and scrub the shell well. Pick out the brown and white meat from the body using a small knife and make sure that there are no shell splinters left. Throw away the mouth and the grey stomach sack along with the intestine that is attached to the top of the shell and the long pointed white gills which are attached to the bony body. The soft tomalley is a delicacy as is the coral which is only found in the female crab.

Chop the meat – both the white and the brown including the flesh from the claws – dress with plenty of olive oil, salt, pepper and lemon juice and sprinkle with finely chopped parsley. Return it, if you like, to the empty shell. Serve chilled.

Variation

The French serve crab salad with mayonnaise (p. 211) or aïoli (p. 212).

Coquilles St Jacques à la Provençale

Scallops Provençal

This makes an exquisite and very grand instant dish.

Serves 4

750 g (1½ lb) scallops
Salt and white pepper
Flour for dredging
3–4 tablespoons olive oil
2 garlic cloves, crushed
2 tablespoons cognac (optional)
Large bunch of parsley, finely chopped

Cut the scallops in half horizontally, leaving any corals attached. Sprinkle with salt and pepper and roll in flour. Heat the oil in a large frying-pan. Add the scallops and garlic and fry for 2–3 minutes, turning the scallops over carefully until they become translucent. Be vigilant – scallops become tough very quickly if overcooked. Add the cognac and parsley towards the end of cooking and serve immediately.

The Wines of Provence

Among the many excellent wines produced in Provence, not all *appellation contrôlée* necessarily but reasonably priced and worth trying, are Côtes du Luberon, Côtes du Ventoux and Coteaux d'Aix en Provence. The reds are warm and generous, the whites fruity and fresh, and all of them admirably complement the herb-fragrant dishes of the region.

In the southern part of the Rhône valley, some villages may call their wines Côtes-du-Rhône-Villages. Bound by strict rules of planting, grape variety and testing, the wines produced are well-rounded, elegant and full of fruit. Other villages to have been granted this right are in the nearby departments of Drome and Gard.

The wines of the Côtes de Provence come from vines grown in an arc that runs from Marseilles to Nice and inland to the foothills of the Alps. One of the loveliest reds from this area is Bandol. Dark red and very smooth, the taste reminds one of violets.

Crevettes à la Provençale

Prawns Provençal

For this splendid dish it is better to use unpeeled prawns and peel them yourself. Better still, buy them raw and cook them in boiling salted water until they turn pink.

Serves 4

1 kg (2 lb) unpeeled prawns, or 350 g (12 oz) peeled prawns, cooked
1 onion, finely chopped
2 tablespoons olive oil
2 garlic cloves, finely chopped
750 g (1½ lb) tomatoes, peeled and chopped
1 small hot chilli pepper, finely chopped (optional)
3 tablespoons cognac
150 ml (5 fl oz) dry white wine
1 teaspoon thyme
1 bay leaf
Pinch of cayenne
Salt and pepper

Garnish:
Large bunch of parsley, finely chopped

Peel the prawns if necessary. Fry the onion in the olive oil till golden. Add the garlic and fry until its aroma rises. Add the tomatoes and the remaining ingredients except the prawns. Simmer uncovered for about 20 minutes or until the sauce is a rich and aromatic purée. Add the prawns and cook for a few minutes longer. Serve hot, garnished with plenty of parsley.

Poulpe à la Provençal

Octopus Provençal

This is incredibly delicious and also extremely easy. The octopus turns a beautiful appetising deep mauve.

Serves 6

1 octopus, weighing about 1 kg (2 lb)
1 onion, chopped
2 tablespoons olive oil
500 g (1 lb) tomatoes, skinned and chopped
35 cl ($\frac{1}{2}$ bottle) dry red or white wine
Salt and pepper
1 tablespoon sugar
2 garlic cloves, chopped
A few parsley stalks
2 bay leaves
A few sprigs of fresh thyme, or 1 teaspoon dried thyme

Garnish:
Small bunch of parsley, finely chopped

Octopus is generally sold cleaned and tenderised. To prepare it for cooking, see opposite. Blanch in boiling water for 1–2 minutes, drain and cut into small pieces.
   Fry the onion in the oil till golden. Add the octopus and stir for a few minutes. Add the tomatoes and wine and cover with water. Season with salt, pepper and sugar. Add the garlic, parsley stalks, bay leaves and thyme and simmer very slowly for between 1 and $1\frac{1}{2}$ hours or until tender (the time varies quite a bit). Serve hot or cold garnished with chopped parsley.

Rosé Wines of the South of France

From Gigondas comes a superb rosé wine with a particularly fresh bouquet, but the top rosé of the area is Tavel, which comes from near Avignon. This is a dry, deep pink-coloured wine for drinking with white meat and poultry. It is best drunk young and chilled.
   Another favourite, from the Côtes de Provence, is Rosé de Provence. Strong and fragrant, it makes a fine summer aperitif and is a perfect accompaniment to Provençal food, picnics, barbecues and indeed any meal, in or out of doors.

Octopus drying in the sun

Gambas al Ajillo

Garlic Prawns

This popular Spanish *tapa* is traditionally cooked in a small earthenware dish over the fire but it works perfectly in a frying-pan. It cooks in an instant and is absolutely delicious.

Serves 4

3 garlic cloves, finely chopped
1 small dried or fresh chilli pepper, de-seeded and chopped, or a pinch of cayenne
4 tablespoons olive oil
250 g (8 oz) shelled prawns
Salt
Small bunch of parsley, finely chopped
Lemon wedges

Fry the garlic and pepper in the oil. Add the prawns as soon as the garlic begins to colour. Season with salt and continue to fry over a high heat for 1–2 minutes. Serve sizzling hot, preferably straight from the pan, sprinkled with parsley and accompanied by lemon wedges.

PREPARING OCTOPUS

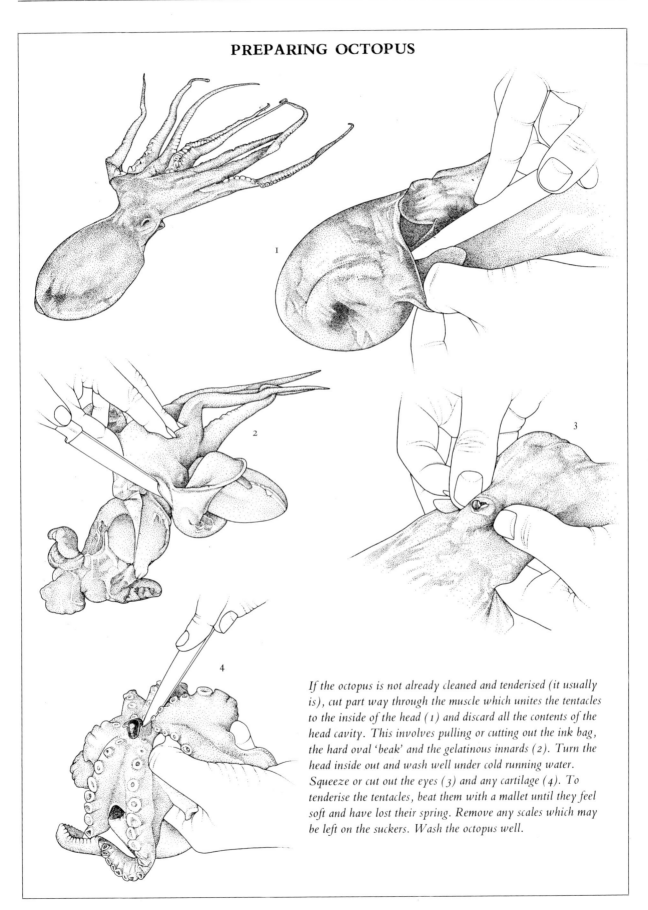

If the octopus is not already cleaned and tenderised (it usually is), cut part way through the muscle which unites the tentacles to the inside of the head (1) and discard all the contents of the head cavity. This involves pulling or cutting out the ink bag, the hard oval 'beak' and the gelatinous innards (2). Turn the head inside out and wash well under cold running water. Squeeze or cut out the eyes (3) and any cartilage (4). To tenderise the tentacles, beat them with a mallet until they feel soft and have lost their spring. Remove any scales which may be left on the suckers. Wash the octopus well.

Oktapothi Vrasto

Octopus Salad

Octopus is a very popular appetiser in Greece. In the winter dried octopus is used and you can see them hanging in the markets. The juices and wine in this salad combine to give the jellied dressing a magnificent flavour and a deep garnet colour.

Serves 6

1 small octopus weighing about 1 kg (2 lb)
200 ml (7 fl oz) red wine
2 tablespoons wine vinegar
2 teaspoons sugar
Salt and pepper
1 teaspoon dried thyme or Greek rigani
5–6 tablespoons olive oil
Small bunch of parsley, finely chopped, to garnish

Octopus is mostly sold cleaned and tenderised. To prepare it for cooking, see p. 143.

Blanch the octopus in salted water for 5 minutes, then drain. Put it in a saucepan, cover and cook over very low heat without any water. Let it cook slowly; it will produce its own liquid. When this liquid has evaporated add the wine, vinegar, sugar, salt, pepper and thyme and a very little water to cover. Simmer gently until it is tender, from 50 minutes up to 2 hours, depending on the size of the octopus. Cut into 2.5 cm (1 in) slices and mix with the cooking juices and the olive oil. Serve cold sprinkled with parsley.

Liftiya bi Mantiq

Squid with Turnips

This peppery stew is from Tunisia where it is made even hotter with harissa (see p. 50).

Serves 6

750 g (1½ lb) baby squid
1 onion, coarsely chopped
2 tablespoons olive oil
500 g (1 lb) small turnips, peeled and quartered
2 fresh chillies, finely chopped
250 g (8 oz) tomatoes, peeled and chopped
Salt
1 tablespoon paprika
Pinch or more of cayenne
500 g (1 lb) spinach or chard, shredded
Small bunch of parsley, finely chopped

Clean and wash the squid (see opposite) and cut it into little pieces. Fry the onion in the oil till golden. Add the turnips, chillies and tomatoes, cover with water, season with salt, paprika and cayenne and simmer for 15 minutes or until tender.

Stir in the spinach and, when it softens, add the parsley and squid. Cook for about 5 minutes or until the squid turns white and opaque. Do not let it over-cook or it will toughen. Serve hot or cold.

Fishing boats on the island of Paros

PREPARING SQUID

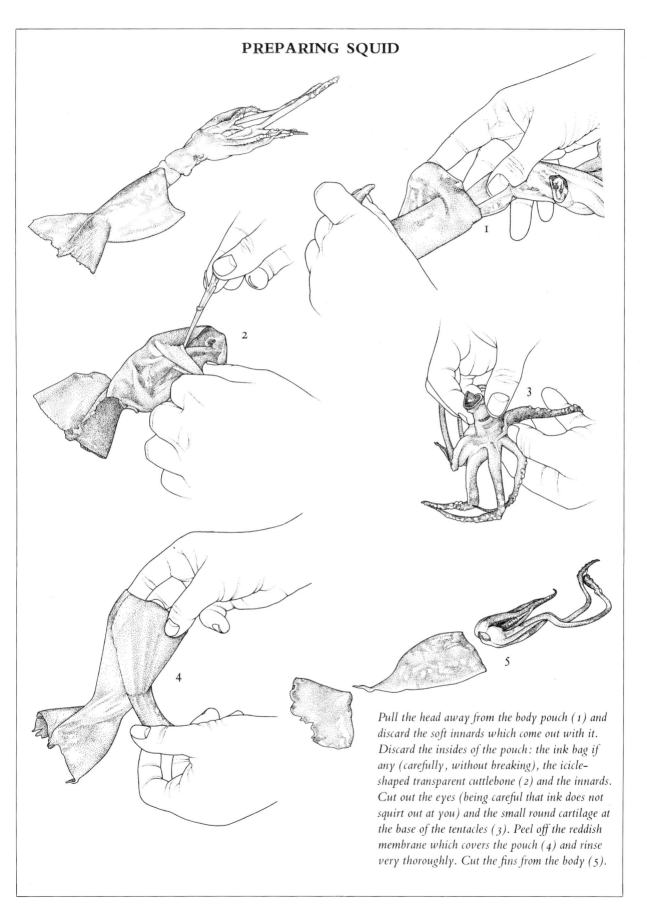

Pull the head away from the body pouch (1) and discard the soft innards which come out with it. Discard the insides of the pouch: the ink bag if any (carefully, without breaking), the icicle-shaped transparent cuttlebone (2) and the innards. Cut out the eyes (being careful that ink does not squirt out at you) and the small round cartilage at the base of the tentacles (3). Peel off the reddish membrane which covers the pouch (4) and rinse very thoroughly. Cut the fins from the body (5).

Kalamarakia Yemista

Stuffed Squid

Although the preparation of squid takes a little time, the filling is easy to make. Yiorgos Vassilenas of Piraeus gave us this recipe.

Serves 12

12 small squid with bodies about 15 cm (6 in) long
1 kg (2 lb) tomatoes, peeled, de-seeded and chopped
Salt and pepper
1 teaspoon sugar (optional)
2 tablespoons olive oil
½ lemon (optional)

For the stuffing:
1 large onion or 5 spring onions, chopped
3 tablespoons olive oil
Large bunch of parsley, chopped
500 g (1 lb) spinach
125 g (4 oz) rice
Small bunch of dill, chopped
Salt and pepper

Clean the squid as described on p. 145. Keep the bodies whole and chop up the tentacles.

To make the stuffing, soften the onions in 2 tablespoons of oil in a large saucepan, add the tentacles and fry until the onion is golden. Wash the spinach and remove the stems, drain and squeeze the water out, cut into ribbons and put into the pan. Stir until the spinach crumples. Add the rest of the ingredients and 250 ml (8 fl oz) of water. Stir well, put the lid on and cook gently for about 10 minutes.

Pre-heat the oven to 180°C (350°F, gas mark 4).

Stuff the squid with the cooled rice and spinach mixture very loosely. They should be less than ¾ full as the rice will expand. Sew up the openings or close them with a toothpick.

Season the tomatoes with salt and pepper and a little sugar if they are sour. Spread half on the bottom of a baking dish, lay the squid side by side on top and cover with the rest of the tomatoes, then sprinkle with oil.

Cover the dish with foil and bake for 10–20 minutes, or until the squid are swollen and firm. Squeeze a little lemon on top and serve.

Variation
Make a sauce with the tomatoes. Add 300 ml (10 fl oz) white wine and simmer in a saucepan for 10 minutes until reduced. Then pour over the squid and bake.

Insalata di Frutti di Mare

Seafood Salad

One year we chose the Isola delle Femmine for our Sicilian holiday because of its romantic name. We discovered on arriving that the hotel was on a motorway adjacent to a cement factory and that the resort was called after the large women's prison there. Nevertheless the holiday was a success. The family of the hotel owner, bent on pleasing their very first customers, took us to all the village festivals in the neighbourhood. My daughter Anna and I were even invited to join the family table with the Sicilian-American relatives because my Egyptian-accented Italian made me sound like a second-generation Sicilian. This *insalata di frutti di mare* was one of my favourite dishes during that stay.

Serves 12

2 kg (4 lb) mussels
1 kg (2 lb) clams
1 small octopus, weighing about 500 g (1 lb)
3 small squid, weighing about 500 g (1 lb)
500 g (1 lb) fresh uncooked prawns

For the dressing:
175 ml (6 fl oz) olive oil
Juice of 3 lemons or to taste
Salt and pepper
Large bunch of parsley, finely chopped

To prepare and cook mussels and clams see p. 138, to prepare octopus see p. 143 and to prepare squid, p. 145. Boil the octopus and squid in salt water – the octopus will take about 1 hour, the squid about 10 minutes. Shell the mussels and clams, cut the octopus into small pieces and the squid into rings and pieces. Boil the prawns until they turn red, then shell them. Combine the seafood in a large bowl.

Beat the dressing ingredients – there should be at least twice as much oil as lemon juice – pour over the seafood and mix gently. Marinate for at least an hour before serving. Sprinkle with chopped parsley.

Variations
France and Spain have similar salads. You can substitute mayonnaise, aïoli, all-i-oli or romesco sauce (see pp. 211–213) for the dressing.

Opposite: Insalata di frutti di mare

Meat and Poultry

MEAT IS THE prestige food in the Mediterranean, but, except for France, the consumption is low and it is made to go far – 125 g (4 oz) being the usual amount for four – because it is expensive. It is cut up into small pieces or minced and rolled into little balls and combined with vegetables, grain and pulses in stews, pilafs or pasta dishes. It is also used in pies and as a stuffing for vegetables and leaves, so look too in other sections in this book for recipes with meat.

The Mediterranean is sheep country. There is not much land suitable for cattle grazing but pastoral life and the transhumance of men and flocks have been part of it since the clearance of the woodland and the domestication of sheep and goats after the seventh millenium BC. Lamb and mutton are the favourite meats, especially in the Islamic countries where the eating of pork is forbidden. There they have adopted the fat-tailed sheep, brought in by the Arabs, whose meat is lean with no marbling and whose fat is concentrated in the tail. This fat is used to moisten the meat when it is cooked by the fierce heat of a charcoal fire. In the western Mediterranean sheep are moved from the winter pastures of the plains to the summer pastures in the hills. They graze on wild herbs which cover the scrub and woodland and this gives the meat a particularly delicious flavour.

In Spain and Italy the cooking of the mountains and the interior is dominated by the pig which can be raised cheaply, but veal, especially milk-fed calves from the high pastures, is also a favourite. Herds of water buffalo are raised for their magnificently rich milk in southern Italy.

Chicken is the popular every day food in the Mediterranean. They are generally thin and scraggy but their flesh is firm, corn-fed yellow and full of flavour. It is not uncommon to buy them live from the market where they are brought, cackling in crates, from the villages. I ate a fat goose in Egypt last year while the hostess entertained us with the story of how she ran after it in the street when it got away. Morocco has particularly good chicken dishes and I have included several.

The Mediterranean sea is the route of millions of migratory birds, the most common being quails and pigeons. Whever they alight on their journey, their arrival in big white clouds is the gastronomic event of the season. It is the huntsman's delight, but really the birds are so tired that you can pick them up like fallen fruit. Wild ducks and geese are part of the scenery around marshlands and rivers, and mountainous regions harbour pheasants, partridge and woodcock. All these, with rabbit, hare and wild boar, produce some of the best delicacies of the Mediterranean. In many dishes, especially the stews, meats are interchangeable and you should use whatever is the best available.

Offal is the poor man's delicacy and it is treated with respect by everyone and cooked with all the usual trimmings of vegetables, herbs and spices. Feet, heads, tripe, intestines, hearts and even ears go into soups and stews. Sweetbreads and testicles, kidneys and livers are fried and grilled, while brains are poached and sautéed.

Right: Athens central market

Djej Matisha Mesla

Chicken with Tomatoes and Honey

In North Africa Moroccan cooking is the one which has most retained its personality because for centuries Morocco remained isolated, sheltered from invasion by formidable mountain ramparts. It is the least Europeanised country and has had the fewest alien influences, early Arab and Andalusian ones being the most important. The Turks stopped at the border and the French colonisation lasted only 44 years.

This wonderful Moroccan dish derives its special flavour from the mountains of tomatoes in which it cooks and from the honey which comes in at the end. Though it is perhaps more elegant to cook and serve the chicken whole, I prefer to cut it into quarters as this ensures that the flesh is well impregnated with the sauce.

Serves 4

1 chicken weighing about 1.5 kg (3 lb), quartered
3 tablespoons butter or sunflower oil
Salt and pepper
1 onion, grated
1 garlic clove, crushed
2 teaspoons cinnamon
¼ teaspoon ginger
Pinch of saffron-coloured powder (optional)
1.5 kg (3 lb) tomatoes, skinned and cut into large pieces
2 tablespoons fragrant honey such as Hymethus

Garnish:
50 g (2 oz) blanched almonds (optional)
Sunflower oil (optional)
1 tablespoon sesame seeds

Put the chicken pieces in a large pot with the butter or oil, salt, pepper, onion, garlic, spices and tomatoes. Cook gently, covered, stirring and turning the chicken frequently, for about 1 hour or until it is so tender that the flesh can easily be pulled off the bone.

Remove the chicken and reduce the sauce further to a sizzling cream until the tomatoes begin to caramelise, stirring often and taking care that the bottom does not stick or burn. Stir in the honey and return the chicken to the sauce to heat through.

Fry the almonds in oil, if using, or toast them and the sesame seeds in a dry frying-pan or under the grill. Serve the chicken hot, covered with the sauce and garnished with the almonds and sesame seeds.

Djej Mqualli

Chicken with Preserved Lemons and Olives

The cooking of all the North African countries derives from Morocco because the empires which spread throughout the area were centred there. Moroccan chicken with preserved lemon and olives is one of the most popular dishes. Lemons which are preserved in salt (see p. 214) lose their sharpness and become soft and mellow. Their flavour is complemented in this recipe by that of olives, soaked in water and then blanched to remove any saltiness or bitterness. As in many Moroccan chicken dishes, the mashed livers are used to give body to the sauce.

Serves 4

1 chicken, including the liver, weighing about 1.5 kg (3 lb)
½ teaspoon ginger
1¼ teaspoons cinnamon
Large pinch of saffron-coloured powder
Salt
White pepper
3 tablespoons sunflower oil
2–3 garlic cloves
1 large onion, finely chopped
Large bunch of parsley, finely chopped
Large bunch of coriander, finely chopped
Peel of 1 preserved lemon or 2 preserved limes, rinsed and cut into small pieces
50 g (2 oz) pinky-green or brown olives, soaked in 2 changes of water for 1 hour

Clean the chicken. Put the ginger, cinnamon, saffron, a pinch of salt and pepper in a large pan with about 700 ml (1¼ pints) of water and the oil. Stir well, then add the chicken with its liver and the remaining ingredients, except the preserved lemon or lime peel and the olives. Cook, covered, for 45 minutes, turning it over occasionally and adding more water if necessary. Add the peel and the drained and rinsed olives. Cook for a further 15 minutes or until the chicken is so tender that the flesh easily comes away from the bone. Remove the liver, mash it, then return it to the pan to thicken the sauce, which should be greatly reduced but not too dry.

Transfer the chicken to a serving plate and pour the sauce over the top. Serve hot.

Djej bil Loz

Chicken with Almonds

In this Moroccan dish the almonds are not added at the end but stewed to softness.

Serves 4

1 chicken, quartered, or 2 poussins, halved, weighing 1.5 kg (3 lb) in total
125 g (4 oz) blanched almonds
1 large onion, cut in half, then thinly sliced
75 ml (3 fl oz) sunflower oil
Salt and pepper
$\frac{1}{2}$ teaspoon cinnamon
$\frac{1}{2}$ teaspoon ground ginger
$\frac{1}{2}$ teaspoon saffron-coloured powder, or a pinch of real saffron
Large bunch of parsley, finely chopped

Put all the ingredients, except the parsley, in a pot. Add about 300 ml (10 fl oz) water and simmer, covered, over a low heat. Turn the pieces of chicken over occasionally and add water if necessary, so that there is always a good amount of sauce. After about an hour or when the chicken is so tender it can be pulled off the bone, add the parsley and cook for a few minutes longer. Serve hot.

Variations
* For an Algerian version, add 4 tablespoons raisins.
* For another from Tunisia, add 2 de-seeded and thinly sliced peppers.

Pollo al Rosmarino

Chicken with Rosemary

This quick and easy dish is a speciality of the region of Naples.

Serves 4

40 g (1$\frac{1}{2}$ oz) butter
1 tablespoon sunflower or olive oil
2 large garlic cloves, cut in half
2 sprigs of rosemary
1 chicken weighing about 1.5 kg (3 lb), cut into quarters
Salt and pepper
175 ml (6 fl oz) dry white wine

Heat the butter and oil in a frying-pan with the garlic and rosemary. When the mixture sizzles, put in the chicken and cook over medium heat, turning the pieces to colour them all over. It is usual to remove the garlic and rosemary at this stage so that they lend only a touch of flavour but I prefer to leave them in. Add salt and pepper and the wine, and simmer, covered, for about 30 minutes or until the chicken is very tender. Serve hot.

Pollo con Pasas y Pinones

Chicken with Raisins and Pine-nuts

This is a Catalan recipe for quail which is also used for chicken. I make it with boned chicken, particularly thighs, but if you have quails do them in the same way, allowing one per person.

Serves 4

2 tablespoons raisins
175 ml (6 fl oz) dry sherry
1–2 tablespoons butter
1$\frac{1}{2}$ tablespoons olive or sunflower oil
750 g (1$\frac{1}{2}$ lb) boned chicken
Salt and pepper
2 tablespoons pine-nuts or slivered almonds

Put the raisins to soak in the sherry. Heat the butter and 1 tablespoon of oil in a frying-pan and, when the mixture begins to sizzle, put in the chicken. Lower the heat and cook gently for a few minutes until lightly browned, turning the pieces over at least once. Add salt and pepper, pour in the sherry with the raisins and simmer very gently over a low heat, covered, for about 20 minutes or until the chicken is done. Make sure that the bottom does not stick and add a little water if necessary. Fry the nuts in the rest of the oil until lightly coloured, drain them on kitchen paper, then stir them in with the chicken. Serve hot.

Hamam bel Ferik

Pigeoncotes are a common sight in Egypt, both in the countryside and in the cities, where they can be seen perched on balconies or precariously hanging out of windows. Pigeons stuffed with green unripe hulled wheat, *hamam bel ferik*, is one of the great dishes of Egypt. You can buy the cooked birds on the train going to Upper Egypt where they are a speciality. The street vendors of Luxor reputedly make the best. Egyptian pigeons are small and tender like the French *pigeonneaux* and the *ferik* is different from the wheat you can buy in health shops as it cooks quickly and becomes very soft. The grain is cooked first and pressed into the pigeons, which are then poached in water flavoured with onions, cardamom and cinnamon, then drained and fried. The puréed onion thickens the sauce.

Let us hope that green wheat becomes available here soon.

Pigeoncote in the Nile delta

Ferakh Maamer

Poussin with Couscous Stuffing

The glittering Moroccan dynasties of the Almoravides, the Almohades and the Merenides, whose realm stretched over North Africa and a great part of Spain for centuries, produced a prestigious cuisine. Young spring chickens (poussins) stuffed with almondy couscous cooked in a honeyed sauce are one of the great delicacies of Morocco. They are served at feasts and celebrations presented on great platters around a mountain of extra stuffing. If you want to make it easier for yourself, do not stuff the birds but prepare and serve the stuffing separately. It will be just as spectacular and just as delicious, and, since the only couscous available here is pre-cooked, nothing could be easier.

The stuffing is sweet, characteristic of the cooking of Fez which boasts the dominant and most refined cuisine of the country. This recipe uses less sugar than they do in Fez where it is added by the glassful. You can leave it out altogether if you prefer but I recommend you try it.

Serves 4

4 poussins
3 tablespoons butter or sunflower oil
1–2 large onions, grated
2 garlic cloves, crushed
2 teaspoons cinnamon
$\frac{1}{4}$ teaspoon ginger
$\frac{1}{2}$ teaspoon saffron-coloured powder
Salt
2 tablespoons honey

For the stuffing:
500 g (1 lb) pre-cooked couscous (see p. 178)
Salt
1–2 tablespoons caster sugar
3 tablespoons sunflower oil
$1\frac{1}{2}$ teaspoons cinnamon
2 tablespoons orange blossom water
3 tablespoons raisins, soaked in warm water for 10 minutes
125 g (4 oz) blanched almonds

To prepare the stuffing, moisten the couscous with a little less than its volume of salted water – about 600 ml (1 pint). Stir well so that it is evenly absorbed. After about 5 minutes, stir in the sugar, 2 tablespoons of the oil, the cinnamon and the orange blossom water. Drain the raisins and add them. Fry the almonds in

Ferakh maamer

the remaining oil, coarsely chop them and stir them into the stuffing.

Fill each poussin with about 3 tablespoons of stuffing. They should not be too tightly packed or the stuffing may burst out. Sew up the skin at both ends using cotton thread (or use cocktail sticks) so that it overlaps the openings. Reserve the remaining stuffing.

In a wide and heavy saucepan put the butter or oil, the onions, garlic, cinnamon, ginger, saffron and salt. Add 300 ml (10 fl oz) water and the stuffed poussins.

Simmer gently, covered, for about 30 minutes or until the birds are tender, adding more water if necessary. Turn them over at least once, ending up breast down, so that they are well impregnated with the sauce and its flavours. Lift one out (to make a little room) and stir in the honey, then return the poussins to the pan and continue to cook until the flesh is at 'melting tenderness' and can be easily pulled off the bone.

Heat up the reserved stuffing in a saucepan, adding a little water if necessary until the grain is plump and

tender. Be careful that it does not stick. Alternatively, heat it up in a covered dish in the oven.

To serve, make a little mountain of the stuffing on a platter and place the birds around it.

Variations

* Add 3 tablespoons coarsely chopped pistachios, a pinch each of ground cloves, allspice and nutmeg to the stuffing.
* At the Hotel Merinides in Fez they stuff 1 large chicken and steam it in the top part of a couscousier, making the sauce separately.
* Baby pigeons (like the French *pigeonneaux*) are the traditional and favourite birds for this dish. Our own wood pigeons will not do.

Bisteeya

Moroccan Pigeon or Chicken Pie

Bisteeya (also pronounced *pastilla*) is the festive jewel in the crown of Moroccan cooking. The crust is made of layers of paper-thin, almost transparent pancakes called *ouarka*. I have watched many people making them but I have never attempted to myself. It takes time and a great deal of patience, skill and expertise. The traditional recipe calls for water to be worked into hard flour with a pinch of salt to make a very soft dough. This is kneaded to a great elasticity and left, covered by a thin layer of water, for an hour. A round tray (tinned on the outside) is placed over a fire. The moist elastic dough is dabbed onto the oiled surface and the thin film which is formed as it touches the hot tray is gradually expanded into a round of about 30 cm (12 in) in diameter.

You can use bought filo dough (see p. 45) instead of *ouarka*.

All the major towns in Morocco have their own cooking styles though Fassi cooking (from Fez) is considered the most prestigious. This is a Fassi recipe from Malika Laraichi, who, with her husband, runs the L'Ambra restaurant in Fez which is renowned for its excellent traditional food and beautiful décor.

Serves 8

2 French pigeonneaux or 1 medium-sized chicken, jointed
Sunflower oil
$\frac{1}{2}$ teaspoon ginger
Salt and pepper
$\frac{1}{4}$ teaspoon saffron-coloured powder
$3\frac{1}{2}$ teaspoons cinnamon
2 large onions, grated or finely chopped
Very large bunch of coriander, chopped
Very large bunch of parsley, chopped
8 small eggs
125 g (4 oz) blanched almonds, coarsely chopped
10 sheets of filo dough
Icing sugar to taste

Put the pigeons or chicken in a large pot with 3 tablespoons of oil, the ginger, salt and pepper, saffron powder, $\frac{1}{2}$ teaspoon of the cinnamon, the onions, and a very little water so that the birds are braised and not boiled. Cook very gently, covered, turning the pigeons or chicken occasionally and adding water if necessary, until they are very tender. The chicken will take an hour while the pigeons will take 30–45 minutes.

Take out the pigeons or chicken, remove the skin and bones and cut the flesh into smallish pieces. It is more traditional to leave the chicken on the bone but this makes it awkward to eat the pie. Add the coriander and parsley to the liquid in the pan and reduce it to a thick, dryish sauce. Beat the eggs, add them to the sauce and scramble them with a fork over a very gentle heat. This constitutes the filling.

Fry the almonds in 1 tablespoon of oil till golden. To assemble the pie, brush a large, shallow, round baking tin about 33 cm (13 in) in diameter and 5 cm (2 in) deep with 3 tablespoons of oil. Drop a sheet of filo in, easing it into the corners with the brush and let the edges hang over the side. Fit 4 more sheets, one on top of the other, brushing each with a little oil.

Spread the pigeon or chicken pieces in the bottom, then cover with the egg mixture. Lay a small or folded sheet of filo on top and sprinkle with the chopped almonds; the filo prevents the almonds being softened by the moist filling. Dust with 2 teaspoons of cinnamon and, if you like, with 1–2 tablespoons of icing sugar. Bring up all the edges of filo and fold them over the almonds. Cover with the rest of the filo, brushing a little oil between the sheets, and tuck the edges into the sides of the tin, under the pie, to wrap it up like a neat parcel. Pour a little oil round the edge of the pie, then put the tin over a very low, even heat and cook it until the bottom is golden brown. Then, very carefully, turn the pie over by dropping it upside down onto a large plate or tray and slipping it back into the pan to cook the other side. You may need a little more oil; pour some down the side of the pan and lift the pie with a spatula to make sure the oil gets underneath. Sieve a dusting of icing sugar over the top and decorate with criss-cross lines using the last teaspoon of cinnamon. Serve hot.

Variation

It is easier to bake the bisteeya in the oven and the result is lighter. Make it in the same way and put it in a 180°C (350°F, gas mark 4) oven for about an hour or until it is crisp and brown.

Bisteeya at the L'Ambra Restaurant, Fez

Pato con Peras

Duck with Pears

Remei Martinez, a beautiful young woman with a short, blonde, punk hair-cut, took over the cooking at her husband's Can Toni restaurant in San Feliú de Guíxols when her mother-in-law died. She uses recipes collected from fishermen and market people and specialises in seafood. Traditionally this dish would have been with goose. The famous Catalan sauce, *picada*, is used to thicken and flavour the broth.

Serves 6

**1 duck weighing about 2.25 kg (5 lb), cut into
  6 pieces or 6 breasts or legs
Olive oil
6 unripe pears, peeled and cut in $\frac{1}{2}$
1 cinnamon stick
2 onions, sliced
1 carrot, sliced
2 ripe tomatoes, peeled, de-seeded and cut into
  pieces
Pinch of dried thyme
Salt
125 ml (4 fl oz) Spanish brandy
300 ml (10 fl oz) meat or chicken stock or water**

**For the picada:
3–4 garlic cloves
50 g (2 oz) blanched almonds, toasted**

Brown the duck pieces in 2 tablespoons of oil in a frying pan. The duck will lose quite a lot of fat which should be discarded. Cover the pears in water and boil them with the cinnamon for about 20 minutes or until tender. Do not let them fall apart. Reserve the cooking liquid.

To make the sauce, cook the onions, carrot and tomatoes in 3 tablespoons of oil until they soften. Add the thyme, salt, brandy and the stock or water plus about the same quantity of cooking liquid from the pears and simmer for about 30 minutes. Transfer the sauce to a blender and blend until smooth. Return the sauce to the pan, add the duck and cook gently for about 45 minutes or until the duck is tender.

To make the picada, pound the garlic and almonds to a paste with a pestle and mortar, or use a blender. Stir this mixture into the duck sauce and cook for 10 minutes longer.

Serve the duck pieces with the sauce poured over them and decorate with the warmed pear halves.

Spanish Red Wines

Many of Spain's most distinguished red wines come from the northern central region known as *La Rioja*. Rioja wine has a characteristic oakey flavour and deep colour. The *clarete*, in its claret-shaped bottle, is considered to be the best.

Most of the everyday Spanish red wine comes from Valdepeñas, south of Madrid, in La Mancha. This is a light red, typically the wine used for making sangria (see p. 208).

There are also some outstanding powerful red wines produced in Catalunya. These are beautifully made, substantial wines that should not be missed. They are perfect with a typical Catalan dish such as the duck with pears described on this page.

Cassoulet de Canard à la Languedocienne

Duck Cassoulet

Cassoulet is a speciality of the Languedoc where beans are cooked slowly together with a variety of meat. It is a very fatty dish but it is the fat which makes the beans so delicious. There are many versions which also include goose or duck confits (see p. 57) and mutton or lamb, or simply sausages and bacon or salt pork.

Historically the Languedoc was closely associated with the Aragonese–Catalan Empire and cassoulet has much in common with the bean and sausage dishes of Catalonia.

Serves 10

1 kg (2 lb) dried white haricot-type beans, soaked
  overnight
250 g (8 oz) pork rind
750 g (1½ lb) piece of bacon or salt belly of pork
  (both unsmoked), soaked overnight
1 onion stuck with 3 cloves, plus 2 onions, sliced
250 g (8 oz) tomatoes, peeled and chopped
3 carrots, sliced
4 garlic cloves, crushed, plus 3 garlic cloves,
  chopped
3 sprigs of thyme
3 bay leaves
Bunch of parsley stalks, plus a bunch of parsley,
  finely chopped
2–3 tablespoons lard
300 g (10 oz) Toulouse or Cumberland-type
  coarse-cut pure pork sausage, cut into pieces
1 duck weighing about 2.25 kg (5 lb), cut into pieces
Salt and pepper
4 tablespoons tomato paste
425 ml (15 fl oz) dry white wine
300 g (10 oz) boiling sausage, preferably garlic-
  flavoured, cut into pieces
50 g (2 oz) or more fine dry breadcrumbs

Drain the beans. Boil the pork rind for 20 minutes, then cut it into 2.5 cm (1 in) cubes. Put them in a large heavy pot with the beans, bacon or salt pork, the onion stuck with cloves, tomatoes, carrots, crushed garlic and the herbs and parsley stalks. Cover with water, bring to the oil, then simmer, uncovered, for 1½ hours or until the beans are tender but still firm. You will need to remove the scum which rises to the surface at the start and to add water from time to time.

Melt the lard in a large frying pan. Brown the Toulouse or Cumberland-type sausage and take it out. In the same fat fry the duck pieces with the sliced onions and chopped garlic for about 15 minutes, turning them to brown them all over. Season with salt and pepper, stir in the tomato paste, add the white wine and barely cover with water. Simmer for 45 minutes or until the duck is tender. Add the fried pork sausage and the boiling sausage for the last 10 minutes.

Pre-heat the oven to 180°C (350°F, gas mark 4). Pour half the beans in a large shallow earthenware pot, place the meats on top and cover with the rest of the beans. The meats should remain half covered. Sprinkle with breadcrumbs mixed with the chopped parsley and bake for 1 hour or until a golden crust has formed. It is usual but not essential to break the crust that forms from time to time. Stir it in and sprinkle lightly with more breadcrumbs each time. Serve hot.

Variations
* Add 1½ kg (3 lb) boned shoulder or breast of lamb. Brown it in the fat at the same time as the duck.
* Use goose instead of duck.

Preparation of cassoulet de canard à la languedocienne

Hünkâr Beğendi

Meat Balls with Creamed Aubergines

This dish is associated with the Empress Eugénie, wife of Napoleon III, when she was the guest of the Turkish Sultan Abdulaziz. According to legend the chef named it 'Her Majesty's Favourite' after her.

Serves 6

1 medium onion, coarsely chopped
3 tablespoons sunflower oil
625 g (1¼ lb) ground lamb or mutton
Salt and pepper
1 teaspoon cinnamon
½ teaspoon allspice
A few sprigs of fresh mint or 2 teaspoons dried
  mint
1 tablespoon pine-nuts
1 red pepper, shredded
500 g (1 lb) tomatoes, peeled and diced
Bunch of parsley, coarsely chopped

For the sauce:
1 kg (2 lb) aubergines
2 tablespoons butter
2 tablespoons flour
300 ml (10 fl oz) milk
50 g (2 oz) Gruyère cheese, grated

In a large frying-pan, fry the onion in oil till golden. Put the meat, salt and pepper, cinnamon and allspice, mint and pine-nuts in a bowl and work them well with your hands. Wetting your hands, roll the mixture into walnut-sized balls and put them into the pan.

Add the red pepper and fry quickly, stirring often, until the meat balls are brown outside but still pink inside and the pepper is soft. Add the tomatoes and parsley and turn off the heat.

To make the sauce, put the aubergines under the grill and turn until the skin is black and blistered and the flesh feels soft. Put the aubergines in a colander, peel them and press the bitter juices out, then purée in a blender. Melt the butter in a saucepan, add the flour, stir well and cook, gently stirring, until well blended. Add the milk, a little at a time, as for a *béchamel* sauce, taking the pan off the heat and stirring vigorously each time. Cook for about 10 minutes until the taste of flour disappears. Add the aubergine purée and the cheese and stir well. Cook a few minutes longer. Heat the meatballs and tomatoes through, spread the aubergine cream on a large, flat serving dish and spoon the meat balls and their sauce on top.

Güveç Kebabı

Lamb Stew

This Turkish peasant stew served with bulgur pilaf (see p. 180) is a meal in itself.

Serves 6

1 large aubergine, cubed
Salt
125 g (4 oz) chickpeas, soaked overnight
2 onions, chopped
3 tablespoons or more sunflower oil
500 g (1 lb) lean tender lamb, cut into cubes
500 g (1 lb) tomatoes, peeled and chopped
1½ teaspoons cinnamon
1 teaspoon allspice
Pepper
5 medium courgettes, cut into thick rounds

Sprinkle the aubergine generously with salt and let the juices drain in a colander for about an hour.

Boil the chickpeas in fresh water for about 30 minutes. Fry the onions in oil till soft and lightly coloured in a large saucepan. Add the aubergine, well rinsed and gently squeezed, and fry, stirring for a minute or so, then add the meat and sauté, turning it over once, until it changes colour.

Add the peeled tomatoes, drained chickpeas, cinnamon, allspice, salt and pepper and about 600 ml (1 pint) water to cover. Simmer gently, covered, for 45–60 minutes or until the meat is very tender. Add the courgettes towards the end of cooking and water, if necessary, to finish up with a reasonable amount of sauce.

Top: Güveç kebabı
Bottom: Bulgar pilavi (p. 180)

Preparation of tagine barragog bis bisela

Tagine Barrogog bis Basela

Lamb Tagine with Prunes

The Andalusian Moors who left Spain after the Reconquest had a great impact on North Africa. Under their stimulus a renaissance of cooking came about in Fez and in Tetouan where they settled. This winter stew was made for us at the Palace Marrakech in Tetouan. In Morocco there are several festive meat dishes in which apples, apricots, pears, quinces, raisins and dates are used together with sugar or honey. This one with prunes is the most common. Large amounts of black pepper and spices provide a delicate balance with the sweetness.

Serves 6–8

1 kg (2 lb) boned shoulder, leg, or neck fillet of
  lamb, cut in large pieces
Salt
2 teaspoons ground black pepper
½ teaspoon saffron-coloured powder
1 teaspoon ground ginger
2 garlic cloves, crushed
1 large onion, grated
Small bunch of parsley, finely chopped (optional)
4 tablespoons sunflower oil
500 g (1 lb) prunes
2 teaspoons cinnamon
1–3 tablespoons orange blossom water
1–4 tablespoons honey or sugar

Garnish (optional):
1 tablespoon sesame seeds
175 g (6 oz) blanched almonds, coarsely chopped
  or left whole

Put the lamb in a pan with salt, pepper, saffron powder, ginger, garlic, onion, parsley and 3 tablespoons of the oil. Add enough water to cover and simmer, covered, for 1½ hours or until the meat is very tender.

Add the prunes and cinnamon and cook for another 15 minutes, then add the honey or sugar and the orange blossom water and cook for a few minutes more until the sauce is quite thick and reduced. Just before serving, toast the sesame seeds under the grill and fry the almonds in the remaining oil. Sprinkle the sesame seeds and almonds over the meat. Serve hot.

North African Wines

Most North African wines used to be rough, strong, blending wines, but better quality wines are now being produced in the foothills of the Atlas mountains. Good Algerian wines have begun to sell here in a small way. Mascara, Medea, Dahra, Zaccar, Tessala and the blended Cuvée du President are full-bodied, strongly flavoured reds while the first three are also fine dryish rosés.

Red wines such as Magon and Sidi Saad from the region of Tebourba and the superior Château Khanguet from Sidi Salem in the north west are the best in Tunisia. The white Muscat de Kelibia is also very pleasant.

Morocco produces some of the best table wines in North Africa. They are particularly proud of their rosés such as Gris de Guerrouane and Gris de Boulaouane.

Safardjaliyya

Lamb with Quince

This is one of the many fruit and meat stews which originate in ancient Persia and which are now common in North Africa. When quinces appear in the autumn take advantage of them to make this wonderful and delicately perfumed dish. Tart cooking apples, apricots and firm pears can be used in the same way and are all worth trying.

Serves 6–8

1 large onion, coarsely chopped
2–3 tablespoons sunflower oil
1 kg (2 lb) boned leg, shoulder or fillet of lamb
Salt and pepper
½ teaspoon powdered ginger
1 teaspoon cinnamon
¼ teaspoon saffron-coloured powder (see p. 52)
2 large tomatoes, peeled and cut into pieces
750 g (1½ lb) quinces

Fry the onion in oil until soft. Add the meat, trimmed of all fat and skin and cut into 3.5 cm (1½ in) pieces. Brown them all over, then add salt and pepper, ginger, cinnamon, and saffron powder. Add the tomatoes, cover with water and simmer, covered, for about an hour or until the meat is very tender.

Scrub the quinces well and cut them in 2 if they are small or in 4 or 8 if large. Core, but do not peel them – much flavour and a gelatinous quality comes from the skin. Cut off any blemishes. Add the prepared quinces to the stew with water, if necessary, and cook for 10–30 minutes, until the quinces soften. You must keep an eye on them as the time they need varies and they fall apart quickly.

Serve the lamb hot on a wide, flat dish garnished with the quinces, skin-side up. There should be some sauce.

Variation
Add the juice of ½ a lemon and 1 tablespoon honey at the same time as the quince.

Sikbadj

Lamb Stew with Dates and Apricots

This is one of the sweet ceremonial dishes of North Africa which could have come out of a tenth-century cookery manual from Baghdad. In Tunisia it is usually made with either dates or sharply flavoured, dark, reddish brown apricots, and a fair amount of sugar. I particularly like this combination of meat with both fruits together, and the sugar omitted.

Serves 12

2 large onions, coarsely chopped
Sunflower oil
1.5 kg (3 lb) boned leg or shoulder of lamb
2 teaspoons cinnamon
1 teaspoon allspice
Salt and pepper
3 medium aubergines, cubed
375 g (12 oz) dried dates, pitted
125 g (4 oz) or more sharp, dried apricots
250 g (8 oz) blanched almonds
2 tablespoons sesame seeds

Fry the onions in a large saucepan in 3 tablespoons oil. Trim the meat of fat and skin, and cut it into 4 cm (1½ in) pieces. Add it to the onion and turn to brown all over. Cover with water, bring to the boil, add cinnamon, allspice, salt and pepper, and simmer, covered, for about an hour. Meanwhile, sprinkle plenty of salt on the aubergines and let them degorge their juices. When the meat is very tender, rinse the aubergines and add them to the stew with a bit of water if necessary. After another 20 minutes add the dates and apricots and cook for another 10–20 minutes until the aubergines and fruits are soft.

Fry the almonds in oil until browned and toast the sesame seeds in a dry frying-pan until lightly coloured. Serve the stew, sprinkled with almonds and sesame seeds, on a large shallow plate.

Variation
A popular and more robust version is made with 125 g (4 oz) chickpeas, soaked in water overnight and put in with the meat. Omit the almonds and sesame seeds.

Marquit Quastal

Lamb with Chestnuts

While Tunisia has been sympathetic to Western ideas and although it was subjected to a massive immigration of French and Italian peasants when it became a French protectorate, it has sustained Arab cooking in its most ancient form. This beautiful and fragrant stew is a typical example. Dried chestnuts are often used, but fresh ones are far better.

Serves 4

1 large onion, coarsely chopped
3 tablespoons olive oil
500 g (1 lb) boned shoulder of lamb, trimmed of fat and cut into pieces
125 g (4 oz) chickpeas, soaked overnight
Pepper
1 teaspoon cinnamon
¼ teaspoon saffron-coloured powder (see p. 52) (optional)
Salt
500 g (1 lb) chestnuts
2 tablespoons raisins
1 tablespoon honey (optional)
1 tablespoon rose water (optional)

Fry the onion in oil in a large pot until soft. Add the meat and turn to brown it all over. Add the chickpeas, cover with water and bring to the boil. Remove any scum, then add pepper, cinnamon and saffron. Cook, covered, for about 1½ hours, or until the meat is very tender and the chickpeas have softened. Add salt when the chickpeas are softening, and water, if necessary.

To shell the chestnuts, make 2 crossed slits on the flat side with a sharp pointed knife, then drop them in a pan of boiling water. Simmer for about 15 minutes, or until the inner skins begin to separate from the nuts, then drain and shell as soon as they are cool enough to handle. Add the chestnuts and raisins to the stew and, if you like, honey and rose water (in Tunisia ground rosebuds are used). Simmer 15 minutes longer and serve hot.

Arni Fricassée

Lamb Fricassée

This is a slightly different version of the dish cooked by Yiorgos Bagia at the Taverna Costoyanis in Athens. (He adds 1 tablespoon of flour to the stew and to the sauce, and cooks the lettuce for much longer, so that it becomes very soft.) Either way, the dish is delicious.

Serves 6

1 kg (2 lb) boned shoulder or neck fillet of lamb
1 large onion or a bunch of spring onions, finely chopped
3 tablespoons olive oil
Salt and pepper
200 ml (7 fl oz) dry white wine
200 ml (7 fl oz) chicken stock
1 large cos lettuce, cut into ribbons
3 tablespoons dill, parsley or mint, chopped

For the sauce:
2 large eggs
Juice of 1–2 lemons

Trim the lamb of fat and cut into serving portions. Put them into a large saucepan together with the onion or spring onions and oil and sauté gently for about 10 minutes. Add salt and pepper, then pour in the wine and stock. Simmer very gently, covered, for about 1½ hours or until the meat is very tender, adding a little water if it becomes too dry. Then add the lettuce and herbs and cook for a few minutes, so that they are still a little crisp.

Just before serving, make the egg and lemon sauce. Beat the eggs with the lemon juice, add a few tablespoons of liquid from the stew, beat very well, then pour this mixture into the saucepan. Stir gently over a very low heat for 1–2 minutes or until the sauce thickens, being careful not to let it curdle. Serve hot.

Gigot Rôti

Roast Leg of Lamb

In Provence they do not believe in piercing a joint to insert pieces of garlic – they prefer to bake whole heads at the same time as the meat.

Serves 6

Small leg of lamb weighing about 2.25 kg (5 lb)
Large bunch of mixed fresh herbs such as thyme,
  oregano, mint, basil, savory and rosemary
Pepper
2 tablespoons olive oil
Salt

Pre-heat the oven to 230°C (450°F, gas mark 8).

Chop up the herbs together with a little pepper. Thyme and rosemary are strong and must be used in small quantities. Using a sharp knife, loosen the flesh around the leg bone and then loosen the outside skin from the flesh to make a pocket. Slip most of the herb mixture between the skin and the flesh and the rest around the leg bone.

Rub the joint with olive oil and sprinkle with salt. Roast for about 10 minutes, then reduce the heat to 190°C (375°F, gas mark 5) and cook for 45 minutes, if you like it rare, up to an hour if you want it pink. Let the lamb rest for 15–30 minutes in a warm place before cutting. Carve at the table and serve with baked garlic heads (see p. 120). Crush them into the gravy with a fork if you like.

Sauces

* For an Arab sauce simmer 125 g (4 oz) dried apricots (the dark, sharp kind, not sweet ones) in 600 ml (1 pint) of water for about 30 minutes or until very soft, then blend to a light smooth cream.
* For an oriental sauce popular in Nice fry 1 coarsely chopped onion in 2 tablespoons olive oil until brown, then add 3 tablespoons pine-nuts and continue frying until the nuts are lightly coloured. Add 3 tablespoons raisins soaked in hot water for 10 minutes, then drained. Finally add the meat juices, skimmed of fat, and cook for another minute or two.

Gigot rôti with ail au four (p. 120)

Variation

For a Moroccan roast leg or shoulder of lamb known as *méchoui*, mix 1 tablespoon paprika, 1 teaspoon cumin, a few finely chopped sprigs of fresh mint, 4 crushed garlic cloves with 4 tablespoons of oil and rub over the meat. Cook in a 190°C (375°F, gas mark 5) oven for up to $2\frac{1}{2}$ hours or until the meat is so tender that you can pull it off with your fingers. Serve with extra cumin to sprinkle on each serving.

Méchoui

Whole lamb roasted on the spit is the Moroccan national dish for grand and festive occasions. Specialists called *chouaye* do the roasting and rush the lamb steaming to the table. They cook it slowly between two charcoal fires for up to $3\frac{1}{2}$ hours, until it is so tender that you can pull moist juicy pieces of flesh off with your fingers. Each morsel is sprinkled with a little salt and cumin.

Top: Navets au sucre (p. 123)
Bottom: Lapin aux oignons

Scaloppine di Maiale al Marsala

Pork with Marsala

This dish couldn't be easier to make. The Sicilian dessert wine used in it, Marsala, comes from the town of the same name. The word is derived from the Arabic *Marsah Allah* meaning 'Port of Allah'.

Serves 6

1 kg (2 lb) pork fillet, cut into medallion slices
4 tablespoons sunflower oil
Salt and pepper
150 ml (5 fl oz) Marsala

Fry the pork quickly in the oil over a high heat and brown both sides. Sprinkle with salt and pepper and pour in the Marsala. Cook for a few minutes until the meat is done and the liquid is reduced.

Lapin aux Oignons de Monsieur Hiély

Mr Hiély's Rabbit with Onions

Pierre Hiély is one of the few great French restaurateurs who is concerned with maintaining traditional Provençal cooking. Rabbit, like all game, is very popular in the interior of Provence.

Serves 4

1 shallot or ½ onion, finely chopped
3 tablespoons olive oil
2 tablespoons butter
1 rabbit with its liver and kidney
Sprig of thyme
Sprig of sage
Salt and pepper
250 ml (8 fl oz) red wine
1–3 tablespoons sherry vinegar

Garnish:
24 baby onions, peeled
1 tablespoon olive oil
2 tablespoons butter
½ tablespoon sugar
Salt and pepper

Make the garnish first. Put the onions with the oil, the butter, sugar, salt and pepper in a frying-pan large enough to contain them in one layer and cover with about 750 ml (1½ pints) of water. Simmer, covered, for about 20 minutes, then take the lid off and cook gently for about 40 minutes more, adding water if necessary, until the onions are tender and golden and the sauce is reduced to a thick syrup.

In the meantime cut the rabbit into pieces, reserving the liver and kidneys. Fry the chopped shallot or onion till golden in 2 tablespoons of the oil and all the butter in a heavy pan. Add the rabbit pieces, sprinkle with salt and pepper, thyme and sage and sauté gently to brown them all over. Add the wine and vinegar to the casserole and simmer for 10 minutes until the sauce is reduced by about half. Adjust the seasoning, cover and cook for about 30 minutes or until tender, adding water if it becomes too dry.

Cut the rabbit liver in slices and the kidneys in half. Fry the liver and kidneys in the remaining olive oil for 30 seconds. Serve the rabbit garnished with the liver, kidneys and the onions.

Stifatho

Greek Meat Stew

This is a rich aromatic Greek winter dish of beef or pork, or rabbit or hare with wine and a large amount of pickling onions. It is very easy to make though the onions take a little time to peel. Either brown the meat and onions in oil before stewing over a low heat with the rest of the ingredients or do as Roula Markris does: marinate the meat overnight in an earthenware casserole which then goes straight into the oven the next day. Roula said that in the countryside *stifatho* used to be cooked slowly all night in an outdoor oven.

Serves 6

1 kg (2 lb) beef or pork cut into pieces, or 1 rabbit
  or hare cleaned and cut into joints
1 kg (2 lb) small whole pickling onions, peeled
4 large tomatoes, peeled and chopped
2–3 garlic cloves, chopped
2 bay leaves
Salt

For the marinade:
500 ml (18 fl oz) red wine
4 tablespoons wine vinegar
4 tablespoons olive oil
6 peppercorns
5 cloves
$\frac{1}{2}$–1 teaspoon allspice

Mix the marinade ingredients in a large earthenware casserole and turn the meat in the mixture. Cover and leave in the refrigerator overnight.

Pre-heat the oven to 160°C (325°F, gas mark 3). Add the rest of the ingredients and barely cover with water. Cover tightly and bake for 4–5 hours or until the meat is very tender.

Top: Stifatho
Bottom: Horiatiki salata (p. 69)

Daube

Provençal Meat Stew

This rustic winter stew is infinitely variable. It derives its name from the *daubière*, the earthenware pot in which it is cooked. I am not entirely sure that it matters if the meat is marinated, but I do this anyway in accordance with tradition. The longer and the slower the stew is cooked with the surface barely moving – the French call this *mijoter* – the better the result. The meat becomes incredibly tender, all the flavours mingle and any harsh wine taste mellows into a wonderful aroma. In Provence, the local wine is used, like Côtes du Ventoux or Côtes du Rhône, but any inexpensive table wine will do.

Serves 10

2 kg (4 lb) stewing beef or lamb, cubed
125 g (4 oz) streaky bacon, cut into pieces
Salt and pepper

For the marinade:
2 large onions, cut in half and thinly sliced
3 carrots, thinly sliced
4 garlic cloves, crushed
1 75 cl bottle red wine
4 cloves
1 teaspoon allspice
2 bay leaves
Bunch of parsley stalks tied together
2 teaspoons thyme
A strip of dried orange peel

Marinate the meat in the marinade ingredients over-night in the refrigerator. The following day put all the ingredients in a large, heavy casserole, add a little water to cover, bring to the boil and remove any scum. Put a sheet of foil under the lid to seal it her-metically, cover and simmer on the lowest possible heat, so that the stew barely trembles, for at least 3 hours, and up to 5. Open the pot at the table to enjoy the aroma. Many prefer the stew re-heated the next day or eaten cold.

Variations
* Add about 4 tablespoons cognac or grappa.
* Add 500 g (1 lb) tomatoes, peeled and chopped, dried *ceps* (boletus mushrooms) or a few stoned black olives.

Right: Parma hams and other Italian cured meats

Fegato Garbo e Dolce

Sweet and Sour Liver

The flavour of this Venetian dish depends on a delicate balance of sweet and sour. As lemons vary so much in size and sharpness it is important to start with a little lemon juice and add more to taste and then decide for yourself just how much sugar is needed. In Italy, liver is usually sliced as thin as bacon but this dish does not benefit particularly from very thin slicing.

Serves 4

2 tablespoons butter
1 tablespoon sunflower or olive oil
500 g (1 lb) calves' liver, thinly sliced
Salt and pepper
Juice of $\frac{1}{2}$–1 lemon
1 teaspoon sugar or more to taste

Heat the butter and oil in a frying-pan. When the mixture sizzles fry the liver for 4 minutes over a high heat, adding salt and pepper and turning the slices over once. Push the liver to one side of the pan to leave room for making the sauce. Add the lemon and sugar to the other side of the pan and blend quickly to dissolve the sugar. Mix with the liver. Cook a few seconds more so that the liver is done but still pink inside. Serve at once.

Moukh M'Charmel

Brains in Tomato Sauce

I adore brains, and so do most people in the Mediterranean. This particular Moroccan recipe is the tastiest way I know of cooking them.

Serves 6

6 lambs' or 3 calves' brains
1 tablespoon wine vinegar
3 garlic cloves, crushed
3 tablespoons sunflower oil
500 g (1 lb) tomatoes, peeled and chopped
Salt
1 teaspoon paprika
Large pinch of cayenne or to taste
Juice of $\frac{1}{2}$ lemon
1 teaspoon sugar (optional)
Large bunch of coriander, finely chopped

The brains must be very fresh and cooked on the day they are bought. Soak in cold water acidulated with vinegar for about an hour. Carefully remove the thin outer membrane and rinse in cold running water.

Fry the garlic in oil in a large pan. When the aroma rises, add the tomatoes, salt, paprika, cayenne and lemon juice. Add sugar if you are serving the dish cold. Stir well and add the brains. Simmer gently, turning over the brains at least once and ladling the sauce over them. After about 10 minutes cut the brains in halves or quarters, stir in the coriander and cook for 5–10 minutes or until firm. Serve hot or cold.

Halaweyaat

Sweetbreads

This is an Arab dish. Lamb's sweetbreads are very much cheaper than calves' and they are easier to deal with. You can buy them fresh in the spring and summer and in the winter they are available frozen.

Serves 4

$\frac{1}{2}$ kg (1 lb) lamb's sweetbreads
25 g (1 oz) butter
1 tablespoon sunflower oil
Salt and white pepper
$\frac{1}{2}$ teaspoon cinnamon
$\frac{1}{4}$ teaspoon ground cardamom
$\frac{1}{2}$ teaspoon paprika
Juice of $\frac{1}{2}$ lemon

Garnish:
Small bunch of parsley, finely chopped

Wash the sweetbreads – there is no need to skin them.

Heat the butter and oil in a frying-pan and when it begins to sizzle put in the sweetbreads. Season with salt and pepper and sprinkle with the cinnamon, cardamom and paprika. Cook for 6 minutes until they become firm. Add the lemon juice and serve garnished with parsley.

Top: Sultan Reshat pilavi (p. 181)
Bottom: Halaweyaat

Grilled Food

GRILLING over the gentle heat of glowing coals or wood embers is one of the most traditional and popular ways of cooking around the Mediterranean and it produces food with a uniquely appetising flavour. You can cook all sorts of things on a simple barbecue and with practice it becomes an art. All you need is a well oiled grill and suitable skewers – flat or twisted for cubes of meat and fish, flat or square for minced meat. Start to cook only when the fire has burned right down, the smoke has gone and a light powdery grey ash covers the glowing coals. If there are flames they will scorch the food before it has had time to cook inside. Wood takes longer to burn to a bed of embers than charcoal so if you are using wood start well before you want to eat.

Different foods require different intensities of heat and different cooking times. The quality and thickness of each item also affects the cooking time. The heat can be regulated to a certain extent by lowering or raising the grill and by fanning the fire. Out of doors, of course, it also depends very much on the weather conditions.

The cooking heat is measured by the distance of the grill from the bed of embers. Searing hot is 2.5–4 cm ($1-1\frac{1}{2}$ in) away, hot is 7.5 cm (3 in), medium is 10 cm (4 in) and low is 13 cm (5 in) away. If you want to, you can also test the heat by putting your hand above the coals where you intend to place the food. If you cannot leave it longer than 3 seconds it is probably too hot. It is medium hot if you can leave it for 4 seconds and low if you can leave it for 5. If you cannot easily adjust the height of the grill, simply move the food away from the hottest part in the middle to the edge of the fire. The best permanent position to have the grill at is a height of 7.5 cm (3 in).

There are several refinements worth trying. Aromatic woods such as bay tree and fruit woods give a delicious aroma and flavour to the food, and dried herbs can be added to the fire near the end of the cooking time to lend their perfume. Vine twigs or prunings give a specially delicate taste and dried fennel stalks make a good bed on which to grill fish. Pieces of garlic and orange peel in the fire also give a delightful aroma. The voluptuous smell of roasting meat with the fleeting one of the aromatics is a great appetite-whetter.

Marinating meat in a mixture of oil and wine, vinegar or lemon juice with herbs and seasonings flavours and tenderises it. Marinating also helps to prevent meat drying out on the grill. It is usual to protect certain lean meats and game by barding them with thin strips of bacon or pork fat tied with string. Vine leaves are used to wrap up quail and red mullet and lend them a distinctive sharp flavour. Most importantly, brushing or basting with oil or melted butter is usually needed to keep grilled food moist and juicy.

If it is not possible to cook on an outdoor grill a very good alternative is to cook under an ordinary oven grill.

Right: Grilling chicken on a Barcelona street

Grilled Fish

Restaurants throughout the Mediterranean serve grilled fish, whole, cut in slices or in cubes, simply accompanied by lemon wedges. There is no better way of cooking really fresh fish.

Red mullet, sardines, herring, mackerel, tuna, bream, turbot, brill, bass, gurnard, sole, grey mullet and flounder – all these and more can be put either on the grill or under it. By the sea they often do not bother to scale the fish. The scales coalesce over a fierce heat and make a protective crust which keeps the flesh soft and juicy. The salt deposit they contain will intensify the tangy flavour of the sea. But if you cook the fish unscaled you will have to take the skin off before eating. If you want a nice, crispy brown skin which permeates the flesh with an agreeable smoky flavour, scale it. Clean, gut and wash the fish but leave the head on. With red mullet do not remove the innards – they are a delicacy. If the fish is large, score in two or three places so that it cooks evenly.

Large fish like hake, turbot and swordfish can be cut into steaks or split in half along the bone, the skin slashed, and the fillets cooked skin-side down without turning. Except for sardines and other oily fish which only need salting, brush inside and out with olive oil and sprinkle inside and out with salt.

Put the fish on an oiled grill over glowing embers or under an indoor grill. A special double-sided fish holder is useful so that the skin does not break when you turn the fish over. Depending on the size and thickness of the fish, put it near the heat, 5 cm (2 in) from the fire if the fish is small, and up to 13 cm (5 in) away if very large. Allow 5–6 minutes for very small fish and fish steaks, and about 10 minutes per $2\frac{1}{2}$ cm (1 in) of thickness for large ones. Turn at least once and brush frequently with oil. Flat fish like brill, skate, sole and place should be cooked white-side up first. The fish is cooked when the flesh flakes away from the bone if cut with the point of a knife.

Serve garnished with sprigs of parsley and lemon wedges.

Variations
* Add fresh or dried herbs such as rosemary, fennel, thyme, bay, tarragon, basil, oregano and marjoram to the basting oil.
* Roll the fish in flour for a more crispy crust.
* Stuff the cavity with a few sprigs of fresh herbs. In the eastern Mediterranean they use parsley, mint, coriander, in the west rosemary, fennel, thyme, bay, tarragon, basil, oregano and marjoram. You may also add a clove or two of crushed garlic.
* Wrap red mullet in vine leaves which give it a tangy flavour. Use fresh leaves or preserved ones soaked in water to remove the salt.

Grilled Shellfish and Seafood
Oysters, scallops, cockles, clams and mussels all open when put on a hot grill. Serve with the lemon sauce on p. 139. Prawns are best grilled in their shells. Grilled small squid and cuttlefish are a Sicilian speciality called *creste di calamari*. Clean them thoroughly (see p. 145) and slice the bag on one side halfway, but not completely through. Brush with olive oil and sprinkle with white wine. Place the squid on a grill pan and put under a hot grill about 7.5 cm (3 in) from the heat. Grill for 8–10 minutes or until they are golden and have opened up. Serve with a dressing of olive oil, lemon juice and garlic seasoned with salt and pepper.

Sauces for grilled fish and seafood
You may like to try one of the following to accompany your fish.
* All-i-oli, see page 213.
* Mayonnaise, see page 211.
* Romesco, see page 211.
* Aïolli, see page 212.
* Vinaigrette, see page 210. Make it sharp and peppery for oily fish.
* To make an oil and lemon sauce beat 3 tablespoons of olive oil with the juice of 1 lemon, 2 crushed cloves of garlic, salt and pepper.
* To make an anchovy sauce put 6 anchovies in the blender with 125 ml (4 fl oz) olive oil and the juice of $\frac{1}{2}$ a lemon.
* To make *chermoula*, a spicy Moroccan sauce, beat 6 tablespoons of olive oil with 2 crushed garlic cloves, 2 teaspoons cumin, 1 teaspoon paprika, a pinch of cayenne, salt and a bunch of finely chopped coriander. If the fish is oily add 2 tablespoons of vinegar.

Poisson aux Herbes

This is a grand French method of grilling worthy of more expensive fish like bass or bream. Clean and scale the fish and, if you like, stuff it with fresh herbs (see opposite). Roll it in flour seasoned with salt and pepper, sprinkle with olive oil and cook on the grill. Make a bed of dry fennel branches or bay leaves or a mixture of dried rosemary, fennel and thyme on a heatproof serving dish. Lay the fish on top and cover it with additional dry herbs. Pour a little heated cognac or other spirit such as marc, armagnac or calvados over it and ignite. Let the alcohol burn off before serving.

Cooking a la Plancha

Cooking very quickly on a *plancha* or hot-plate greased with oil is a traditional way of cooking in Spain. Seafood more than anything is remarkably good brushed with olive oil, put on the plancha, lightly seasoned and served sizzling hot. *Pescado* or *marisco tapas* bars do much of their seafood like this, sometimes in front of their customers. But other things too are cooked in this way. The most memorable food I had in Spain was sliced baby artichokes *a la plancha* in Valencia. Light portable planchas (see p. 59) can be bought for home use on top of a gas hob or over an electric or charcoal grill, but you can always use a heavy frying-pan or griddle instead.

Here are a few things which can be cooked on the plancha. They need to be brushed with, or dipped in oil and turned over once. The plancha must be very hot.
* Prawns (preferably raw unshelled ones) – sprinkle with salt and squeeze a little lemon juice on top.
* Tiny baby squid and cuttlefish – wash and remove ink bags and central bone, place on the plancha for less than a minute until they seize up. Sprinkle with salt, pepper, garlic, paprika and parsley.
* Small fish – clean and scale, stuff with parsley or other fresh herbs and sprinkle with salt and pepper.
* Large firm fish such as swordfish – cut into steaks and sprinkle with salt and pepper.
* Liver and fillet of pork cut in thin slices and kidneys split in half – sprinkle with salt.
* Mussels, clams, oysters and all kinds of shellfish can be put on the plancha. They open very quickly. Eat them with a dressing of olive oil and lemon juice with a faint touch of garlic, if you like.

Red mullet wrapped in vine leaves (opposite)

Kebab Samak

Fish Kebab

Use a firm fish such as swordfish, monkfish, tuna or halibut which will not fall apart on a skewer.

Serves 4

1 kg (2 lb) firm fish
Juice of $\frac{1}{2}$ lemon
4 tablespoons olive oil
$\frac{1}{2}$ onion, grated
Salt and pepper
Bay leaves (optional)

Garnish:
Bunch of parsley, coarsely chopped
Lemon wedges

Grilled fish steaks and prawns (p. 168) and kebab samak

Cut the fish into cubes 4 cm ($1\frac{1}{2}$ in) thick. Mix the lemon juice, oil, onion, salt and pepper in a bowl and leave the fish in this marinade for at least an hour, turning the pieces over occasionally. Thread onto skewers with a flat or twisted blade so that the pieces do not slide when you turn them over. Put a bay leaf, if you like, between each piece to lend its fragrance. Cook the kebabs over a gentle fire for 8–10 minutes, or until only just done, brushing them from time to time with the marinade and turning them over to brown all sides. Serve at once, garnished with parsley and lemon wedges.

Variations
* For a Turkish flavour add 1 teaspoon paprika to the marinade.
* For an Alexandrian flavour add 2 teaspoons ground cumin.

Involtini

Stuffed Meat Rolls

Every region of Italy has its favourite *involtini*. They can be made with beef, veal, lamb or pork, stuffed with all kinds of fillings and be grilled, baked, fried or stewed. This Sicilian recipe comes from the restaurant La Botte in Monreale, Sicily.

Serves 4

Veal escalopes or slices of tender beef, lamb or
  pork weighing about 350 g (12 oz)
1 onion, cut into wedges
A few bay leaves
Olive oil
Salt and pepper
Fine breadcrumbs

For the filling:
1 small red onion
Large bunch of parsley
A few sprigs of mint (optional)
A few sprigs of basil (optional)
Pinch of oregano
75 g (3 oz) fresh, mild, soft 'Milano'-type salame
50 g (2 oz) cooked ham
125 (4 oz) mild cheese, such as bel paese, fontina,
  provolone or toma
75 g (3 oz) dry breadcrumbs
25 g (1 oz) grated Parmesan
2 small eggs, lightly beaten
Pepper

Put the meat slices between two layers of wax paper and beat them with a meat hammer or cutlet bat as thinly as you can without breaking the meat. Cut into rectangles 8–10 cm (3–4 in). Finely chop the onion in a food processor, then add the herbs, salame, ham and mild cheese and process until you obtain a coarse but not too soft mixture. Turn into a bowl, add the breadcrumbs, grated Parmesan, eggs and pepper and stir well.

Place a tablespoon of filling on each slice near one of the longer edges, shape into a thin sausage and roll the meat up over it. Thread the little rolls onto skewers, interspersing them with bay leaves and pieces of onion. Then brush with oil, sprinkle with salt and pepper and dust lightly with breadcrumbs.

Place the skewers on an oiled grill over the embers of a charcoal fire or on a tray under an indoor grill for about 10 minutes, turning them over once, until the rolls are browned all over and cooked through. Alternatively you can cook the meat rolls on a lightly oiled griddle.

Carne ai Ferri

Italian Mixed Grill

A very common way of cooking meat in southern Italy is *ai ferri*, *alla griglia* or *alla brace* – on the grill. Tiny lamb, pork and veal chops, veal escalopes, pieces of chicken, pork sausages, slices of bacon and raw ham, lamb's liver cut into slices, lamb's kidneys split in half – all these are done over wood embers. When they are put onto skewers they are called *spiedini*. *Rosticini* are little kebab-type cubes.

The meats are marinated in olive oil with pepper and herbs such as rosemary, sage, oregano, basil and mint. Sometimes there is red or white wine in the marinade or a small amount of wine vinegar. Salt is sprinkled on before putting the meat on the fire and a bunch of rosemary is used to brush more oil on as the meat cooks. For instructions on cooking on embers or under the grill see p. 166.

A version of *involtini* consists of thin slices of veal, lamb or pork brushed with oil, sprinkled with herbs such as oregano and basil, rolled up and threaded on skewers. Often there is a slice of mozzarella inside which melts a little as the meat roasts.

Verdura Arrosto

All kinds of vegetables acquire a remarkable flavour when cooked on the grill. Onions, courgettes and aubergines cut in slices lengthwise and whole mushrooms must be constantly brushed with olive oil. Whole peppers and tomatoes can be turned on the fire until they soften, and then skinned.

Djaj Meshwi

Grilled Spring Chicken

Restaurants along the Nile such as the Casino des Pigeons are famed for grilled young pigeons and quail which are great delicacies in Egypt. Baby chicken is the standby when pigeons and quail are out of season. Pigeons in this country are different birds altogether and not suitable for grilling. Quail are excellent and you should use them when you can, but this recipe is for spring chicken (poussin), which is readily available and which is at its best when cooked this way. If you cannot cook on a charcoal or wood fire do them under the grill.
 Warm bread and salad are the usual accompaniments.

Serves 2

2 poussins
4 tablespoons olive oil
Juice of 1 lemon
1–4 garlic cloves, crushed
Pepper
2 tablespoons butter (optional)
Salt
Bunch of parsley, finely chopped

Lay the poussins breast down and split them open all along the backbone. Crack the breastbone and open the birds out. Cut the wing and leg joints just enough to spread them out. Turn the poussins over and pound each one flat so that they cook evenly.

  Mix the oil and lemon juice with the garlic and pepper in a bowl. Marinate the poussins in a cool place for an hour or two, turning them over once.

  Place the birds on an oiled grill 7.5 cm (3 in) from the fire, skin-side down, and cook for 8–10 minutes until the skin has turned brown. Brush with the marinade or with melted butter, sprinkle the poussins with salt and turn them over. Cook for about 15 minutes and turn again, if necessary, until the juice from a thigh when you prick it with a fork is no longer pink. Serve sprinkled with parsley.

Note about quails

Split quails down the back, marinate and cook as above but only for 5–6 minutes. You can also wrap the quails in vine leaves – fresh ones or preserved in brine – as a protection against drying out. The leaves give them a distinctive flavour. (Leaves in brine should be soaked in water first.)

Marinade variations
* Syrians like to add 1 tablespoon thyme.
* Omit the lemon juice, but add 2 teaspoons paprika, 1 teaspoon cumin and a pinch of cayenne, and serve sprinkled with chopped coriander for a Moroccan flavour.
* One of my favourites is also Egyptian: put 1 onion in a blender with 1 teaspoon cumin, $\frac{1}{2}$ teaspoon coriander, $\frac{1}{2}$ teaspoon cinnamon, a pinch each of allspice, ginger and nutmeg, and salt and pepper. Blend to a paste and spread this on the meat.

Grilled spring chicken and quails
Grilled pork and lamb chops (p. 171)

Kofta alla Shish

Minced Meat on Skewers

For this type of kebab the minced lamb is worked to a paste and the flavourings are fully incorporated. There are many versions of this recipe and many ways of serving it. The following one, which is the most usual, should be very green with herbs. When cooked directly over a fire, the minced meat needs fat to keep it moist and juicy, and you must be careful not to overcook it. Serve with warm pitta bread and salad.

Serves 6

1 kg (2 lb) fat lamb, preferably from the leg
  or shoulder
250 g (8 oz) lamb fat (optional)
2 onions, grated
Large bunch of parsley, finely chopped
Salt and pepper

Garnish:
Parsley sprigs
2 lemons, cut in wedges

If the meat is lean and you are going to cook it on a charcoal grill, include the lamb fat. (Don't be put off; it will melt in the heat of the fire and drip out.) Blend all the ingredients to a paste in a blender or food processor. Alternatively, ask the butcher to mince the meat for you and work it to a soft consistency with your hands. Leave the mixture to rest for an hour.

Wet your hands, take portions of meat and wrap them around a skewer. (The type with a square section or wide flat blade are particularly good for this.) Shape the meat into a flat sausage about 13 cm (5 in) long on the skewer and press firmly so that it holds to-gether. The technique will become easy once you have got the feel of it. If you do not have skewers, shape the meat into burgers. Place the skewers or burgers on an oiled grill and cook over hot charcoal for 5–8 minutes, turning them over at least once. You can also cook them under the grill. Serve immediately garnished with parsley and lemon wedges.

Variations
* Use fresh mint, very finely chopped, instead of, or together with the parsley.
* Add 2 teaspoons dried thyme.
* Add 1 teaspoon cinnamon, 1 teaspoon paprika and a good pinch of cayenne.
* For a Moroccan flavour, add 1 teaspoon ground cumin, 1 teaspoon cinnamon, 1 teaspoon paprika, a pinch of cayenne and a large bunch of coriander instead of the parsley, finely chopped.
* For a Lebanese flavour, sprinkle with sumac.
* For kofta Antablia which is from the region of Antab in Turkey, prepare the following sauce: fry 2 coarsely chopped onions in 3 tablespoons olive oil till soft. Add 750 g ($1\frac{1}{2}$ lb) peeled, chopped tomatoes and a large bunch of finely chopped parsley. Season to taste with salt and pepper and add the juice of 1 lemon, or 2 tablespoons sumac (see p. 53). Warm up 3 pitta breads, open them out into halves, spread each half with the sauce and place the kofta on top.
* For kofta snobar toast 50 g (2 oz) pine-nuts, take por-tions of meat paste the size of a small egg, press a few pine-nuts into the centre of each and shape into long, thin ovals. Wrap around skewers and grill.

Şiş Kebab

Skewered Meats

Everyone knows şiş kebab as the chief item on the menu of Middle Eastern restaurants, which are really kebab houses. Or they may have bought it in the street in a pocket of bread filled with salad and pickles. The grander style of the Turkish *et locantasi* (meat restaurant) came about more than 70 years ago. When the Ottoman Empire crumbled the hundreds of cooks employed by the sultan at the palace of Topkapi in Istanbul (they all came from the same area of Bolu in central Anatolia) opened restaurants to survive. The grilled meats and appetisers which are still on offer are called *saray* (seraglio) cooking.

The preferred meat for şiş kebab is lamb, but tender beef or veal are also used and make an excellent alternative. I was told in Turkey that the tradition of interspersing pieces of tomato, onion and pepper with bay leaves between cubes of meat threaded onto skewers came as a result of chefs wanting them to capture the interest of foreigners. In reality it is usual, as it is in the rest of the oriental Mediterranean, to cook the meat alone on skewers because that way it cooks better.

Serves 6

1 kg (2 lb) tender lamb, preferably from the leg

For the marinade:
150 ml (5 fl oz) olive or sunflower oil
2 onions, grated
2 bay leaves, crushed
2 tablespoons mint, marjoram or thyme
Salt and pepper

Garnish:
2 lemons cut in wedges
Bunch of parsley or mint

Remove any fat and cut the meat into cubes about 2.5 cm (1 in) thick. Mix the marinade ingredients in a bowl and marinate the meat, leaving it in the refrigerator for at least an hour or overnight, turning the pieces over once.

Thread the cubes of meat on wide, flat-bladed or twisted skewers, and place on an oiled grill about 7 cm (3 in) from the embers of a wood or charcoal fire or under the grill. Cook quickly for 7–10 minutes, turning the meat over once, so that the outside is well browned and the inside is pink and juicy.

Transfer the skewers straight onto a plate garnished with lemon wedges and sprigs of parsley or mint. Accompany by an Arab mixed salad (see p. 68) and warmed pitta bread.

Variations
* If you use beef – porterhouse, sirloin, fillet or rump steak – cook it closer to the fire and for a shorter time. It is best when rare inside. Veal (use fillet) is best cooked a little longer on a gentler fire.
* Add the juice of 1 lemon to the marinade, to tenderise the meat and give it a slightly tart flavour.
* Add 1 teaspoon cinnamon and $\frac{1}{2}$ teaspoon allspice for an aromatic marinade.
* For a Moroccan marinade add 1–2 teaspoons cumin or 2 teaspoons ground caraway seeds, 1 teaspoon paprika, a pinch of cayenne and 2 or 3 garlic cloves, crushed.

Right: Şiş kebab
Left: Kofta alla shish (p. 173)

Yogurtlu Kebab

Kebab with Yogurt

The alternative name for this refreshing dish is *Iskander kebab* after the man who invented it 60 years ago. It is a favourite on Turkish kebab house menus but can easily be done at home.

Serves 4

4 skewers of şiş or kofta kebab (pp. 173 and 174)
500 g (1 lb) tomatoes, peeled, de-seeded and chopped
4 tablespoons olive oil
Salt and pepper
1 pitta bread
600 ml (1 pint) thick ewe's milk yogurt or strained yogurt (see p. 213), at room temperature
1 teaspoon paprika
4 small green peppers, finely sliced (optional)
Bunch of parsley, finely chopped

Prepare the kebabs. Simmer the tomatoes with 1 tablespoon oil, salt and pepper for a few minutes until they reduce to a light sauce.

Open out the bread into 2 halves, brush the smooth side with 2 tablespoons oil and toast under the grill until crisp and brown. Break the bread into small pieces and put them in the bottom of a serving dish or on individual plates. Pour the hot tomato sauce over the bread, then cover with yogurt. Slide the meat from the skewers on top. Beat the remaining oil with the paprika and dribble over the dish. Garnish with the green pepper and parsley.

Variation
Some Turkish chefs, like Hüseyin Özoguz at the Divan Hotel in Istanbul, make the sauce with finely chopped onion, tomatoes and shredded green pepper.

Yogurtlu kebab

Grains and Pulses

THE TRADITIONAL ways in which the Mediterranean combines grain with pulses, vegetables, fruits and nuts, and also with fish or meat, represent what nutritionists today recognise as the ideal combination for a healthy diet. Grains and pulses – like preserves and dried fruit – are the simple basic products of the Mediterranean larder. While rice is generally a city dish, pulses, wheat and other grains are peasant foods. In rural areas you can still see the wheat being washed in the river and spread out to dry on sheets in the fields. And you can still find all kinds of pulses such as chickpeas, beans and lentils drying on rooftops beside trays of tomato paste, strings of red peppers and mountains of grapes.

All these things have been part of the internal trade within the Mediterranean for centuries since the slow sailing ships took weeks to arrive at their destination and consequently grains and pulses are to be found everywhere. Pasta is not confined to Italy, nor couscous to Morocco. The poor man's street foods of Egypt are a mixture of rice, lentils and short macaroni called *koshari*, and a sweet couscous with nuts and raisins. Just as grand court cuisines have been transported from one seat of power to another during the great empires, there have also been culinary exchanges on the peasant level. The Moroccan soldiers recruited by the Arab armies who went on to conquer Sicily introduced couscous dishes there. When France colonised North Africa the immigrants who came to work the land were peasants from southern Italy as well as from southern France and Spain. The Italians brought their ways of cooking pasta. But the pasta dishes of the eastern Mediterranean have a personality of their own and belong to the old Arab cuisine which originated in Persia. Southern Italian pasta is the best and most varied in Italy and no region can match the brilliant Sicilian marriages of pasta with fish and vegetables.

With rice every country has its own cooking methods, some preferring the grains to be separate and firm, others liking them soft and mushy. But rice is at its best in Turkey. I once met a woman there who had researched pilafs and she had discovered a hundred different recipes.

Right: Izmir grain and pulse stall

Couscous

Couscous is a many-splendoured North African Berber dish which I think is at its best in Morocco. The name applies both to the grain (a type of semolina) and to the whole garnished dish, and is said to come from the French pronunciation of the word *suksoo* which describes the sound the vapour makes when it passes through the grain as it steams. It is the *face*, as the stew or garnish is called, which is infinitely variable.

Couscous is by tradition a Friday lunch meal and also a festive dish. It is usual to use up all the vegetables which are left in the house at the end of the week. At a banquet it is served at the end, after several courses, to make sure that guests cannot eat any more, and the dish is likely to return to the kitchen barely touched, to be eaten by the cooks.

Couscous is served in a large round shallow dish. The grain is heaped in a mountain with a shallow depression on top. Pieces of meat or chicken are placed in the well and the vegetables on top or down the side. Alternatively, the grain is dressed with almonds or raisins and sometimes dates, and accompanied by the stew in a separate dish. The dish is placed in the middle of the large tray which serves as a table. Everyone helps themselves by rolling small lumps into a bite-sized ball with three fingers of the right hand.

Couscous

Almost all the couscous available here is commercially pre-cooked. The 'real thing' – a coarsely ground hard wheat which is moistened and rolled in flour by hand – needs to be steamed for 35–40 minutes and taken out at least once to be sprinkled with water and rubbed between the palms so that the grains do not stick together in lumps. It is usually steamed in the aromatic vapours of a meaty stew. Pre-cooked couscous, which is widely used even in Morocco, only needs water adding and heating through and if it is treated with care the result can be perfectly good.

Serves 10 or more

1 kg (2 lb) pre-cooked couscous
A little under 1.2 litres (2 pints) salted water
4 tablespoons sunflower oil
2–4 tablespoons butter or sunflower oil

Put the couscous in a large bowl. Pour in about half the quantity of slightly salted water and stir well until evenly absorbed. Leave for 10 minutes. Add the rest of the water and the oil. Rub the grain between your palms and make sure that it is not sticking together in lumps. After about 10 minutes the grains should be swollen and tender but separate. Steam it, uncovered, in the top half of a couscousier (see p. 59) or in a steamer over boiling water or a bubbling stew. When the steam begins to come through the grain it is ready to serve. Transfer into a serving dish and break up any lumps. Stir in the butter or oil before serving.

Alternative cooking methods:
* Add a little extra water to the swollen couscous and warm through in a saucepan over a low heat. Stir often to make sure that the bottom grains do not burn.
* Place the swollen couscous, covered, in an oven pre-heated to 200°C (400°F, gas mark 6) for 10 minutes or until heated through.

Couscous aux Sept Légumes

Couscous with Seven Vegetables

Couscous is the national dish of Morocco. There it is more delicate and less hot and spicy than the Tunisian and Algerian versions now found in France. Seven is the traditional number of vegetables used in this recipe (seven, like five, is considered a lucky number), but the choice usually depends on the season. Choose seven from those listed below. Any combination can be used, the important thing being to add them in the right order.

This is a one-pot meal, easy to make for large numbers. The sauce is light, like a broth, and you may need to keep adding water as it cooks. See the instructions opposite for cooking the couscous grain. It may seem to you from looking at the recipe that everything is optional but that reflects the very personal way of working to taste.

Serves 10 or more

1.5 kg (3 lb) (boned weight) stewing beef, shoulder or fillet of lamb, or knuckle of veal
250 g (8 oz) chickpeas, soaked for at least an hour (optional)
2 large onions, quartered, then thickly sliced
3 garlic cloves, chopped
½ teaspoon saffron-coloured powder (p. 52)
2 teaspoons cinnamon
1 teaspoon paprika (optional)
A good pinch of cayenne (optional) or 2 small chilli peppers, finely chopped
½ teaspoon ground ginger (optional)
Salt

Choose 7 vegetables (plus the raisins) from:
500 g (1 lb) carrots, cut in half lengthways
1 medium white cabbage, cut into 8 pieces
6 artichoke hearts
2 medium aubergines, quartered
500 g (1 lb) small potatoes
500 g (1 lb) turnips, quartered (left whole if baby ones)
500 g (1 lb) broad beans, shelled
250 g (8 oz) raisins (preferably large Malaga)
500 g (1 lb) piece of orange pumpkin, cut into 5 cm (2 in) pieces
500 g (1 lb) courgettes, cut in half lengthways
4 tomatoes, quartered

Couscous aux sept légumes (opposite)

Large bunch of parsley, chopped
Large bunch of fresh coriander, chopped
4 tablespoons oil

Remove as much fat from the meat as possible and put it, together with the chickpeas, in a large pot or the bottom half of a couscousier (see p. 59). Cover with 3 litres (5 pints) of water, bring to the boil and remove the froth. Add the onion, garlic and spices and simmer for at least an hour. Add the salt when the chickpeas begin to soften.

Add the carrots, cabbage, artichoke hearts, aubergines and potatoes, and more water if necessary, and cook for 20 minutes. Add the turnips, broad beans and raisins and cook for 10 minutes. Add the pumpkin, courgettes and tomatoes and, after 5 minutes, while they are still firm, add the herbs and cook for 5 minutes longer. While the vegetables are cooking prepare the couscous as described opposite, putting it to steam when the turnips, broad beans and raisins are added.

Turn out the couscous onto a large round serving dish and crush with a fork to separate the grains. Stir in the oil and ladle on a little broth – just enough to moisten it – then shape into a mound with a well in the centre. Cut the meat into pieces, taking out some of the bones, and place the meat in the well. Lift the vegetables out using a perforated spoon and place on top of the meat or on the sides of the couscous mound. Serve at once with the broth in a separate bowl.

If you expect to have left-over couscous, serve the stew in a separate bowl so that you can re-heat it. In this case a good way to garnish the grain is: with boiled dates or chickpeas; fried or toasted blanched almonds; boiled raisins or currants; a sprinkling of cinnamon; or a combination of 2 or more of these things.

Variations
* For a fiery Tunisian version which is very popular in France mix 2 teaspoons of harissa or 2 teaspoons paprika and ¼–½ teaspoon cayenne into a bowl of the broth and pass it round for everyone to take just a little.
* Bury dates in the couscous while it is steaming or warm them up in a little broth.
* Add dried brown broad beans (soaked overnight) at the same time as the chickpeas.
* In Tetouan they fry the meat and vegetables before stewing them.

Bulgur Pilavi

Cracked Wheat Pilaf

Cracked wheat is the rural alternative to rice in the eastern Mediterranean, especially in Turkey.

Serves 8

500 g (1 lb) coarse-ground cracked wheat
4 tablespoons sunflower oil
900 ml (1½ pints) meat or chicken stock
Salt and pepper

Rinse the cracked wheat in cold water in a colander. Put the oil and the stock in a large saucepan and season with salt and pepper. Bring to the boil, add the cracked wheat and cook, covered, for about 25 minutes or until the cracked wheat is tender, but not mushy, and the liquid is absorbed. Turn off the heat and let the cracked wheat rest for a few minutes while it grows plump.

Variations

* Add 500 g (1 lb) ripe tomatoes, peeled, de-seeded and chopped, to the saucepan. Reduce the amount of stock to 600 ml (1 pint) as the tomatoes will provide juice.
 * Cook down 500 g (1 lb) peeled tomatoes with the oil to a thick sauce, then add the stock.

Butifarra amb Mongetes

Black-eyed Beans with Sausage

Catalan cooking can be rich, complicated and sophisticated but it can also be simple and rustic. While the cooking of the coast is dominated by fish, the cooking of the interior is dominated by pork.

Serves 6

500 g (1 lb) black-eyed beans
2 garlic cloves
1 bay leaf
2 teaspoons cinnamon
Pinch of nutmeg
Salt and pepper
125 g (4 oz) bacon, cut in small pieces, plus its fat
6 butifarras or large, spicy, pure pork sausages

Simmer the beans in water with the garlic, bay leaf, cinnamon and nutmeg until soft, adding a pinch of salt, if necessary, and pepper towards the end. There should be a little water left. Melt the bacon fat and fry the bacon in it until crisp and brown. Prick the sausages with a fork to prevent them bursting and fry in some of the bacon fat, or grill or bake them in a hot oven until browned. Add to the beans and cook a few minutes longer. Serve hot.

Roz bil Ful

Rice with Broad Beans

Malak Mawaldi gave us this lovely summer dish when the Cairo vegetable markets were spilling over with broad beans.

Serves 6

500 g (1 lb) long-grain rice
2 kg (4 lb) broad beans, unshelled
65 g (2½ oz) butter
Salt
900 ml (1½ pints) chicken or other meat stock

Garnish:
Split almonds
250 g (8 oz) fried minced meat

Soak the rice in water for 30 minutes, then rinse and drain in a colander. Shell the beans and simmer in salted boiling water until tender.

Heat the butter in a pan and throw in the beans, then the rice, and stir until the rice becomes transparent. Add salt and enough stock to cover. Bring to the boil and simmer, covered, for about 20 minutes or until the rice is tender and the broth has been absorbed. Stir the rice and let it rest, still covered, while the remaining moisture is absorbed and the grains become separated.

Toast the almonds under the grill and sprinkle them over the dish with the fried minced meat before serving.

Roz bil Zafran

Saffron Rice

Almost every Mediterranean country has a saffron rice in its repertoire. In this Arab version saffron is the only flavouring used and there are no conflicting aromas, so it is one of the few dishes where it is important to use real saffron pistils.

Serves 4–6

750 ml (1 pint 7 fl oz) water or stock
½ teaspoon saffron pistils (see p. 52)
500 g (1 lb) long-grain rice
3 tablespoons sunflower oil
Salt
2 tablespoons butter (optional)

Garnish (optional):
50 g (2 oz) pine-nuts, almonds and pistachio nuts, or a mixture

Bring the water or stock to the boil. Crush the saffron pistils a little with a small pestle and mortar or with the back of a spoon and stir into the boiling liquid. Turn off the heat and leave to infuse.

Heat the oil in a large heavy-bottomed pan. Add the rice and stir for a minute or so until the grains become transparent. Pour in the saffron liquid, add salt and stir well. Bring to the boil, then reduce the heat to as low as possible and cook, covered, for about 15 minutes or until the rice is tender. You may like to stir in the butter at this point. Take the pan off the heat and let the rice rest for a few minutes so that the grains become more separate.

Serve garnished with the nuts if you like. Pistachios need to be coarsely chopped, pine-nuts lightly toasted and almonds toasted and chopped.

Sultan Reshat Pilavi

Turkish Pilaf

Many classic Turkish dishes are associated with the Ottoman Sultans. Stories abound of their eating whole sheep at one sitting so as to be able to satisfy the wives in the harem, and of the little slave apprentices procured by the pastry cooks. This pilaf, Sultan Reshat's favourite, is on record in the archives of the palace of Topkapi. He is said to have buried a golden chickpea in the rice to add excitement to the meal.

Serves 4

1 large aubergine, cut into cubes
Salt
1 large onion, coarsely chopped
Sunflower oil
350 g (12 oz) long-grain rice
650 ml (1 pint 3 fl oz) meat or chicken stock
500 g (1 lb) minced lamb or veal
½ teaspoon allspice
1–2 tablespoons pine-nuts
2 tablespoons blanched almonds
1–2 tablespoons pistachio nuts, cut in half
2 tomatoes, cut into wedges

Sprinkle the aubergine with plenty of salt and let the juices degorge in a colander.

Fry the onion in 3 tablespoons oil until soft and lightly coloured. Add the rice and stir for a minute or so until it becomes translucent. Bring the stock to the boil, pour over the rice, add salt, stir well and cook, covered, for 18–20 minutes, or until the liquid is absorbed and the rice is tender. You may need to add a little more water.

Season the meat with salt and pepper to taste, add the allspice and knead well. Roll into balls the size of large hazelnuts.

Fry all the nuts quickly in oil in a large frying-pan, stirring and turning them over until lightly coloured, then drain on kitchen paper. Wash the aubergines to remove the salt and pat dry, then fry quickly in hot oil. Drain on kitchen paper and press gently to remove excess oil. Fry the meat balls quickly until brown outside and still slightly pink but cooked inside. Lastly, fry the tomatoes quickly until they soften slightly, then drain. Mix all the fried ingredients into the rice and heat through, or serve them piled on top of the rice. Both presentations are attractive.

Paella a la Valenciana

Valencian Paella

The cooking of *paella* in Spain is a social or family celebration. The name of the dish is derived from the large shallow double-handled pan, the *paellera* (see p. 59) in which the rice is cooked. It is a peasant dish cooked out in the open on a charcoal fire. The burning wood gives the rice an exceptionally delicious aroma. When paella is cooked indoors a specially large gas ring with several concentric circles joined to a butane cylinder gives the desired spread-out heat. Without this you cannot attempt a paella for more than six people. It is also useful to use a mat which disperses the heat. *Paella a la valenciana* is versatile and the ingredients change according to the season. In Spain small snails called *vaquetas* are used for the flavour of the wild rosemary they feed on. The small hard Spanish rice is not generally available here and the closest you can get is Italian risotto rice. Because this rice can get mushy if overcooked, you will have to watch it; it needs about twice its volume of liquid but you will have to measure with your eye and add as required in this recipe. Otherwise you achieve good results with a medium grain rice which does not fall apart.

Glamorous versions of paella, one more spectacular than the next, combining lobster, crab, prawns and mussels with rabbits and chicken have become very popular abroad under the name *valenciana* but this is the traditional classic recipe. It was given to me by Maria Amal, the family cook of Mas Carmen, a large country house outside Valencia.

Serves 6

$\frac{1}{2}$ **chicken weighing about 750 g ($1\frac{1}{2}$ lb)**
1 rabbit or 750 g ($1\frac{1}{2}$ lb) lean pork or lamb
4–5 tablespoons olive oil
1–2 ripe tomatoes, peeled and chopped
125 g (4 oz) large dry white Spanish beans
  (garrofon) or butter beans, soaked overnight
250 g (8 oz) green beans, topped and tailed, strings
  removed and cut into pieces
1–2 teaspoons paprika
2 sprigs of rosemary
$\frac{1}{2}$ **teaspoon saffron**
Salt
750 g ($1\frac{1}{2}$ lb) short- or medium-grain rice

Cut the chicken and rabbit or meat into small pieces. Fry in the oil in a *paellera* or large frying-pan until lightly browned. Add the tomatoes, drained butter beans and green beans. Sprinkle with paprika, rosemary, saffron and salt, cover with water and simmer for 45–60 minutes until the meat is very tender.

Add the rice, stir well and cover with enough water to make up about 1.75 litres (3 pints) of liquid and cook first on a high heat for about 10 minutes, then reduce the heat and cook until the rice is tender but still relatively firm and separate, adding water if it becomes absorbed too quickly or turning the heat up to dry it out if it is still wet at the end. Cover it with a lid and let it rest for 5 minutes before serving.

Note
You can put the pan to cook in a 160°C (325°F, gas mark 3) oven, uncovered, for about 20 minutes.

Sangria (p. 208)
Paella a la valenciana

Arroz a Banda

Rice Cooked in Fish Stock

The most flavourful rice I have ever eaten was in a modest restaurant called El Trampoli by the sea near Denia in the Alicante region of Spain. It was cooked by Luisa Puigcerver. We were first served a selection of simply cooked, magnificent seafood and then this rice, accompanied by a very garlicky all-i-oli sauce (see p. 213). What makes *arroz a banda* so delicious is the fish broth it is cooked in. In Spain they used a variety of fish and crabs to make the stock but the fish stock on p. 216 makes a very good alternative. At El Trampoli dried red peppers, onions and garlic fried together start off the fish stock, but cayenne and paprika added later will provide the authentic piquancy. *A banda* means 'apart' because traditionally you serve the rice first, then the fish and seafood, which are poached in the stock, separately as a second course with the all-i-oli.

You can serve the rice with any kind of fish (see variation).

Serves 4–6

1.2 litres (2 pints) fish stock (see p. 216)
75 ml (3 fl oz) olive oil
4 garlic cloves, crushed
2 tomatoes, peeled, de-seeded and chopped, or
 1 tablespoon tomato purée
1 teaspoon paprika
Pinch of cayenne
Salt and pepper (optional)
500 g (1 lb) short-grain rice
$\frac{1}{4}$ teaspoon saffron or saffron-coloured powder (see
 p. 52)

All-i-oli sauce (see p. 213)

Make a stock as described on p. 216 but without wine. Heat the oil in a paella pan (see p. 59) or casserole. Put in the garlic and when it just begins to colour, add the tomatoes or tomato paste. Cook the tomatoes for about 10 minutes until they are reduced to a paste and the oil begins to separate. Add the paprika and cayenne.

Add the rice and cook, stirring constantly, for a minute or two. Add the saffron (and salt and pepper if the stock is not already seasoned) and stir well. Then pour in the strained stock. If using Spanish or Italian short-grain rice, the amount of stock has to be double the volume of rice. Cook over a high heat for 5 minutes, then lower the heat and cook gently for another 15 minutes or until the rice is tender but separate. Take it off the heat and let it rest, covered, for a minute or two so that any slightly underdone rice has time to soften. Alternatively, bake the rice in a covered ovenproof dish at 160°C (325°F, gas mark 3) for 30 minutes. Serve accompanied by the all-i-oli sauce.

Variations

* For a meal of fish to serve with this recipe poach 500 g (1 lb) unshelled prawns until they turn pink, then lift them out, shell them and return the shells to the stock to give it more flavour. Poach 1 kg (2 lb) cod, halibut or monkfish and take it out very quickly just as soon as it begins to flake. Keep the shelled prawns and fish aside, covered with a little stock. Heat up before serving.
* A lovely alternative is *fideua* which is made in the same way but using vermicelli instead of rice.

Arroz a banda with all-i-oli (p. 213)

Yufkalı Pilav

Pilaf Pie

Mrs Neşet Eren of Istanbul serves this filo-encased chicken pilaf with her aubergine salad (see p. 70).

Serves 10–12

1 chicken, with giblets, weighing 1.5 kg (3–3½ lb)
2 carrots, diced
2 onions, quartered
Salt
6–8 peppercorns
4 sprigs of parsley
2 tablespoons pine-nuts or slivered almonds
125 g (4 oz) butter
Pepper
500 g (1 lb) long-grain rice
250 g (8 oz) filo pastry (see p. 45)
250 g (8 oz) cooked green peas

Wash the chicken and reserve the heart and liver from the giblets. Put the chicken in a pan with water to cover and add the carrots, onions, salt, peppercorns and parsley. Simmer, covered, for about 45 minutes or until the chicken is tender, then lift it out of the pan. When it is cool enough to handle, remove the skin and bones and cut the meat into 5 cm (2.5 in) strips.

Strain the stock, reserving the carrot pieces separately. Fry the pine-nuts or almonds in 1 tablespoon of the butter until golden, then remove with a slotted spoon. Cut the chicken heart and liver into small pieces and fry in the same butter for 5 minutes, adding salt and pepper.

Now make a rice pilaf. Bring 900 ml (1½ pints) of the strained stock to the boil in a saucepan, add the rice and stir. Bring to the boil again, then simmer, covered, for about 10 minutes or until little holes appear on the surface of the rice. Remove from the heat before all the stock has been absorbed. Stir in the nuts and the heart and liver with 50 g (2 oz) of the remaining butter.

Pre-heat the oven to 180°C (350°F, gas mark 4). Grease a 4.5 litre (1 gallon) ovenproof dish or bowl. Melt the rest of the butter. Line the bowl with 6 sheets of filo so that they overlap and hang over the rim, brushing lightly with melted butter between the sheets. Spread with 2 layers each of the rice mixture, chicken pieces, carrots and peas, then cover with a final layer of rice.

Bring the hanging pastry edges up and fold them over the rice, brushing with a little butter. Cover with 4 more sheets of overlapping pastry, brushing each with melted butter. Trim the corners and fold the edges down into the sides of the dish to close the pie.

Bake for about 30 minutes or until the top is golden brown. Serve hot, using a sharp knife to cut through the crust.

Ezo Gelin

Lentils with Rice and Pasta

Like many Turkish dishes this one has a romantic name – *ezo gelin* means 'young girl'.

Serves 4

1 large onion, coarsely chopped
2 tablespoons sunflower oil
500 g (1 lb) tomatoes, peeled and cut into pieces
Salt and pepper
125 g (4 oz) green lentils
125 g (4 oz) rice (optional)
125 g (4 oz) fettuccine
2 tablespoons butter
1 tablespoon dried mint

In a large pan, fry the onion in oil until golden. Add the tomatoes with a little salt and pepper and turn off the heat.

Boil the lentils, rice and fettuccine separately in pans of salted water. (Don't add the salt to the lentils until they have softened a little.) Drain, add to the onion and tomato and heat through.

Heat the butter with the mint until it sizzles and pour over the dish before serving.

Roz wa Shaghria

Rice with Vermicelli

This is often served instead of plain rice in the Arab world. You can vary the proportions and use more vermicelli. Yogurt makes a nice accompaniment.

Serves 4

125 g (4 oz) vermicelli
250 g (8 oz) long-grain rice
Salt
3 tablespoons butter or sunflower oil

Using your hands, crush the vermicelli into small pieces. Toast them on a tray under the grill until they are lightly browned, stirring them once or twice so that they colour evenly. (The old way was to fry them in butter.) Tip the rice and vermicelli into a pan of rapidly boiling salted water. Boil about 10 minutes or until the rice is still a little hard when you bite it. Drain quickly in a colander.

Put the butter or oil in the saucepan, add the rice and vermicelli, stir well, then cover and steam in their own moisture on a very low flame for about 10–15 minutes. Be careful that the rice and vermicelli do not burn. Serve hot.

Variation
Add 50 g (2 oz) cooked chickpeas to the dish five minutes before serving.

Spaghetti Aglio e Olio

Spaghetti with Garlic and Oil

There is a marked contrast of cuisines in the north, centre and south of Italy because the historic context of each was very different until the unification only a century ago. The north–south gastronomic boundary at Campania and the Abruzzi is also the poverty line. The historic insecurity and social problems have left their imprint on the cooking of the south which is simple and austere.

Serves 6

500 g (1 lb) spaghetti
Salt
3–4 garlic cloves, finely chopped
1 small hot chilli pepper, finely chopped (optional)
6 tablespoons olive oil
Pepper
A few mint leaves, finely chopped
Very large bunch of parsley, finely chopped

Cook the pasta *al dente* (see below).

Very gently fry the garlic together with the chilli pepper in 2 tablespoons of oil until the garlic only just begins to colour but does not brown. Stir into the drained pasta and add the pepper, the remaining oil and the mint and parsley. The garlic and chilli pepper are usually discarded so that there is only a hint of their flavour left in the oil, and the parsley and mint are then fried in it. But to my taste it is better to retain the garlic and chilli and to eat the herbs fresh.

How to Cook Pasta

500 g/1 lb serves 4 to 6

Bring plenty of water (about 4.8 litres/8 pints) to the boil in a large saucepan and add salt. Put in the pasta, stirring well to prevent it from sticking. If it is long, do not break it, but force it under water by bending it gradually as it softens. Some people add 1 tablespoon of oil to keep the pasta separate but I have never found it necessary. Cover the pot to bring it quickly to a fast boil, then uncover and continue at a bubbling boil, stirring occasionally so that the pasta does not stick together. Begin to taste for doneness when it starts to swell and rise to the surface. When it is only just tender but still firm, *al dente*, it is done. The time depends on the type of pasta. Do not overcook – it should not be soft and mushy.

Drain at once and serve quickly in a warm bowl. While in northern Italy they melt in a good dollop of butter so that the cooked pasta slithers smoothly, in the south a little olive oil or – and this is one of the little secrets to which everyone confesses – a few tablespoons of the cooking water are added. Part of the beauty of southern cooking is its simplicity and economy and the way nothing is lost. The cooking water is often also the water in which the vegetables or fish for the sauce have been boiled. Reserve a little as you drain the pasta or simply do not drain the pasta too thoroughly. Serve very hot.

Trenette al Pesto

Pasta with Genoese Basil Sauce

Pesto is a simple sauce – a mixture of pounded fresh basil, pine-nuts, garlic and cheese with olive oil – but it has the power to transport you. It is the extraordinary fragrance of the mingled odours which works the magic. You will enjoy making pesto by hand with a pestle and mortar and the result will be better, but it is easier to do it all in the blender. Pesto is usually eaten with a kind of fettuccine pasta called trenette.

Serves 4–6

500 g (1 lb) thin pasta such as trenette, fettuccine or
  linguine
Salt
Extra grated Parmesan or pecorino

For the pesto:
Large bunch of basil leaves weighing about 50 g
  (2 oz)
3 tablespoons pine-nuts, lightly toasted
2–4 garlic cloves, crushed
125 ml (4 fl oz) virgin olive oil
3 tablespoons Parmesan, grated
2 tablespoons pecorino, grated

To make the pesto in a processor or blender, blend all the ingredients except the cheese to a smooth paste then stir in the cheese. If you are doing it by hand, first pound and grind the basil, a handful at a time, then add the pine-nuts and garlic and pound to a paste. Stir in the cheese and then beat in the olive oil.

 Boil the pasta in plenty of salted water until *al dente*. If it is fresh it will only take a few seconds. Drain, reserving a little of the cooking water, and serve on a warmed plate with a few tablespoons of the water or 2 tablespoons of oil. Serve accompanied by the pesto and grated cheese.

Note
It is quite common to add a handful of parsley if you do not have quite enough basil.

Pasta alla Crudaiola

Pasta with Uncooked Sauce

Different kinds of pasta such as fusilli, orecchiette, bucatini and spaghetti (see p. 47) can be used with this delightfully simple uncooked sauce. Much depends on the quality of tomatoes, which should be ripe but firm. The dish is also called *alla carrettiera*.

Serves 4

1 kg (2 lb) sweet tomatoes, peeled, de-seeded and
  roughly chopped
2–3 garlic cloves, crushed (optional)
Large bunch of basil, coarsely chopped or torn
4 tablespoons extra virgin olive oil
Salt and pepper
400 g (14 oz) pasta
50 g (2 oz) salty ricotta or Parmesan, grated
  (optional)

Put the tomatoes in a bowl together with the garlic, if you like, basil, olive oil, salt and pepper. Mix thoroughly, then let them stand an hour for the flavours to infuse. Cook the pasta until *al dente*. Drain and mix with the tomato sauce. You can hand the cheese round separately but it is not essential.

Top: Spaghetti con cozze (p. 188)
Centre: Orecchiette alla crudaiola
Bottom: Trenette al pesto

Bucatini con Broccoli

Bucatini with Broccoli

In Sicily they often call their variety of cauliflower 'broccoli'. Either can be used in this recipe.

Serves 4–6

1 large broccoli or cauliflower head, weighing
  about 500 g (1 lb)
Salt
1 large onion or 6 spring onions, finely chopped
3 tablespoons olive oil
60 g (2½ oz) pine-nuts
60 g (2½ oz) currants
4–5 anchovy fillets in oil, cut into small pieces
300 ml (10 fl oz) dry white wine
Pepper
¼ teaspoon or 1 packet saffron (optional)
500 g (1 lb) bucatini or any long pasta
Grated Parmesan or pecorino

Trim and wash the cauliflower or broccoli, cut into small pieces, then boil in salted water until tender. Drain, reserving the water.

Fry the onion in 2 tablespoons olive oil until soft, then add the pine-nuts and currants. When the pine-nuts are golden pour in the wine and cook, uncovered, for 5 minutes or until reduced. Add the broccoli, the salt, pepper and saffron, if using, and a ladleful of the reserved water. Cook for 10 minutes, gently crushing the broccoli into the sauce with a wooden spoon. In a separate pan heat the anchovies in the remaining oil. Crush them with the spoon and, when they have dissolved, add them to the sauce. Meanwhile cook the bucatini in plenty of boiling water until *al dente*. Drain and mix with the sauce. Serve hot with grated Parmesan or pecorino.

Pasta alla Norma

Sicilian Pasta with Aubergines

On weekends the Sicilian seaside is packed with people from the towns installed table to table on the beaches and in the woods. If you pass between the tables you can see the pasta sauces bubbling over primus stoves. This one was offered to us when we looked into a large saucepan and it was wonderful.

Serves 4

400 g (14 oz) aubergines
Salt
1 medium onion, finely chopped
2 tablespoons olive oil
2 garlic cloves, finely chopped
350 g (12 oz) ripe tomatoes, peeled and chopped
Black pepper
1 teaspoon sugar (optional)
A few basil leaves, coarsely chopped, or torn, or
  finely chopped parsley
Sunflower or olive oil for frying
400 g (14 oz) spaghetti or rigatoni
40 g (1½ oz) salty ricotta or provolone, grated

Dice the aubergines, salt them and leave them for about an hour to degorge their juices.

To make the sauce, fry the onion in oil till golden. Add the garlic and, when the aroma rises, add the tomatoes, salt and pepper and a little sugar, if using. Cook for 15 minutes or until the tomatoes are soft and the juice reduced, then add the basil.

Wash and dry the aubergines and fry in hot oil until lightly browned and tender, then drain on kitchen paper and add to the sauce. Cook the pasta until *al dente*, drain quickly and mix with the sauce. Stir in the cheese and serve.

The Wines of Sicily

Sicily produces some excellent wines, both dry and sweet. One of the best whites, Bianço d'Alcamo, comes from the hills between Palermo and Trapani. This is a dry wine, light and fresh, perfect with the many local fish dishes.

The famous Corvo wines, red and white, come from the province of Palermo itself. The red is soft and perfumed, the white clean and dry.

For a softer, more fragrant white wine, look for Regaleali, which comes from further inland.

From the slopes of Etna, near Catania, comes Etna Bianco, a delicate, pale straw-coloured wine which is both cool and smokey.

The most famous of all Sicilian wines is Marsala, from the far west coast of the island. Invented almost by accident in 1773 by John Woodhouse, an Englishman from Liverpool, it is a fortified wine which you can buy dry or sweet and drink it chilled as an aperitif or at room temperature as a dessert wine.

Linguine alla Puttanesca

Linguine with Olives and Capers

Like most restaurants in southern Italy, Don Salvatore in Naples is a family-run concern. This famous recipe was given by the present owner, Antonio Aversano. The name of the dish comes from *puttana*, the Italian word for prostitute – the reason why remains mysterious.

Serves 4

2 tablespoons capers
3 garlic cloves, finely chopped
3 tablespoons olive oil
2–3 anchovy fillets in oil, chopped (optional)
About 16 small pitted black olives, preferably from Gaeta
4 small ripe tomatoes, roughly chopped
Salt and pepper
Large bunch of parsley, finely chopped
A few basil leaves, roughly torn or chopped (optional)
400 g (14 oz) linguine or spaghetti

First soak the capers to remove any brine or vinegar. To make the sauce, gently fry the garlic in the oil until the aroma rises. Add the anchovies, if using, and crush them with a wooden spoon, then add the capers, olives, tomatoes, a little salt and a few grinds of pepper. Cook gently for about 5 minutes or until the tomatoes are soft and the anchovies have blended into the sauce. Then add the herbs and cook for a little longer.

Cook the pasta in rapidly boiling salted water until *al dente* then drain. Serve mixed with the sauce and with a generous sprinkling of additional parsley.

Spaghetti con Cozze

Spaghetti with Mussels

The typical pasta dish of southern Italy is fish and vegetables. Restaurants on the Adriatic side offer a huge variety of fish and seafood, none more so than Da Tommaso, a restaurant just outside Bari right on the seashore. The food is *cucina povera, semplice e espresso* – simple ingredients quickly prepared. The following dish is an excellent example of this.

Serves 4

1 kg (2 lb) mussels
400 g (14 oz) spaghetti
3 garlic cloves, finely chopped
2 tablespoons olive oil
250 g (8 oz) ripe tomatoes, peeled and chopped
Salt and pepper
1 teaspoon sugar (optional)
Small bunch parsley, finely chopped

Clean and cook the mussels as described on p. 138. Remove the cooked mussels from their shells and reserve. Strain and boil the cooking liquor until reduced by half.

As the sauce takes only a few minutes to cook, start cooking the tubettini first in plenty of rapidly boiling salted water. Then make the sauce. Fry the garlic in the oil and, when the aroma rises, add the tomatoes, salt and pepper, add a little sugar (if you need it) and the reduced cooking liquor. Add the parsley and cook for a few minutes or until the tomatoes soften. Then add the reserved mussels and immediately take the sauce off the heat as the mussels will not need any further cooking.

As soon as the spaghetti is *al dente*, drain and add to the sauce. Stir briefly over a high heat and serve immediately.

Variation

For *spaghetti alle vongole*, substitute clams for the mussels.

Fresh Italian anchovies

Pasta con Alici e Pangrattato

Pasta with Anchovies and Breadcrumbs

On my last visit to Sicily I spent much time on the beach of the Saracen Hotel at the Isola delle Femmine. The people there joked that they were the only Arabs who did not fight Israel. It crossed my mind that in looks and in character they had much that was Arab. The Saracens, as the Arabs of the ninth-century Sicily were called, remained the dominant influence on the cooking of the island. A sprinkling of pine-nuts and currants is one of the main characteristics of this Saracen influence and in this recipe they are combined with a common local ingredient, anchovies, to make a most interesting pasta dish.

Serves 6

3 garlic cloves, finely chopped
5 tablespoons olive oil
10 anchovy fillets, chopped
Pepper
Large bunch of parsley, finely chopped
500 g (1 lb) spaghetti
Salt
3 tablespoons pine-nuts
3 tablespoons currants
4 tablespoons fresh breadcrumbs

Fry the garlic in 3 tablespoons of olive oil till the aroma rises, then add the anchovies and squash them with a wooden spoon so that they practically melt. Add the pepper.

Cook the spaghetti until *al dente*, then drain. Meanwhile, gently fry the pine-nuts, currants and fresh breadcrumbs in the rest of the oil until the breadcrumbs are brown. Mix the pasta well with the anchovy sauce and stir in the parsley. Serve hot sprinkled with the pine-nuts, currants and breadcrumbs.

Pasta all'Uovo

Egg Pasta

The art of making egg pasta by hand lies in rolling the dough very thin without breaking it.

Serves 4

350 g (12 oz) or more plain flour, plus extra for flouring
Large pinch of salt
4 large (size 2) eggs, lightly beaten
1½ tablespoons olive oil

Place the flour and salt in a bowl, make a well in the centre and pour in the eggs. Gradually work the flour into the eggs, using a fork, then continue with your hands until they are well mixed. Add a tablespoon or more of flour, if necessary, so that the mass holds together well, then knead for 10–15 minutes or until the dough is smooth and elastic, adding a little more flour if it is too sticky. Rub the dough with ½ tablespoon of oil and wrap it in a polythene bag to prevent a dry skin forming. Let it rest for an hour at room temperature.

Divide the dough into 2 balls for easier handling. Roll each out as thinly as possible on a lightly floured board with a lightly floured rolling pin. With experience you should be able to roll the dough almost paper-thin before it becomes dry.

To make noodles, carefully transfer the two sheets of dough to a teacloth and leave to dry out for 20 minutes. Fold the sheets over and over and, using a sharp knife, cut into ribbons about 0.5 cm (¼ in) wide to make tagliatelle and narrower for fettuccine (see below).

To cook the noodles, drop them into a large pan of salted boiling water and add the remaining oil. They will take only a few seconds to cook *al dente*.

Preparation of pasta all'uovo

Sweets

THE ARAB legacy is all-important in sweet-making throughout the Mediterranean. Cakes made with ground almonds, pastries filled with chopped nuts or marzipan (the name is derived from the Arabic *martaban*), fritters, milk puddings, sweets made with dried and preserved fruits or garnished with pine-nuts or bathed in sugar syrup, those perfumed with cinnamon, orange zest and honey, rose and orange blossom water, these are all attributed to Saracens, Moors and Turks. Often they have names such as 'caliph's hats' or 'sultan's ears'.

The Mediterranean inherited from the Arabs a love of ritual and celebration as well as a sweet tooth. Many dishes are associated with religious festivals and public holidays but none so much as sweets which have a ritual role and are eaten on special occasions such as saints' days and historic events. They are prepared at the beginning or the end of a fast, to honour the dead or to celebrate an event such as a betrothal, the birth of a child, a first tooth or a home-coming. They may be given to the poor or thrown from the top of a minaret or they may be eaten as a charm to bring happiness or ward off the evil eye or to cast a spell – for the Mediterranean has also inherited from the Arabs a fascination with magic and superstition.

Another factor which is responsible for the development of little sweets that keep, like sweetmeats, spoon jams, fruit preserves and compotes, is the legendary hospitality of the area. People live to entertain and guests are encouraged to drop in unexpectedly. One of the most delightful social rituals is the offering of sweet things set out on a beautiful tray with coffee or tea or a fruity syrup.

It is usual to buy certain sweets from specialists. In the countries which were part of the Ottoman Empire there are guilds of milk-pudding makers and pastry makers. The trade is jealously guarded and remains in the hands of the same families for generations. In the Christian Mediterranean many sweets are the creation of convents and monasteries; some are produced to mark specific saints' days, others are sold the year round. I visited a convent, the Monasterio de San Geronimo in Granada, where the nuns are famous for their featherlight *suspiros* (sighs) and other pastries. They explained that the tradition of convent pastry-making started in Granada when it was regained from the Moors by the Catholic kings. It was a way for the Church to repay its noble benefactors. Daughters of noblemen who did not marry were sent to convents and they each brought with them four or five Moorish servants who introduced Arab pastries into the convents. Selling pastries helped these religious establishments to survive during the Civil War and later the Pope asked them to continue as a populist gesture to please the people. The pastry recipes of the convents have remained a secret to the outside world and even the measuring cups and weights have special coded symbols so that the nuns themselves do not know the exact amounts.

Right: Filo pastry makers in Istanbul

An Arrangement of Fruits

A selection of fruit can be turned into a fabulous and most alluring party piece if they are cut up and arranged in a beautiful composition. The idea is to mix all kinds of fruit, some cheap and well known, some expensive and exotic. The choice is large – use pp. 28–31 for inspiration.

First prepare the serving dish – a large plate, a flat basket or a tray. Line it with vine or fig leaves or any decorative leaves you like. Cut the fruit into thin slices or wedges or separate it into segments. Drop any that discolour into a bowl of water with plenty of lemon juice. Leave figs unpeeled and small fruit such as cherries, plums, apricots and tiny mandarins whole. Soft fruits such as strawberries should be very briefly washed, if at all. If possible, leave stems, calyces and leaves on.

Salade d'Oranges

Orange Slices

An orange salad is a perfect conclusion to a Mediterranean meal. This Moroccan one is delicately scented.

Serves 6

8 oranges
4 tablespoons orange blossom water
1 tablespoon or more cinnamon

Peel the oranges and remove all the pith. Slice them thinly and lay them out on a large serving plate.

Sprinkle with orange blossom water and garnish with a dusting of cinnamon.

Bademli kayısı

Apricots Stuffed with Almond Paste

These fresh apricots stuffed with marzipan are usually poached in a sugar syrup, but it makes for a lighter delicacy to bake them as they are.

Serves 6

1 kg (2 lb) apricots
125 g (4 oz) ground almonds
125 g (4 oz) caster sugar
2–3 tablespoons orange blossom or rose water

Pre-heat the oven to 180°C (350°F, gas mark 4).

Make a slit in each apricot and remove the stone. Work the ground almonds, sugar and orange blossom or rose water to a firm paste with your hand. Take small portions, roll them into little balls and stuff the apricots. Lay in a shallow ovenproof dish, cover with foil and bake for 30 minutes.

Serve hot or cold.

Variation

If you want to try the apricots with syrup, boil 500 g (1 lb) sugar and 300 ml (10 fl oz) water with a squeeze of lemon until it is thick enough to coat a spoon. Add the apricots and cook very gently, being careful that the stuffing does not fall out.

An arrangement of fruits

Ensalada Levantina

Citrus, Almond and Honey Salad

This is a speciality of Alicante and of the nearby hills. A winter dessert, it is fragrant and lovely after a hot stew or a rice dish. It is usually accompanied by almond pastries and served with sweet muscatel wine. This dish is best made the day before so that the flavours have time to mingle.

Serves 6

6 oranges, peeled and thinly sliced
2 grapefruits, peeled and thinly sliced
Juice of ½–1 lemon
6 tablespoons clear honey
2 tablespoons orange blossom water
200 g (7 oz) blanched almonds

In a bowl arrange layers of orange and grapefruit slices. Sprinkle each layer with the lemon juice, honey and orange blossom water mixed together. Macerate for at least an hour and, if possible, overnight.

Toast the almonds under a grill, chop them coarsely and sprinkle over the salad just before serving.

Fraises au Châteauneuf-du-Pape

Strawberries in Wine

Pierre Hiély of Avignon makes a grand dessert by macerating strawberries in this blackish, gentle wine with its powerful scent of soft fruit. Another red wine will do, of course, but it will not be the same.

Serves 6

1 kg (2 lb) strawberries
5 tablespoons caster sugar or to taste
Châteauneuf-du-Pape or another red wine

Hull the strawberries, then rinse them briefly and drain well. Put them in a bowl, dredge with sugar and only just cover with the wine. Let them macerate, covered, in the refrigerator for about an hour. Serve in wine glasses.

Top: Preparation of tarte aux abricots (p. 194)
Left: Poires au vin
Right: Amandine (p. 202)

Poires au Vin

Pears in Wine

Comice pears turn a beautiful, deep, rich burgundy colour and become deliciously tender when they are cooked slowly in red wine.

Serves 6

6 large firm pears, peeled and left whole
A 75 cl bottle inexpensive dry red wine
125 g (4 oz) sugar or to taste
4 cloves
1 vanilla pod or 3 drops real vanilla essence

Put the pears in a pan with the remaining ingredients. Add water, if necessary, to cover the pears completely. Bring to the boil and simmer, uncovered, for about an hour until they are very tender but still hold their shape. Carefully lift them out and arrange in a bowl. Reduce the syrup further if necessary and pour over the pears. Serve cold.

Clafoutis

Fruit Flan

Clafoutis is the perfect dessert for the French Midi with its scattered orchards and great variety of fruit. Depending on the seasons and the *pays* (regions) different fruits are dropped into a creamy batter or, as in this recipe, an egg custard, and baked in the oven.

Serves 6

500 g (1 lb) cherries, plums, apricots, pears or a
  mixture of 2 or more of these
4 eggs
2 egg yolks
3 tablespoons sugar
600 ml (1 pint) milk
4 tablespoons kirsch or cognac, or a few drops of
  real vanilla essence
Icing sugar

Pre-heat the oven to 170°C (325°F, gas mark 3).

Peel pears, cut them in half and remove the cores. Halve plums and apricots and remove the stones. Leave cherries as they are. Spread in a buttered, shallow 30 cm (12 in) ovenproof dish.

Beat the eggs and yolks with the sugar, then beat in the milk and add the kirsch, cognac or vanilla. Pour over the fruit and bake for 45–60 minutes or until browned. Serve warm, sprinkled with sugar.

Tarte aux Abricots

Apricot Tart

Tarts, usually creamless, are made with every kind of fruit in the Midi region of France. This one, with fresh apricots and a peach sauce, is delectable.

Serves 6–8

For the pastry:
250 g (8 oz) flour
Pinch of salt
2 tablespoons caster sugar
125 g (4 oz) unsalted butter
2 egg yolks
2–4 tablespoons water or milk
A little egg white for the glaze

For the sauce:
5 peaches, peeled, halved and stoned
75 g (3 oz) sugar
Juice of 1 lemon
4 tablespoons kirsch

For the filling:
1.1 kg (2½ lb) ripe apricots, halved and stoned
3 tablespoons apricot jelly (optional)

Mix the flour with the salt and sugar in a bowl. Rub in the butter. Add the egg yolks and just enough water or milk to bind the dough, stirring with a knife and then, briefly, with your hands. Cover and leave in a cool place for an hour.

To make the sauce, put the peaches through a blender together with the sugar and lemon juice. Transfer the mixture to a saucepan and simmer over a low heat until it has reduced a little, then stir in the kirsch.

Pre-heat the oven to 200°C (400°F, gas mark 6). Roll the dough out on a floured board with a floured rolling pin. Gently lay the dough into a 30–35 cm (12–14 in) tart dish or flan tin and pat it into place, pressing it into any fluted sides. Trim the edges, prick with a fork and bake for 10 minutes. Take it out of the oven, brush with egg white to seal the crust and prevent it becoming soggy. Return to the oven for 5 minutes longer. Pour the sauce on the pastry, then arrange the apricots on the sauce, skin-side down, and bake for about 20 minutes or until they are tender. If you like, brush with an apricot glaze made by melting the jelly with a little water. Serve warm or cold.

Tarte aux abricots

Tourte de Blettes

Tourte de blettes is Nice's most celebrated sweet pastry. It is amusing and odd – but surprisingly pleasant. The filling for the short crust pastry is Swiss chard leaves or spinach with raisins, pine-nuts and apples, and eggs to bind it all. The basic recipe is sometimes embellished further with the local spirit marc, rum, redcurrant jelly or grated cheese.

Although usually a sweet pastry, it can also be served as an hors d'oeuvre.

Panade

Apple Tart

Mountains of grated apples make a fruity, soft and moist filling for this easy Provençal tart. Henri Fontin of Séguret provided the recipe.

Serves 6

Pastry as for the previous recipe

For the filling:
9–10 Golden Delicious apples
Juice of 2 lemons (optional)
1 tablespoon cinnamon
3–5 tablespoons caster sugar

Make the pastry and leave in a cool place for an hour. Pre-heat the oven to 230°C (450°F, gas mark 8). Roll the pastry out on a floured board with a floured rolling pin. Lay the dough gently into a 30–35 cm (12–14 in) tart dish or flan ring, reserving a little for decoration. Press the pastry into place and trim the edges.

Grate the apples, sprinkling them with lemon juice to stop them discolouring and to sharpen the flavour, and spread over the pastry. Sprinkle with cinnamon and, if you like, make a criss-cross pattern over the top with the remaining pastry. Bake for 45–60 minutes or until golden. Sprinkle the tart with sugar as it comes out of the oven. I like it best hot but you can also serve it cold.

Pommes au Riz Meringué

Apple with Rice Meringue

This homely Provençal dessert is usually made with russets or reinette apples, but bramleys are to me a better choice, their sharpness contrasting well with the sweet and creamy bed of rice.

Serves 10–12

For the apple and rice:
125 g (4 oz) short-grain rice
1.2 litres (2 pints) milk
Piece of vanilla pod or a few drops of real vanilla extract
150 g (5 oz) caster sugar
5 bramley apples, weighing about 1.1 kg ($2\frac{1}{2}$ lb), peeled and thinly sliced
2 teaspoons cinnamon

For the meringue:
4 large egg whites
175 g (6 oz) caster sugar

Pre-heat the oven to 150°C (300°F, gas mark 2). Simmer the rice in milk with the vanilla, uncovered, for about 15 minutes, then add 75 g (3 oz) sugar and cook until soft and creamy and the milk is almost absorbed. Remove the piece of vanilla pod and pour the rice and milk mixture into a large, round flat oven dish. Arrange the apple slices on top in layers, sprinkling each layer with cinnamon and sugar.

To make the meringue, whisk the egg whites until stiff. Sift half the caster sugar across the surface and lightly beat it in, retaining as much air as possible, then gradually and gently fold in the rest by hand.

Cover the apples with the meringue and bake for an hour, or until the apple slices feel tender when you cut into them with a pointed knife. Serve hot or cold.

Dessert Wines

Beaumes de Venise, from the village a few miles east of Orange, in the South of France, is a very special dessert wine, naturally sweet and full of perfume. A Mistela is a sweet Spanish wine from around Valencia and Alicante which will complement any dessert. Another is Moscato de Pantelleria, from the Italian island of the same name. All are equally good with fruit or with coffee after a meal.

Ayva Tatlisi

Baked Quince

I have travelled in Turkey when quinces were in season and I was insatiable for them. Wherever we stopped and however much we ate I found room for a quince dessert. There is no more perfumed fruit than the quince. From Egypt to Spain all kinds of compotes, jams and pastes are made with them, but they are at their best simply baked in foil. Make the most of them when they come into the shops in the autumn.

Serves 6

6 small or 3 large quinces
25–40 g (1–1½ oz) unsalted butter
About 250 g (8 oz) sugar or to taste
300 ml (10 fl oz) double cream, whipped, or
  strained yogurt (optional)
1 tablespoon rose water (optional)

Pre-heat the oven to 200°C (400°F, gas mark 6).

Wash the quinces well. Cut them in half along the core (they are very hard so use a large strong knife) and cut out the cores and seeds. Put each quince half, cut-side up, on a square of foil. Put a sliver of butter on each and cover with about 2 tablespoons of sugar or to taste – they are quite sharp and need plenty of sugar. Wrap them in the foil and place the parcels in a baking dish, still cut-side up. Bake for about an hour or until very tender. The time varies depending on their size and quality.

Serve this sweet hot or cold, topped, if you like, with the cream or yogurt. Either can be scented with a little rose water.

Arnadi de Carabassa

Pumpkin Dessert

This classic dish of Xativa in Valencia is found all around the region and is said to be very old and of Arab origin. It is made in the first cold days of autumn and right through the winter. I was told that it can be shaped like a pyramid but I found the mixture too soft and collapsible for that. Alicia Ríos gave me the recipe and it is the best pumpkin dessert I have eaten.

Serves 10

A piece of pumpkin weighing about 1.5 kg (3 lb)
2 eggs
Grated rind of ½ lemon
1 teaspoon cinnamon
250 g (8 oz) sugar or to taste
200 g (7 oz) ground almonds

Decoration:
50 g (2 oz) blanched almonds
2 tablespoons pine-nuts (optional)
Icing sugar
Cinnamon

Pre-heat the oven to 200°C (400°F, gas mark 6).

Cut the pumpkin into large pieces and scrape out the seeds and loose fibres. Place the pieces in a baking dish, cover with foil and bake for 20 minutes or until the pumpkin feels tender when you pierce it with the point of a knife. Cut away the skin and mash the flesh, then put it in a colander and squeeze out as much of the juice as you can. Lower the oven temperature to 150°C (300°F, gas mark 2).

Beat the eggs with the lemon rind, cinnamon and sugar and mix in the ground almonds. Add the mashed pumpkin and mix very well. Oil a large ovenproof dish and pour in the mixture. Bake for 1 hour or until it feels firm and the top is gently coloured.

Stick the almonds, pointing upwards, into the dessert. Scatter pine-nuts, if you like, over the top and dust with icing sugar and cinnamon. Serve cold.

Variation
Mix peeled, boiled chestnuts, cut into small pieces, into the mashed pumpkin.

Sunday market in San Feliù de Guixóls, Catalunya

Crema Catalana

Catalan Cream

This light aromatic cream is popular in the region of Catalunya in Spain. I had my first taste of it in the fishing village of San Feliú de Guíxols for breakfast in a café which caters for market stall-holders. I was served it again as a delicate dessert at the end of a grand meal of Spanish *nouvelle cuisine*.

Serves 6

1 litre (1¾ pints) milk
1 vanilla pod and/or 1 cinnamon stick
Peel of 1 lemon
8 egg yolks
200 g (7 oz) sugar
3 tablespoons cornflour

Bring the milk to the boil with the vanilla and/or cinnamon stick and lemon peel and simmer, uncovered, for 5–10 minutes. Then let it rest for a few minutes while the flavours infuse.

Beat the yolks with 125 g (4 oz) of the sugar and all the cornflour until pale and creamy. Remove the vanilla pod and/or cinnamon and lemon peel from the milk and beat a ladleful into the egg mixture. Then pour the egg mixture into the milk, beating well. Cook slowly over a low heat, stirring vigorously, for 5–10 minutes or until it turns gradually into a thick custard. Be careful that it does not boil or it will curdle. Pour into a shallow earthenware dish or individual heatproof bowls and refrigerate.

When you are ready to serve, sprinkle the rest of the sugar evenly over the top of the cream and put under a hot grill for a minute or so until the sugar is brown and caramelised. (In Spain they run a sizzling hot branding iron over the sugar to do this.) It will form a brittle crust when it cools.

Zabaglione

This Italian sweet is one of my favourites. Serve it hot or cold in wine glasses. It is so rich that you only need a little for each serving.

Serves 6

8 large egg yolks
75–125 g (3–4 oz) sugar
250 ml (8 fl oz) Marsala

Beat the egg yolks with the sugar until they are pale, then beat in the Marsala. Pour into a large saucepan and heat gently by standing the pan in a larger pan of barely simmering water. Beat constantly – an electric beater is a help – until the mixture swells to a thick foam. Ladle into warm glasses and serve at once, or refrigerate.

Variation
Add 2–3 drops of vanilla essence or a little grated orange or lemon peel.

Mel i Mato

Ricotta with Honey and Pine-nuts

This is a simple Spanish sweet that is usually made with a bland Spanish cheese called *requeson*. Ricotta is a good substitute.

Shape a mound of about 100 g (3½ oz) ricotta on each person's plate. Dribble 2 tablespoons or more of clear honey on top and sprinkle with toasted pine-nuts.

Mel i mato

Bademli Muhallebi

Milk Pudding with Almonds

Neşet Eren made this milk pudding and served it in her Istanbul apartment with the first crop of strawberries in May. You can use ready-ground almonds but grinding or chopping them yourself gives a more attractive texture.

Serves 6

1.2 litres (2 pints) milk
75 g (3 oz) sugar
Pinch of salt
2 tablespoons cornflour
2 tablespoons ground rice
75 g (3 oz) blanched almonds
1 teaspoon almond essence

Bring the milk slowly to the boil with the sugar and salt. Mix the cornflour and ground rice to a paste with about 4 tablespoons of water and pour the paste into the milk, stirring constantly to avoid lumps forming, until the mixture thickens. Then leave for about 30 minutes, stirring occasionally, on the lowest possible heat.

Grind the almonds or chop them very finely in a food processor and stir them into the liquid. Cook to a thick consistency for another 15 minutes. Stir in the almond essence and pour into a serving bowl or individual bowls. Serve chilled.

Variations
* Add 1–2 tablespoons of rose water or orange blossom water or a mixture of the two instead of the almond essence.
* You may like to brown the top under the grill, in which case use heatproof bowls.

Roz bi Halib

Rice Pudding

There are all kinds of rice puddings in the Mediterranean made with whole or ground rice. A faint touch of mastic (see p. 51) and orange blossom water gives this one an Arab flavour.

Serves 6–8

75 g (3 oz) short-grain rice
1.5 litres (2½ pints) milk
75 g (3 oz) sugar or more to taste
3 tablespoons honey
3 tablespoons rose or orange blossom water
2 small grains of mastic, pulverised
2 tablespoons pistachio nuts, finely chopped
75 g (3 oz) pistachio nuts, almonds or hazelnuts, toasted and finely chopped

Boil the rice in plenty of water for 4–5 minutes, then drain. Bring the milk to the boil in a large saucepan, add the rice and simmer, stirring often, over a very gentle heat for about 45 minutes or until the milk is almost absorbed and the mixture is creamy.

Add sugar, honey, rose or orange blossom water and mastic. Mastic is very strong so you must only use very little and it must be very finely pulverised with a pestle and mortar. Simmer for about 5 minutes longer, check for sweetness and pour into a serving bowl. Sprinkle with the chopped nuts – in a pattern if you like. Serve hot or cold.

Om Ali

Milk and Pastry Pudding

This creamy Egyptian dessert whose name means 'mother of Ali' is very rich. When I asked a friend if the pudding could be made lighter by omitting butter or cream he said with a disgusted look that some people did so but that he would spit it out! This recipe is a compromise; instead of frying the pastry in plenty of butter it is baked with only a little.

Serves 6

5 sheets of filo (see p. 45) weighing 100 g (3½ oz)
1½ tablespoons butter, melted
150 g (5 oz) mixed nuts, such as pistachios, almonds, hazelnuts and walnuts, coarsely chopped
50 g (2 oz) raisins
1 litre (1¾ pints) milk
4 tablespoons sugar or to taste
300 ml (10 fl oz) double cream

Pre-heat the oven to 240°C (475°F, gas mark 9).

Brush the sheets of filo with butter and bake them on separate shelves or loosely, one on top of the other, for 3 or 4 minutes or until they are crisp and very slightly golden. Lower the heat to 180°C (350°F, gas mark 4). Break the filo into pieces and place in a baking dish or individual ovenproof bowls with the nuts and raisins. Heat the milk with the sugar and add the cream, then pour over the filo and nut mixture. Bake for 20–30 minutes or until browned. Serve hot.

Dolci Siciliani

Weddings are more important in Sicily than anywhere else. It seems that every other shop sells either sugared almonds or wedding dresses. And women are forever embroidering and crocheting for a trousseau.

A hotel where I once stayed near Palermo had banqueting rooms which were given over to weddings four times a week. Part of the ritual was an incredibly elaborate wedding cake made out of plaster and sporting angels and colonnades. On each occasion it was wheeled in to thunderous applause, then wheeled back to the kitchen where acres of frosted sponge, cut up into hundreds of small squares, replaced the cake on the trolley for a second triumphal *entrée*. The sponge was distributed at the same time as *pasta reale* – brightly coloured marzipan flavoured with brandy or lemon juice and shaped into miniature fruits, flowers and animals; *frutta candita* – fruit candied in a way that magically preserves their real flavour; and *cannoli* – crisp, brown, cigar-like tubes stuffed with scented ricotta and the same finely chopped crystallised fruit. I did not try to obtain the recipes for these as they are sold by specialist pastry-makers who usually are not willing to reveal their secrets.

Granita all' Arancia

Orange Water Ice

With the export of Italian ice cream parlours and vendors' carts, *cassata*, *gelato* and *granita* ices have become well known all over the world.

Orange water ice is ideal after a meal, and now that you can buy freshly squeezed orange juice at the supermarket it is extremely easy to make. Make it a day in advance.

Serves 6

1 lemon
450 ml (15 fl oz) water
250 g (8 oz) sugar
700 ml (1¼ pints) fresh orange juice (or the juice of 7 oranges)
2 tablespoons orange liqueur

Pare the peel of the lemon finely and put it to boil with the water and sugar for 10 minutes. Take out the peel and let the syrup cool, then stir in the orange juice, juice of the lemon and the liqueur. Pour into a freezer tray, cover and freeze for several hours until set to a frozen slush. Blend in a blender or food processor to break up the ice into finer particles and return to the freezer to set. Take out 10 minutes before you are ready to serve.

Top: Frullati di frutta (p. 207)
Centre: Cassata siciliana (p. 200)
Bottom: Granita all'arancia

Cassata Siciliana

Sicilian Cheese Cake

This speciality of Palermo is not the famous ice cream of the same name but a rum-flavoured sponge and ricotta cake. This party dish is extremely rich and a little goes a long way.

Serves 20

1 kg (2 lb) unsalted ricotta
100 g (3½ oz) icing sugar or to taste
4 drops of vanilla, or 1 teaspoon grated orange or lemon zest
100 g (3½ oz) bitter chocolate, grated
300 g (10 oz) mixed candied fruit, including if possible pumpkin and orange peel, chopped small
300 g (10 oz) sponge fingers or slices of sponge cake
175 ml (6 fl oz) rum or to taste

Beat the ricotta with about 65 g (2½ oz) of the sugar and the vanilla or zest, then fold in the chocolate and candied fruit, leaving a few tablespoons to use as decoration.

Line a 25 cm (10 in) cake tin or mould with cling-film so that you can turn the cake out easily. Dip the sponge fingers or cake in rum for a few seconds, just enough to slightly moisten and soften them, and use them to line the bottom and sides of the tin or mould. Spread the ricotta mixture evenly inside and cover with the rest of the sponge fingers dipped in rum. Cover with a piece of cling-film and press down hard. Put in the refrigerator for at least 1 hour to become firm. When you are ready to serve, remove the cling-film cover, then turn the cake out upside down, and remove the rest of the cling-film. Sprinkle the cake with icing sugar and decorate with the remaining chopped fruit.

Diplomatico

Chocolate Cream Cake

I discovered this cake many years ago in Italy. It looks complicated but is extremely easy and can also be put in the freezer and served as a *semi-freddo*, a type of ice-cream cake.

Serves 16

400 ml (14 fl oz) double cream
400 g (14 oz) good quality bitter chocolate
400 g (14 oz) sponge fingers
600 ml (1 pint) cooled espresso or very strong black coffee
5 tablespoons rum

Beat the double cream until thick. Melt the chocolate in a bowl over a pan of hot water and let it cool a little, then beat it into the cream. Use a cake tin with a detachable bottom or line an ordinary tin with foil or cling-film, so that the cake can be lifted out easily. Mix the coffee and rum together and dip the sponge fingers into the mixture for a few seconds, so that they are moist but not soggy. Line the bottom of the tin with the fingers. Spread a layer of cream on top and repeat with 2 more alternating layers of sponge and cream. Serve chilled or frozen. It defrosts in a few minutes.

Konafa maker in Alexandria

Konafa bi Jibn

Konafa with Cheese

This Arab version of the pastry known as *kadaif* in Greece and Turkey makes one of the best Arab desserts. Eat it hot from the oven, first pouring the cold syrup through the crisp sizzling pastry into the bland cream cheese. Forget the ubiquitous commercial pastries of the same name and make your own – an entirely different experience.

Serves 10 or more

500 g (1 lb) konafa (also called kadaif) (see p. 45)
250 g (8 oz) unsalted butter, melted
1 kg (2 lb) unsalted ricotta

For the syrup:
500 g (1 lb) sugar
300 ml (10 fl oz) water
1 tablespoon lemon juice
2 tablespoons orange blossom or rose water or both

Decoration:
75 g (3 oz) pistachio nuts, finely chopped

Konafa bi jibn

Pre-heat the oven to 180°C (350°F, gas mark 4).

Put the raw konafa in a large bowl, then pour the melted and slightly cooled butter over it. Pull out and separate the strands and mix them well with your hands so that they do not stick together and are all thoroughly coated with butter.

Spread half the pastry out evenly in the bottom of a large round tray or ovenproof dish, crumble the ricotta evenly over it and cover with a layer of the remaining pastry. Press down firmly with your hands so that it all holds together compactly. Bake for 45 minutes then turn up the oven to 230°C (450°F, gas mark 8) and bake for 15 minutes longer or until it is a light golden colour.

Prepare the syrup as soon as you put the pastry in the oven so that it has time to cool. Boil the sugar and water with the lemon juice for about 15 minutes or until it is thick enough to coat a spoon, then add the orange blossom or rose water, and simmer for 30 seconds longer. Let it cool, then put in the refrigerator to chill.

When the pastry is cooked, immediately cut around it using a sharp knife and turn it out onto a large round serving plate. Pour over the syrup and sprinkle with pistachios. You can also serve it from the tray and you can use less syrup – even half the quantity if you prefer. Serve warm.

Variations

* *Konafa bil loz* (konafa with nuts) should be eaten cold and is more of a pastry than a dessert. Instead of ricotta use: 1 kg (2 lb) ground or finely chopped walnuts, mixed with 2 tablespoons cinnamon and 3 tablespoons sugar; or 1 kg (2 lb) minced or very finely chopped almonds mixed with 2 teaspoons ground cardamom; or 1 kg (2 lb) minced or finely chopped pistachio nuts.

* *Konafa bil eishta* (konafa with cream) has a soft creamy filling made with 1.2 litres (2 pints) of milk. It should be eaten hot. Mix 3 tablespoons ground rice and 3 tablespoons cornflower with a little of the milk into a paste, then bring the rest of the milk to the boil in a pan with 4 tablespoons sugar. Beat some of it into the paste and pour this back into the pan. Let it simmer, stirring constantly, so that lumps do not form. (If they do, put the liquid through the blender.) Be careful not to let the mixture burn and continue stirring for 10–15 minutes or until it thickens. Stir in 150 ml (5 fl oz) double cream.

Tarta de Naranja

Orange and Almond Cake

This moist almond cake bathed in orange-flavoured syrup is more of a dessert than a pastry and it is best eaten the day after it is made. The recipe comes from our Spanish travel companion Maria José Sevilla Taylor.

Serves 6–8

4 eggs, separated
125 g (4 oz) sugar
Grated zest of 1 orange
50 g (2 oz) ground almonds
50 g (2 oz) blanched almonds, finely chopped

For the syrup:
Juice of 3 oranges (about 300 ml/10 fl oz)
75 g (3 oz) sugar
1 cinnamon stick
1 tablespoon orange liqueur

Pre-heat the oven to 180°C (350°F, gas mark 4).

Mix the egg yolks with the sugar, orange zest and all the almonds. Beat the egg whites until stiff and fold them in. Pour the mixture into a greased and floured 20 cm (8 in) non-stick cake tin or one with removable sides or bottom and bake for 45 minutes. Let it cool, then transfer to a serving plate.

To make the syrup, simmer the orange juice with the sugar and cinnamon for a few minutes until the sugar has melted, and add the liqueur. Pour over the cake after piercing the top with little holes so that the syrup seeps in. It will take some time for the cake to become well impregnated. Leave the cinnamon stick on top for decoration.

Amandine

Almond and Pine-nut Pastry

This recipe is from Jean Testanière, a baker from the village of Lumière in Provence. Ground almonds make it a very rich confection which keeps well for several days.

Serves 10–12

6 eggs
500 g (1 lb) ground almonds
500 g (1 lb) caster sugar
200 ml (7 fl oz) milk
5 drops of real vanilla essence
50 g (2 oz) pine-nuts
150 ml (5 fl oz) apricot jelly to glaze (optional)

Pre-heat the oven to 180°C (350°F, gas mark 4).

Combine all the ingredients, except the pine-nuts and jelly. Line a large, shallow baking tin or pie dish with foil. Butter the foil and pour in the mixture. Sprinkle the pine-nuts on top and bake for $1\frac{1}{4}$–$1\frac{1}{2}$ hours or until the top is brown and the pastry feels firm. While it is still warm, if you wish, melt the jelly with a little water, then brush it over the top.

Buñuelos de San Feliú

Little doughnut-like fritters called *buñuelos* have crossed the borders of Andalusia and are made all over Spain. They also went all the way to Egypt with the Jews who fled the Inquisition in the 14th century and I know them as a speciality of Jewish Hannukah. So it was particularly exciting for me to see them being made at the Patisseria del Puig in San Feliú de Guíxols, up the coast from Barcelona. After showing us puff, choux and sponge pastries filled with pumpkin purée and pine-nuts, and all kinds of lemon creams, egg flans and almond pastes, the owner made an aniseed-flavoured yeast dough with egg, butter and wine. He let it rise, shaped it into rounds, pushed his thumb through the middle, then threw the rings into bubbling oil. We watched them puff up and turn brown, then ate them with a dusting of icing sugar while they were still burning hot.

Baklawa

Baklawa is the most popular pastry of the eastern Mediterranean. You will find it everywhere made with a variety of nut fillings depending on what grows locally.

500 g (1 lb) filo pastry (see p. 45)
350 g (12 oz) unsalted butter, melted
750 (1½ lb) blanched almonds, pistachios or
  walnuts, finely chopped or ground

For the syrup:
500 g (1 lb) sugar
A squeeze of lemon juice
2 tablespoons rose water

Make the syrup first because you must give it time to cool. Boil the sugar and 300 ml (10 fl oz) water with the lemon juice, uncovered, for about 10 minutes. Then add the rose water and cook for a few seconds longer. Let it cool, then put it in the refrigerator.

Pre-heat the oven to 180°C (350°F, gas mark 4). Brush a large rectangular roasting tin – a little smaller than the size of the sheets of filo – with butter. Lay half the sheets carefully in the tin, one on top of another, brushing melted butter between each sheet and folding them up around the edges. Spread the nuts on top and cover with the rest of the filo, brushing each sheet, including the top one, with melted butter. Trim the edges if necessary.

Using a sharp knife, cut the pastry into parallel lines about 3.5 cm (1½ in) apart and then again diagonally to form lozenges, making sure that you have cut the pastry right through to the bottom. Bake for 25 minutes, then reduce the heat to 150°C (300°F, gas mark 2) and bake for 25 minutes longer or until crisp and golden.

Take the baklawa out of the oven and pour the syrup evenly all over. Cool, then cut over the same lines again, using a sharp knife, before serving.

Variations

* Use only half the amount of syrup given for a less sugary taste.
* You can add 2 teaspoons of cinnamon to a walnut filling and the seeds of 2 cardamom pods to an almond one.

Karythopitta tis Maritsas

Maritsa's Walnut Cake

This nutty Greek cake given by Sue Tassios can be served on its own or, as here, turned into a syrupy dessert.

Serves 12

100 g (3½ oz) plain flour
1 teaspoon baking powder
Pinch of salt
350 g (12 oz) walnuts, chopped
6 eggs, separated
350 g (12 oz) caster sugar
1 teaspoon vanilla essence

For the syrup:
500 g (1 lb) sugar
600 ml (1 pint) water
1 teaspoon cinnamon

Pre-heat the oven to 180°C (350°F, gas mark 4).

Mix the flour, baking powder, salt and walnuts. Beat the egg yolks with 150 g (5 oz) of the caster sugar until pale, thick and creamy, then stir into the walnut mixture. Add the vanilla essence and stir well. Beat the egg whites until they stand in firm frothy peaks. Pour the remaining sugar on the surface of the whites, a little at a time, and beat it in, retaining as much air as possible, until the mixture is shiny. Add a little of the whites to the walnut mixture to loosen it before folding the rest gently into the egg and sugar mixture.

Pour into a greased and floured cake tin about 28 cm (11 in) in diameter and bake for 45–50 minutes, or until it is firm to the touch. Meanwhile make the syrup. Simmer the sugar and water with cinnamon for about 10 minutes. When the cake is done, pour the syrup over the cake and make little holes in the top so that the syrup can seep in. Serve when cooled.

Tarta de naranja (opposite)

Kaab el Ghzal

Gazelle's Horns

The most popular Moroccan pastries are best known abroad by their French name *cornes de gazelles*. They are stuffed with ground almond paste and curved into horn-shaped crescents.

Kaab el ghzal were prepared for a wedding party at the Villa Slaoui. The wedding went on for a week with a series of ceremonies and receptions for the women at the bride's home, and receptions for the men on a grander scale at the groom's house.

The horns were served at the pre-nuptial ceremony when the women's hands were hennaed. Salty and sweet briouates (p. 91), ghoriba (right) and cake-like bread rings called *fkakes* were also served as guests arrived. Eating and dancing continued until the early hours of the following day when the bride was finally taken to her husband.

Makes about 16

For the filling:
200 g (7 oz) ground almonds
100 g (3½ oz) caster sugar
½ teaspoon cinnamon
3 tablespoons orange blossom water

For the pastry:
200 g (7 oz) flour
Pinch of salt
2 tablespoons sunflower oil
Scant 175 ml (6 fl oz) orange blossom water

Icing sugar for dusting

Pre-heat the oven to 180°C (350°F, gas mark 4).

Mix the ground almonds, sugar, cinnamon and orange blossom water and knead with your hands into a stiff paste. It will seem dry at first but will soon stick well together as the almonds give out their oil.

To make the pastry, mix the flour and salt with the oil and add just enough orange blossom water to

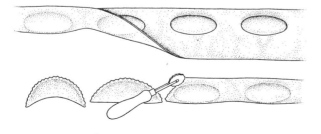

make it hold together in a soft dough. Knead vigorously for about 15 minutes until the dough is smooth and elastic. Roll the dough out with a floured rolling pin as thinly as possible on a floured board and cut into long strips about 8 cm (3 in) wide.

Take lumps of the almond paste filling about the size of a large walnut and roll them into thin sausages about 8 cm (3 in) long and with tapering ends. Place them end to end in a row along one side of each strip of pastry about 3 cm (1¼ in) apart. Wet the pastry edges slightly with water, then fold the pastry over to cover the almond paste and press the edges together to enclose the 'sausages' completely (see illustration).

Cut round the 'sausages' with a pastry wheel or a sharp knife and pinch the edges firmly together. Curve the pastries gently into crescent or horn shapes. Prick the tops with a fork or make a design with a sharp knife. Put the pastries on a greased baking tray and bake for about 20–25 minutes or until lightly coloured. Let them cool, then dust with icing sugar.

Ghoriba

Almond Biscuits

These cracked-looking biscuits of marzipan bound with egg are very popular in Morocco.

Makes about 30

2 small eggs
200 g (7 oz) icing sugar plus a little more to garnish
2 teaspoons baking powder
Grated rind of ½ lemon
A few drops of vanilla essence
400 g (14 oz) ground almonds

Pre-heat the oven to 180°C (350°F, gas mark 4).

Hold back half the white from one egg – and you can add extra later if necessary. Beat the sugar and eggs well together. Add the baking powder, grated lemon rind, vanilla and almonds and mix well. Knead well with your hands until it becomes a soft, moist, workable paste.

Wash your hands and oil them. Take lumps of paste the size of a small walnut, roll into egg-shaped balls and flatten on a plate covered with icing sugar. Place on oiled baking trays about 3 cm (1½ in) apart. Bake for 15 minutes until golden.

Sweetmeats

In very little time you can make up an elegant plate of different coloured and delicately perfumed Arab sweetmeats with almond, apricot and date pastes.

For the almond drops
Mix 100 g (3½ oz) ground almonds with the same weight of caster sugar and work into a stiff dryish paste with 2–4 tablespoons orange blossom or rose water. Shape into small balls the size of a large marble and roll in icing sugar. Stick a split almond on the top of each.

For the apricot drops
Put 250 g (8 oz) of the sharp, brownish dried apricots in a food processor. The pale, sweet and moist kind more commonly available will not have the right flavour. Add a little water at a time by the tablespoon and blend to a firm paste adding about 2 tablespoons icing sugar, or to taste. Shape into small balls and roll in icing sugar. Stick half a pistachio on top of each.

For the date drops
Put 250 g (8 oz) pitted dried dates in a food processor and, adding water by the tablespoon, blend into a stiff paste with 1 teaspoon cinnamon and ½ teaspoon ground cardamom. Using your hands, work in 100 g (3½ oz) of coarsely chopped walnuts, shape into little balls and roll in icing sugar.

Left: Karythopitta tis Maritsas (p. 203)
Right: A plate of sweetmeats

Drinks

T HE MEDITERRANEAN is wine country and some of the greatest wines of the world come from here. Spirits – in particular, anis-flavoured spirits – distilled from grapes are widely taken as aperitifs. In the eastern Mediterranean they are also often drunk throughout the meal, while beer is especially appreciated for open-air eating and charcoal-grilled food.

Naturally, non-alcoholic drinks are important in hot countries and particularly so in Islamic countries where alcohol is forbidden. All kinds of fresh fruit juices, syrups and infusions are popular, as are sweet tea, strong black coffee and yogurt diluted with water.

Above: Drinking tea in Cairo

Tisanes

Infusions of fresh or dried leaves, flowers or roots are drunk for their soothing and medicinal properties as well as their fragrance and refreshing qualities. Mint leaves, camomile flower heads, lime blossom, lemon balm leaves, boldo, rose hips and petals, sage leaves, thyme leaves, orange petals, lime flowers, vervain, lemon verbena leaves, karkade (hibiscus) leaves and raspberry leaves are popular. You can mix them if you like.

Make *tisanes* in a teapot in the same way you make tea, warming the pot and pouring on boiling water, but let it infuse for about 10 minutes. Sweeten, if you like, with sugar or honey and put a slice of lemon or lime in the cup.

Etzai

Mint Tea

The popular drink of Morocco is made with green China tea and fresh spearmint. It is very light and very sweet. Serving it is a traditional ritual of hospitality, and the equipment – silver teapot, sugar bowl and tray with ornately painted glasses and tea table and samovar – can be quite magnificent. To prepare mint tea in the ritual manner warm a 900 ml ($1\frac{1}{2}$ pint) teapot and put in $1\frac{1}{2}$ tablespoons of green tea. Pour in a glassful of boiling water and immediately pour it out to wash the leaves. Add 3 tablespoons of sugar or to taste and a handful of fresh mint leaves. Pour in boiling water from a height of 30 cm (12 in) in order to catch some oxygen, mix well and serve very hot, pouring out from the same height.

Orange blossom and rose petals or a piece of tangerine peel may be added for extra fragrance.

Frullati di Frutta

Fresh Fruit Crush

My aunt who lives in Italy started my son on bananas and orange juice blended with yogurt when he was three weeks old. As my children grew up I added crushed ice to all kinds of fruit concoctions and turned them into sweets.

Try using such fruits as cantaloupe and honeydew melon, watermelon, banana, apricot, peach, strawberry, raspberry, pear, apple, plum and even mango and date. You can use one kind of fruit alone or a mixture.

Peel or wash and pit the fruit as necessary and put them in a blender together with plenty of ice and a little fruit liqueur or spirit. Add sugar if you wish and process for a short time until the fruit is well blended and the ice is crushed. The mixture should not be mushy. Serve at once.

Another way of making a *frullato* is with added milk or yogurt and no liqueur. This turns it into more of a drink.

Ayran

Yogurt Drink

This popular and wonderfully refreshing drink is sold both in restaurants and in the street in Turkey and Lebanon. You can make it up easily in a glass. Fill it $\frac{1}{3}$ with yogurt and beat in ice-cold water or soda water. Add a little salt if you like. A usual embellishment is a sprig of fresh mint which lends a delicate aroma and you can drop in a cube of ice.

Top: Etzai
Centre: Salade d'oranges (p. 194)
Bottom: Ghoriba (p. 204)

Horchata

Tiger Nut Milk

I knew almond milk as a child in Egypt, but this tiger nut drink I had in Valencia was a surprise. It is a lovely refreshing drink with an unusual taste. You can buy the nuts at health food shops.

Makes 4

250 g (8 oz) tiger nuts
About 1 litre (1¾ pints) iced water
50 g (2 oz) sugar or to taste

Wash the tiger nuts, then soak them in fresh water for 12 hours. Rinse and drain, then put them in a blender with some, but not all of the measured water, so that you start with a very thick drink and then dilute it to taste. Strain and add as much sugar and water as you like. Serve chilled.

Kahve

Turkish Coffee

Black coffee is boiled up in long-handled pots in a large part of the Mediterranean. A certain mystique surrounds the process, which varies a little from one country to another. This is the way it is made in Turkey where the pot is called a *jezve*. You can use any medium or dark roast coffee beans but they must be ground to a fine powder.

Serves 1

1 heaped teaspoon pulverised coffee
1 teaspoon sugar or to taste

Put the coffee, sugar and a small coffee cup of water in a pot. Heat, stirring, and when the coffee starts to rise – it should not actually boil – remove from the heat immediately. Give a quick stir, bring just to the boil again and pour into the cup.

If you make several cups of coffee at once, it is a good idea to share the froth among the cups, skimming it off after the first boil. Capturing the elusive froth is an important part of coffee making.

Variation
Lebanese and Egyptians sometimes drop a cardamom pod in the pot at the start.

Chocolate

Chocolate Drink

Spanish hot chocolate made with melted chocolate pieces is incredibly rich and luxurious. It is drunk at breakfast accompanied by sweet deep-fried fritters called *churros*.

Makes 4 small or 2 large cups

150 g (5 oz) plain dark chocolate
600 ml (1 pint) milk

Break the chocolate into the top of a double boiler or a saucepan placed in a pan of boiling water so that the chocolate melts without burning. Bring the milk to the boil in another pan, then pour it into the melted chocolate, a little at a time, beating vigorously. Put the pan of chocolate directly over the heat and whisk until it becomes smooth and frothy. With plain chocolate you should not need any sugar. Serve very hot.

Sangria

Red Wine Punch

This is a refreshing Spanish drink to serve in the summer.

Serves 8–10

2 ×75 cl bottles of red wine
Juice of 1 orange
1–2 tablespoons sugar
2–3 tablespoons cognac (optional)
1 lemon, thinly sliced
1 apple, sliced
1 peach, sliced
½ bottle or more of soda water or fizzy lemon
A few ice cubes

Pour the wine into a large jug and add the orange juice, sugar, cognac, lemon, apple and peach. Cover and leave to macerate for at least 2 hours. Before serving, add the soda water or lemonade and ice cubes.

Sauces and Basics

IN TURKEY I asked a few people how they would describe their cooking. Comparing it to French cuisine, they replied that they had no sauces and in fact this could be said of the entire Mediterranean. Sauces are not prepared separately to pour over a dish but come as a result of it, like the liquor in a stew. A broth is thickened with egg yolk beaten with lemon or with breadcrumbs, ground almonds or walnuts. Mashed chicken livers are used to thicken the sauce in chicken dishes. Meat juices are enhanced with boiled or roasted garlic mashed in with a fork or with a spirit added in at the end.

The exception is the all-pervading tomato sauce. It was born in Spain where it is called *sofrito* and it is one of the chief sauces which defines Catalan cooking. It usually comes in at the start, then other ingredients are added, but it can also be the final touch to a dish. Another great Catalan sauce is the famous *picada*, an almond and garlic paste which is worked in at the last stage of a stew. (Catalans like nothing more than to do a dish in stages.) They take out the pestle and mortar and pound away with passion at the toasted almonds, fried bread and garlic until it is a very smooth paste, then they beat in a little liquid from the stew and stir the *picada* into the sauce. Occasionally pine-nuts or hazelnuts are used instead of almonds.

Otherwise Mediterranean sauces are cold sauces such as versions of mayonnaise with garlic or herbs or of vinaigrette, sometimes enlivened with tiny bits of chopped olives, raw vegetables and pickles. In the eastern Mediterranean, yogurt as it is or scented with a touch of garlic and mint or dill, is poured over all kinds of things like vegetables, omelettes, rice and kebabs. There are many North African relishes based on the Catalan *romesco* theme of puréed tomatoes and peppers, and as many Greek, Arab and Ottoman sauces based on the *tarator* theme of mashed nuts or bread beaten into a cream with olive oil. Put these cold sauces on the table in a bowl for dipping into or for spreading on bread.

Gathering herbs on Paros

Salsa Verde

Sicilian Green Sauce

This Sicilian sauce has all kinds of optional ingredients such as capers, anchovies and mustard, but the simplest version is the best for pasta. It is a very good alternative to pesto sauce (see p. 186). Large quantities can be made and kept in a jar.

Pound or blend equal quantities of basil, parsley and mint with enough olive oil to make a fluid paste, adding salt and pepper and a few crushed garlic cloves. Pour into a jar, add a little olive oil to seal and cover with a lid.

Serve with pasta adding grated pecorino or Parmesan.

Salsa Verde Agrodolce

Sweet and Sour Green Sauce

Vary the quantities of the ingredients of this sauce according to your taste. It is excellent spread on toasted bread to make a strongly flavoured bruschetta (see p. 62). It is also good served with cold meat, fish or boiled vegetables.

3 tablespoons mixed herbs, such as basil, mint and parsley, chopped
1 slice of white bread, weighing about 25 g (1 oz), crusts removed
3 tablespoons wine vinegar
1 tablespoon sugar
3 anchovy fillets (optional)
4 tablespoons or more olive oil
Salt and pepper

Blend all the ingredients together.

Vinaigrette

There is a Provençal saying that you need four people to make an oil and vinegar dressing: a miser for the vinegar, a wise man to add salt and pepper, a spendthrift to pour on the olive oil and a madman to beat them together.

Throughout the Mediterranean the conventional ratio of 1 tablespoon of vinegar to 3 of oil is not usually respected. There is always less vinegar and often none at all, so that the good olive oil which is kept for salads can be properly savoured. Lemon juice is frequently used instead of vinegar.

Chopped onions or crushed garlic and plenty of chopped fresh herbs are frequent ingredients added to vinaigrette. In Provence a few de-salted anchovies are often mashed with the garlic.

Salsa Romesco

Pepper Sauce

Romesco – I love the name – is one of the great
Catalan sauces. The name comes from the mildly
hot, medium-sized dried red peppers which are
used. The sauce was originally a fish stew which
evolved into an accompaniment to fish and
seafood and is now served with many different
dishes including salad and boiled vegetables.
Although it is so common that you find it on almost
every table in Catalunya, it was the most difficult
recipe to obtain because everyone was so secretive
about it. One imagines that they improvise every
time they make it. This one is fresh and light
because the ingredients are roasted rather than fried.
You will not find the romesco peppers easily but
you can substitute a combination of chilli peppers
and fresh red pepper instead.

**2 dried romesco peppers, or 1 small hot red chilli
 pepper, soaked in cold water, and 2 fresh red
 peppers**
250 g (8 oz) ripe tomatoes
3 large garlic cloves, unpeeled
50 g (2 oz) blanched, peeled almonds or hazelnuts
3 tablespoons wine vinegar
300 ml (10 fl oz) olive oil
Salt and pepper

De-seed the romesco peppers, if using, and soak them
in water for 30 minutes. Put the fresh red peppers,
tomatoes, garlic and almonds or hazelnuts in a hot –
240°C (475°F, gas mark 9) – oven. Watch them carefully and remove as soon as each is done – the almonds
when they are lightly brown, the tomatoes and garlic
when they are soft, and the peppers when they are
brown and soft. (Peppers take about 30 minutes.) Peel
the peppers, tomatoes and garlic. Pound the nuts and
garlic to a paste in a mortar or put them through a
food processor. Then add the drained romesco peppers
or the roasted red pepper and the soaked chilli pepper
and tomatoes and blend well. Gradually beat in the
vinegar and oil and season with salt and pepper.

Variation
A toasted slice of white bread, crusts removed, can be
used with half the quantity of nuts.

Mayonnaise

The secret of successful mayonnaise lies in having
all the ingredients and the bowl at room temperature and in stirring in the oil very gradually.

2 egg yolks
**1½ tablespoons or more white wine vinegar or
 lemon juice**
Salt
Pinch of white pepper
300 ml (10 fl oz) olive oil

In a warm bowl, using a wooden spoon or a whisk,
beat the egg yolks until they are pale, thick and sticky.
Add a drop of vinegar or lemon juice and a little salt
and pepper, then add the olive oil, first drop by drop,
then in a thin stream, stirring vigorously all the time.
As the oil becomes absorbed the sauce will thicken to a
heavy, creamy consistency. If it becomes too firm, add
a little more vinegar or lemon juice or a tablespoon
of warm water to prevent it separating. (If the mayonnaise separates, it can be saved by starting again with
a new yolk and using the sauce as if it were the oil.) I
enjoy making it by hand but a blender or food processor will do the work very quickly. Simply blend
the yolks with the salt, then add the oil in a thin stream
while the blades are running. Add the lemon juice,
then taste and adjust the seasonings.

Variations
* For a green mayonnaise, add plenty of finely
chopped fresh herbs, such as chives, chervil, basil,
parsley, tarragon and watercress.
* For a good sauce for fish, mix in 3 or 4 mashed
anchovies or the red eggs of sea urchins, beaten.
* For *rouille*, the fiery mayonnaise served with soupe
de poisson (p. 126) and bouillabaisse (p. 132) add 3
crushed garlic cloves, 1–2 teaspoons paprika, cayenne
to taste and, if you like, 1–2 tablespoons tomato paste
or ½ teaspoon saffron-coloured powder (see p. 52).

Sylva Gauthier's Grande Aïoli

Every Provençal village holds a yearly festival, a *fête de la grande aïoli*. At this celebration the aïoli sauce is served with great quantities of boiled salt cod, hard-boiled eggs and a huge assortment of seasonal boiled vegetables.

Sylva Gauthier, who cooks at a *maternelle* (nursery school) in Marseilles, makes the aïoli for the saint's day festivities at the village of Lacoste. She makes the sauce with a tiny bit of mustard and no lemon. I was there for two fêtes at which rows of trestle tables were set up in the village square while a band played, tricolor flags flew and people flocked in from neighbouring villages. When we had finished eating we all danced and played games.

Aïoli

Garlic Mayonnaise

The amount of garlic used in aïoli depends on how much you like garlic and on the size of the cloves. The mayonnaise is served with bourride (p. 128), crudités (p. 64) or with plain boiled vegetables.

8–15 garlic cloves, pounded or crushed to a paste
3 egg yolks
Salt
600 ml (1 pint) olive oil
Juice of 1–2 lemons (optional)

All the ingredients must be at room temperature. Put the garlic in a large, warmed bowl. Add the yolks and a little salt and beat for a minute until the paste is thick and sticky.

Pour in the oil, drop by drop, beating with a wooden spoon or a whisk. When the sauce thickens, which it should do by the time $\frac{1}{3}$ of the oil has been added, you can pour the oil in a thin trickle but keep beating all the time and make sure that it is being properly absorbed. When about $\frac{1}{2}$ the oil has been incorporated add a little lemon juice or a tablespoon of warm water, then continue beating in the oil until the aïoli is very thick. Add the rest of the lemon juice to taste.

If the sauce is too solid or there is a risk of it curdling, 1 or 2 tablespoons of warm water will help. If the oil is added too quickly, the aïoli may separate, but you can easily save it by starting again with a fresh yolk in a new bowl and slowly beating in the separated sauce.

You can also make the sauce in a food processor. Blend the garlic and yolks with the salt, then add the oil in a thin stream while the blades are running. Add lemon juice, then taste and adjust the seasonings.

Variation
For Sylva Gauthier's aïoli substitute 2 teaspoons of prepared French mustard for the lemon juice.

The height of the Provence garlic season

All-i-Oli

Catalan Oil and Garlic Sauce

You can make this sauce more or less potent, according to taste. Serve with fish, meat or vegetables and with all kinds of grilled foods. If the sauce separates or refuses to thicken, add a small slice of white bread, crusts removed, and pound or blend it into the liquid.

4–10 garlic cloves, peeled and crushed
Salt
About 200 ml (7 fl oz) olive oil

Pound the garlic to a paste together with a little salt in a mortar and gradually beat in the oil until you have a thick cream.

Variations

* To this classic recipe you can add the juice of ½–1 lemon.
* Many Spaniards now make a sauce identical to the French aïoli (see opposite) as an alternative.

Top left: All-i-oli
Top right: Fried fish (p. 133)
Bottom: Squid and prawns à la plancha (p. 169)

Yogurt

Bring to the boil 1.2 litres (2 pints) milk and let it simmer for a minute or two, then let it cool so that it just stings when you dip your little finger in. Beat two tablespoons of plain live yogurt in a bowl, add the hot milk a little at a time, beating well. Cover the bowl with cling-film or with a plate, and wrap it up in a rug or something that will keep it warm. Leave it in a warm place with an even temperature, away from draughts, for 12 hours. By then it should have set. Do not leave it any longer as it becomes progressively more acid.

Store in the refrigerator, but yogurt is best eaten at room temperature, not chilled.

Notes

* For a smaller quantity it is simpler to make it in a wide-necked thermos flask.
* You can thicken the yogurt by draining it through a fine cloth placed in a colander. It gets thicker the longer you leave it and eventually it becomes a soft cheese. This is very good mixed with olive oil, seasoned with salt and pepper or paprika and sprinkled with mint or dill. The yogurt cheese can also be rolled into little balls and preserved in olive oil.

Tarator

Walnut Sauce

Alya Halici made this cold Turkish walnut sauce for us in Izmir. Old walnuts often taste rancid, so make sure that they are fresh. Serve the sauce over cold chicken, boiled vegetables or seafood.

Serves 6

1 garlic clove, crushed
125 g (4 oz) shelled walnuts
Salt
1 slice of white bread, crusts removed and soaked
  in water
150 ml (5 fl oz) chicken stock
Juice of 1 lemon

Pound the garlic and walnuts with a pestle and mortar or put them through a food processor. Add salt and then the bread, squeezed dry. Pound or blend to a paste, then beat or blend in the stock and lemon juice, adding more stock if necessary to obtain a smooth light sauce the consistency of mayonnaise.

Variation
Hazelnuts are a common substitute for walnuts in Turkey. In Syria, pine-nuts are usually used.

Chicken or Meat Stock

Stock is used in soups and for cooking rice and cracked wheat. In many households it is more important than the meat and chicken that go to make it, but it is really just as good to use a chicken carcass or meat bones and a few good scraps. Put some in a saucepan with an onion, a carrot, a few celery stalks, a bouquet garni (optional) and a tomato. For a dark-coloured stock, split the onion in two and let it burn split-side down in a dry frying pan. Cover the ingredients with water, add salt, bring to the boil and remove the scum, then put the lid on and simmer very gently for two or three hours, adding water as required. Then strain. You can keep the stock in the refrigerator for four days. It also freezes well.

Variation
For a Spanish flavour add 2–3 tablespoons dry (fino) sherry.

Opposite: Different quality olive oils in Toulon market

Fragrant Vinegars

You can enhance vinegar by infusing it with herbs and other flavourings. Buy good vinegar made from red or white wine, sherry or cider and push a small bunch of herbs, preferably fresh, into the bottle. The most obvious herb to use is tarragon but thyme, mint, basil, fennel, dill, rosemary, oregano, marjoram, savory, sage, bay and hyssop, or a mixture of these all give very pleasing results.

Distinctive flavours are obtained from elder blossom and mustard seeds. For a garlic flavour add unpeeled whole cloves. Raspberries and rose petals, orange peel and juniper berries all give sweet, delicate perfumes and one or two chillies give a peppery kick. You may also like to try an exotic eastern touch with 2–3 tablespoons of orange blossom or rose water.

Fragrant Olive Oils

Scented olive oils for salad dressing can be made by pushing a few sprigs of fresh thyme, rosemary, mint, fennel, sage, basil or bay leaves, alone or in combination, into the bottle.

Frying oil also benefits from flavourings. One of the secrets of the art of deep-frying is to drop aromatics such as a whole chilli, a clove of garlic or a piece of lemon peel into the bubbling oil to give just the faintest breath of flavour to the food.

Hamad M' Rakad

Preserved Lemons and Limes

This preserve gives a mellow lemony flavour to many North African dishes and is easily made. Choose ripe unblemished lemons or limes. Wash them and make two deep vertical cuts in a cross, almost, but not quite through them, so that they still hold together at the stem. Sprinkle plenty of salt inside on the cut flesh – about 125 g (4 oz) for 1 kg (2 lb) fruit – then close them and put them in a sterilised jar so that they are jammed tightly together. Squeeze enough fresh lemon juice over them to keep them covered. The salt will draw out the juices and the peel will soften within a week. They will be ready to use in 3 or 4 weeks. Rinse off the salt before using and discard the flesh; it is the peel alone that is used for flavouring.

It is cheaper and easier, but not as good, to cover the salted lemons or limes with strong brine, or a mixture of sunflower oil and water.

Fish Stock

In the Mediterranean small bony rock fish which are no good for eating are added together with other fish heads and bones to make the stocks which are the basis of fish soups, stews and sauces. The rock fish give an incomparable flavour, but you can use fish heads, bones and trimmings instead. If you have conger eel, crab and prawn trimmings or, better still, tiny shrimps, they will bring you closer to the real Mediterranean flavour. Make sure that everything is absolutely fresh and add bits of vegetables and herbs and white wine which lend a special perfume.

1 kg (2 lb) fish heads, bones and shellfish trimmings
1 onion, chopped
1 garlic clove
2 carrots, chopped
A few celery leaves, chopped
1 leek, chopped
2 bay leaves
A sprig of thyme, marjoram or oregano
A few parsley stalks
2 tablespoons white wine vinegar or lemon juice
Pinch of salt
A few black peppercorns
1.5 litres (2½ pints) water or a mixture of up to ½ and ½ with dry white wine

Wash the fish pieces. Simmer all the ingredients for about 30 minutes, skimming off any foam at the start. Strain through a very fine sieve and reduce further, if you like, to intensify the flavour. This stock freezes well.

Variation

* For a touch of the Midi add a piece of dried orange peel.
* For a Spanish flavour add 2–3 tablespoons dry (fino) sherry.

Salsa Bolognese

Meat Sauce

This meat sauce is known all over the world and is very good with fresh tagliatelle. Some people prefer to use peeled tomatoes, others will only use tomato paste. In Sicily pork and pork sausage are used. Everyone has his or her own secret recipe.

Serves 6

1 onion, chopped
1 carrot, finely chopped
1 stick of celery, finely chopped
3 tablespoons olive oil
500 g (1 lb) lean minced pork or beef or a mixture
Salt and pepper
A pinch of nutmeg
2 bay leaves
1 teaspoon marjoram
A few parsley stems
300–400 ml (10–14 fl oz) red or dry white wine
2 tablespoons tomato paste
820 g (1 lb 12 oz) tin of peeled tomatoes
Grated Parmesan or pecorino for serving

Fry the onion, carrot and celery in oil until soft. Add the meat and fry gently, crushing it with a fork, until it changes colour. Season with salt, pepper and nutmeg, and add the bay leaves, marjoram and parsley stems. Add the wine (red is used in Sicily) and stir in the tomato paste. Cook over high heat, stirring occasionally, until the wine has evaporated. Add the peeled tomatoes and simmer very slowly, half covered, for 1–3 hours. Stir often and add water if necessary, so the sauce does not stick.

Pour the sauce over the pasta and serve, accompanied by the grated cheese.

Variation

For a Neapolitan *ragù* gently cook 1 onion, 1 carrot and a few sage leaves, all chopped, in 3–4 tablespoons olive oil until soft. Flatten 6 veal cutlets off the bone as thinly as you can and cut into 7.5 cm (3 in) squares. Sprinkle each with finely chopped parsley, a little grated Parmesan and some pepper, then roll up and secure with a tooth pick. Add to the onion and carrot and fry, turning them to colour them all over. Add 750 g (1½ lb) peeled, de-seeded and chopped tomatoes and salt and pepper and simmer, covered, for 2 hours, adding a little water if necessary. Serve the sauce with pasta, and the meat separately.

Coulis et Sauce de Tomates

Fresh Tomato Sauce

If you asked if there was a theme to Mediterranean cooking I would say it was tomato sauce. The sweetish aroma of onion frying in oil with tomatoes which was born in Catalunya belongs as much to the medieval Provençal hill towns as to squalid bustling Naples and the mud house villages on the banks of the Nile. Every Mediterranean country has its own versions of raw fresh pulp and jam-like paste which sizzles in its oil, but France and Italy have made gastronomic poetry with theirs.

Raw pulp: Remove the stalks of very ripe tomatoes and pour boiling water over them. Leave for a few seconds, then peel, halve and press them to squeeze out the seeds and excess juice. Chop the flesh, sprinkle with salt and pepper and drain in a sieve.

Cooked pulp: Soften 1 finely chopped onion in 1 tablespoon olive oil. Add the raw pulp of 1.5 kg (3 lb) tomatoes, 2 whole garlic cloves and a *bouquet garni* consisting of 2 sprigs of thyme, a sprig of marjoram, 2 bay leaves and a few parsley stalks. You may need a pinch of sugar if the tomatoes are a little sour or tasteless. Cook gently for 30 minutes, stirring occasionally until all the juice has evaporated and you have a thick pulp. Remove the garlic and herbs.

Sugo di Pomodoro

Italian Tomato Sauce

There are many ways of making tomato sauce. This one is quick, easy and fresh tasting. It can be served with any kind of pasta – for six people you will need 500 g (1 lb) – and freshly grated Parmesan or pecorino cheese.

Serves 6

1 large onion, finely chopped
3 tablespoons olive oil
1–2 garlic cloves, crushed
1 kg (2 lb) ripe tomatoes, peeled, de-seeded and chopped, or 1 × 820 g (1 lb 12 oz) tin of peeled or chopped tomatoes
Salt and pepper
1 teaspoon sugar (optional)
2 bay leaves
A few sprigs of rosemary, thyme, parsley, marjoram, oregano or basil or a mixture of these

To make the sauce, fry the onion in oil till golden. Add the garlic and, when the aroma rises, add the tomatoes, salt and pepper and a little sugar, if using. Add the herbs and simmer gently for 15–20 minutes or until the sauce is reduced.

Variation
A hot tomato sauce can be made with 2–3 chilli peppers and no onion. Put them in at the beginning and remove just before serving. Served only with chopped parsley, this makes the pasta *all' arrabiata*. The *penne* pasta shape is the most traditional for this sauce.

Tomato-growing in Provence

Favourite Cookery Books
Covering the Mediterranean

FAYEZ AOUN, *280 recettes de cuisine familiale libanaise*. Paris: Jacques Grancher, 1980.

FETTOUMA BENKIRANE, *La nouvelle cuisine marocaine*. Paris: J. P. Taillandier, 1979.

LATIFA BENNANI-SMIRES, *Moroccan Cooking*. Casablanca: Al Madariss, 1975.

ADA BONI, *Italian Regional Cooking*. Godfrey Cave Associates, 1982.

ARABELLA BOXER, *Mediterranean Cook Book*. Penguin Books, 1983. Distributed in the U.S. by Biblio Distributors, 1981.

PENELOPE CASAS, *The Foods and Wines of Spain*. Penguin Books, 1985. Published in the U.S. by Alfred A. Knopf, 1982.

——— , *Tapas: The Little Dishes of Spain*. New York: Alfred A. Knopf, 1985.

FRANCESCO PAOLO CASCINO, *Cucina di Sicilia*. Palermo: Lorenzo Misuraca, 1980.

ELIZABETH DAVID, *A Book of Mediterranean Food*. Penguin Books, 1970. Published in the U.S. by Penguin Books, 1986.

——— , *French Provincial Cooking*. M. Joseph, 1965; Penguin Books, 1970. Published in the U.S. by Penguin Books, 1986.

——— , *Italian Food*. Penguin Books, 1970. Published in the U.S. by Penguin Books, 1986.

ALAN DAVIDSON, *Mediterranean Seafood*. Penguin Books, 1972. Published in the U.S. by Louisiana State University Press, 1981.

NESET EREN, *The Art of Turkish Cooking*. Izmir, 1982.

M. GRANOUX, *Recueil de la gastronomie provençale*. SAEP Colmar, 1983.

JANE GRIGSON, *Charcuterie and French Pork Cookery*. Penguin Books, 1970. Published in the U.S. as *The Art of Making Sausages, Pâtés, and Other Charcuterie* by Alfred A. Knopf, 1976.

——— , *Fish Cookery*. Penguin Books, 1975.

——— , *Fruit Book*. M. Joseph, 1982; Penguin Books, 1983. Published in the U.S. by Atheneum, 1982.

——— , *Vegetable Book*. M. Joseph, 1978; Penguin Books, 1980.

ZETTE GUINEAUDEAU-FRANC, *Fès vu par sa cuisine*. Rabat: J. E. Laurent, 1966.

——— , *Les secrets des cuisines en terre marocaine*. Paris: J. P. Taillandier, 1958.

MARCELLA HAZAN, *The Classic Italian Cookbook*. London: Macmillan, 1981. Published in the U.S. by Alfred A. Knopf, 1976.

ZEINAB KAAK, *La sofra, cuisine tunisienne traditionnelle*. Tunis: STD, 1982.

RENE KHAWAM, *La cuisine arabe*. Paris: Albin Michel, 1970.

MOHAMED KOUKI, *La cuisine tunisienne d'Ommok Sannafa*. Tunis: STD, 1974.

——— , *Poissons méditerranéens*. Tunis: STD, n.d.

AHMED LAASRI, *240 recettes de cuisine marocaine*. Paris: Jacques Grancher, 1978.

ANNA MACMIADHACHAIN, *Spanish Regional Cookery*. Penguin Books, 1976.

THEONIE MARK, *Greek Islands Cooking*. Batsford, 1978.

JACQUES MÉDECIN, *Cuisine niçoise*. Penguin Books, 1972.

KHADIDJA OBEIDA, *253 recettes de cuisine algérienne*. Paris: Jacques Grancher, 1983.

RICHARD OLNEY, *Simple French Food*. Penguin Books, 1984. Published in the U.S. by Atheneum.

GEORGE N. RAYESS, *L'art culinaire libanais*. Beirut: Librairie du Liban, 1957. Published in the U.S. by the International Book Center.

J. B. REBOUL, *La cuisinière provençale*. Marseille: Tacussel, 1970.

WAVERLEY ROOT, *The Food of France*. Macmillan, 1983. Published in the U.S. by Random House, 1977.

——— , *The Food of Italy*. Time-Life Books, 1969. Published in the U.S. by Random House.

RENA SALAMAN, *Greek Food*. Fontana, 1983.

ANNE WILLAN, *French Regional Cooking*. Hutchinson, 1983. Published in the U.S. by William Morrow, 1981.

PAULA WOLFERT, *Couscous and Other Good Food from Morocco*. New York: Harper & Row, 1973.

EDMOND ZEITOUN, *250 recettes classiques de cuisine tunisienne*. Paris: Jacques Grancher, 1977.

Index

Page numbers in italics indicate a colour illustration